TEACHER

DENNIS LITTKY'S FIGHT FOR A BETTER SCHOOL

SUSAN KAMMERAAD-CAMPBELL

A PLUME BOOK

PLUME
Published by the Penguin Group
Penguin Books USA Inc., 375 Hudson Street,
New York, New York 10014, U.S.A.
Penguin Books Ltd, 27 Wrights Lane,
London W8 5TZ, England
Penguin Books Australia Ltd, Ringwood,
Victoria, Australia
Penguin Books Canada Ltd, 2801 John Street,
Markham, Ontario, Canada L3R 1B4
Penguin Books (N.Z.) Ltd, 182-190 Wairau Road,
Auckland 10, New Zealand
Penguin Books Ltd, Registered Offices:
Harmondsworth, Middlesex, England

Published by Plume, an imprint of New American Library, a division of Penguin
Books USA Inc. This is an authorized reprint of a hardcover edition published by
Contemporary Books, Inc. Previously titled *Doc: The Story of Dennis Littky and His Fight
for a Better School.*

First Plume Printing, February, 1991
10 9 8 7 6 5 4 3 2 1

 REGISTERED TRADEMARK—MARCA REGISTRADA

LIBRARY OF CONGRESS CATALOGING-IN-PUBLICATION DATA
Kammeraad-Campbell, Susan.
    Teacher : Dennis Littky's fight for a better school / Susan
Kammeraad-Campbell.
        p.   cm.
    Rev. ed. of: Doc. 1989.
    Includes bibliographical references.
    ISBN 0-452-26573-8
    1. Littky, Dennis.   2. High school principals--New Hampshire-
-Biography.   3. Thayer High School (Winchester, N.H.)   4. School
boards--New Hampshire--Winchester (Town)   5. Winchester (N.H. :
Town)   I. Kammeraad-Campbell, Susan. Doc.   II. Title.
LA2317.L68K46   1991
373.12'012'092--dc20   90-20669
[B]   CIP

Printed in the United States of America

BOOKS ARE AVAILABLE AT QUANTITY DISCOUNTS WHEN USED TO PROMOTE PRODUCTS
OR SERVICES. FOR INFORMATION PLEASE WRITE TO PREMIUM MARKETING DIVISION,
PENGUIN BOOKS USA INC., 375 HUDSON STREET, NEW YORK, NEW YORK 10014.

Susan Kammeraad-Campbell is an award-winning journalist who has worked for newspapers in the Midwest and New England, where she originally covered Littky's story for the Keene, New Hampshire, *Sentinel*. In addition to writing, she is an educational consultant at Miami University in Ohio.

To the people of Winchester

"The list of ways to get involved is endless. What is important is that you begin. Someone must take the first step."—*Dennis Littky*

Contents

Preface

F. J. AMAROSA JR. & SON'S Hardware, Small-Eaze Grocery, Don's Barber Shop, the Pisgah Diner, two churches, a bank, a library, town hall, a couple of gas stations, and a place called Fat Chance Antiques. Sounds like a lot, but the unwitting driver passing through Winchester, New Hampshire, might not notice any town at all. It's there. It's all on Main Street, a road better known to motorists and truckers as State Route 10. Nothing unusual. Nothing much different from any other New England mill town, of which there are legion.

I am an outsider telling a story that happened to happen in Winchester. Working as a newspaper reporter for the *Keene Sentinel*, I stumbled on a hot story one December night in the library of the town's elementary school.

It was the first school board meeting I covered there. Board meetings can be painfully dull; school board meetings often top the list. But this being my first assignment in Winchester, I drove toward town with butterflies in my belly.

The parking lot was packed. This time of year that could mean a basketball game, except that the gymnasium was empty. It was the elementary school library that was loaded with people. Something was awry. Just a regular monthly school board meeting, I had been told by the assignment editor. The agenda had indicated nothing noteworthy:

minutes of November's meeting, citizen's comments, principals' reports, and so on. None of that explained the crowd, nor the tension, pungent as cooking cabbage.

I had entered a room that was like the rest of the building, spare and economical, with exposed steel beams and concrete block walls. Leaves pasted on construction paper decorated a wall above several rows of book cases. A man in the audience was addressing the board members and other officials sitting at the line of tables facing the crowd. He wanted to know why the high school had been removed from an organization called the Coalition of Essential Schools—without notice. His question was framed and delivered politely.

"That business was handled at last month's meeting," said one of the officials. The speaker, unlike most of the men in the audience, wore a business suit. Fat and domineering, he had a pendulous lower lip and massive gut.

"Yes, I know," the man in the audience answered evenly. "I just think you owe us an explanation for why that was done."

The board member jerked to his feet, leaned across the table, and aimed his finger at the man's throat. "We don't owe you anything. If you couldn't see fit to attend last month's meeting when the issue was decided, then we're not going to spend time with you now!"

"It wasn't on the agenda," the man protested. "You gave us no advance notice that the topic was even going to be discussed."

"That's not my problem," the board member shouted. "The board discussed it in executive session, and it's been decided. It's done. We owe you *nothing*."

In my half-dozen years as a reporter, I'd never witnessed a public official being so surly and abusive to a member of the voting public for politely inquiring about a board decision; I'd never heard a public official flatly refuse to explain his actions; I'd never seen a man quite as ponderously unpretty as he. The man's name, I would later learn, was Francis Gutoski.

That was also the night I met Dennis Littky.

When the board left the room mid-meeting to conduct a long closed-door session, the entire crowd waited until the board returned. Some left the room to smoke. Some milled about the library, moving from group to group, fuming about Gutoski's conduct. A reporter from *New England Monthly*, a slick, upscale magazine, sought me out.

"Pretty incredible stuff," he said, shaking his head.

I agreed.

"Who was that man?"

"I was hoping you could tell me who he was."

"This is my first meeting."

"Mine too."

Then the magazine reporter explained why he was there: Winchester had this "super-innovative" high school principal who had "transformed the school" and a suspicious board that wanted him out. It was a hot story, he said, about ready to boil over.

The super-innovative principal was across the room, leaning against a bookcase—alone. His reddish beard was untrimmed, ragged, tinged with gray. It erupted from his face, starting at his cheek bones and mixing with the hairs at the neck of his button-down shirt. His hair fell in loose curls above his shoulders, not quite covering the top of his head. He struck me as the kind of guy who hummed mantras instead of Top 40. Behind John Lennon wire-rimmed glasses, his eyes were soft, philosophical, laugh lines dug deep. But he was not laughing just then.

I introduced myself and got down to business.

"So what the hell's going on here?"

For a second he said nothing. Then he spoke:

"I tell you," he said, "I'd like to talk with you, but it seems that anytime something is printed about me, even when it's favorable, it gets turned against me."

"I don't understand."

"I just can't talk to you. Maybe later. But not now."

That was my first real introduction to Winchester, my first glimpse of a story that would divide a town, grip the attention of the region, and attract national publicity, film crews, book and movie contracts. It is a story that cries out to be told, a story that pushed people to take sides. It alienated families, sabotaged businesses, and changed lives. It is about education, social change, political intrigue, hatred, love—life.

The passion that drove people to support Littky, even at great personal sacrifice, was no less than the passion of those who actively opposed him. There were the power brokers, a handful of people in town who'd called the shots for decades and weren't about to lose their turf to a hippie outsider. There were those who were frightened into thinking Littky's new-fangled ideas meant their taxes would skyrocket and they would lose their homes. And then there were the ideologues, people who made a determined study of Dennis Littky and genuinely believed he was a subversive. In some cases, the groups overlapped.

One of Littky's ideological detractors steered me to the Plymouth Rock Foundation, an especially discrete organization in neighboring Marlboro, New Hampshire, that operates as a kind of national information clearinghouse for ultraconservative, Christian literature such as that produced by Samuel L. Blumenfeld.

From the Plymouth Rock Foundation I acquired several of Blumenfeld's books and tapes, including *NEA: Trojan Horse in American Education* and *Is Public Education Necessary?* Both books describe how a cadre of nineteenth-century secularists spearheaded the drive toward public education in an effort to destroy religion and moral sanity.

Blumenfeld describes today's National Education Association as the most politically powerful and dangerous organization in America that has as its aim converting America into a socialist society. He points to John Dewey, the turn-of-the-century founder of progressive education, as the one "who began to fashion a new materialist religion in which humanity was venerated instead of God. This is basically the religion of Secular Humanism, and this is what has become the official religion of the United States, for it is the only religion permitted in its public schools. . . . John Dewey gave education a social mission of exalted revolutionary proportions: the transformation of American society from capitalism to socialism."

Blumenfeld would call Dewey a scourge. Dennis Littky would call him the ultimate education philosopher. The one book Littky gives every teacher who works with him is Dewey's *Experience and Education*.

I've had the luxury of recording firsthand many details of this story during the past two years, though much of the tale took place long before I had ever heard of Winchester or Dennis Littky. In such cases, I've relied on the memories and writings of those involved. In instances where I was not present to record dialogue, or where a situation was not recorded in some other way, I corroborated the information with at least one direct source, usually several more than that. In the case of a few minor characters, names have been changed. In such instances, only a first name or initial is used.

In exchange for my sharing copyright with Dennis Littky, I hold the exclusive literary rights to his story. He afforded me unlimited access to him and, whenever appropriate, the school. I spent untold hours with him talking, listening, dogging his heels at school, at education conferences, in close moments with students, teachers, and friends, at his cabin, in his jeep. While Dennis Littky emerges as the book's main character, he would not have become "Doc" without the confluence of human forces that rose to both support and oppose him.

This book is an effort to give voice to all sides of the story. But because of the thrust of the narrative, Littky is more fully fleshed out than any other characters. I have, however, tried to fairly represent their substantive positions. To that end, I spent hundreds of hours with those closely associated with the story. The people of Winchester—Littky supporters and detractors alike—opened up their homes, minds, and, occasionally, their hearts to me. The point of view of the book and the words are solely my own.

About no subject were people's opinions and points of view more varied than about Dennis Littky himself. Lumped together, they form a pretty odd picture: Dennis Littky the outgoing recluse, Dennis Littky the honest actor, Dennis Littky the manipulating educator, Dennis Littky the persecuted paladin, Dennis Littky the archetypal misfit. Same man, different man. One man's poetry is another man's peccadillo. It's all point of view.

A seventh-grade boy skips school for the second time in a week. Littky tries talking and reasoning with the boy, but to no avail. He wants him to know the seriousness of his infraction, so this time when the boy enters his office, Littky scowls and slams the door hard to let the student know he means business. Littky isn't really mad, but he knows a young student will be sufficiently unnerved if he thinks he made the principal that angry. That will help correct the student's behavior. Such tactics will work with a seventh grader, but Littky knows they'll likely fizzle on an older student.

When the boy enters the principal's office, Littky winks at his secretaries, warning them to brace themselves for the inevitable slam of the door. He's done this before, and they know why he's doing it. Someone just happening on the scene might be offended by the principal's display of anger and surmise he's too emotional, too unstable, or simply a showman. Someone else hearing what Littky did and the rationale behind it might label him a manipulator, a psychological tactician, a brainwasher. Littky would call himself an effective principal.

Winchester is important to this story because it happens to be where Sheldon Dennis Littky—a.k.a. Dennis, Denny, Doc—became principal. Littky didn't choose Winchester; he stumbled on it by way of a mountaintop cabin more than a decade ago. Winchester didn't choose Dennis Littky. It didn't ask for him; it got him by chance. And while it's true that wherever Dennis Littky deigns to hang his hats he seems to engender conflict, Winchester made it happen on a scale and with an ardor that is rare in these days of good-natured apathy.

Acknowledgments

DURING THE NEARLY THREE years I spent researching and writing, I came to know many of Winchester's people well. They spent hours with me in formal interviews, casual talk, telephone conversation, letters. I watched them in moments of tenderness, triumph, and anguish. They offered me personal letters, journals, and diaries. They suffered my probing questions and exposed themselves in ways that run against the grain of Yankee sensibilities in the belief that this story needed to be told.

I will always be amazed and touched by the warmth and kindness of the people of Winchester. Intruder that I was, they opened their homes and hearts to me.

The sheer number of people who shared their stories with me is quite big, but a few deserve special thanks: Marcia Ammann, Barb Eibell, Karen (Thompson) Marsh, Terri Racine, and, of course, Dennis Littky.

I am also grateful to Val Cole, Marian Polaski, Jimmy Karlin, Don Weisburger and the kids in his advisory who showed me how they make it work, Frankie, Winnie and Frank Amarosa, Cindy Nelson, Robin Carey, Cyndy Ryder, and Erica Ryll.

Thanks also to Melanie Zwolinski, Betty Hall, Jan and Lee Gamache, Althea Nelson, Ed Zitta, Bud Baker, Roger Sundstrom, Dick McCarthy, Bob Findlay, Ben Nicholson, Phil Hamm, Judy Knox, Jack Ainsworth, James Beaman, Billy Higgins, Diane and Ross Burkhardt, Robbie Fried, Jim Harrison, John Meyer, Bucky Jones, Carol Poole, and Henry Parkhurst.

I also want to thank those who stood on the other side of the Littky issue for providing me invaluable dimension to the story. I thank Ernie Royce, Howard Spaulding, and, especially, Marilyn Nolan for their candor, time, and energy in helping me understand their point of view.

For the use of excerpted material, I thank the *Boston Globe*, *Keene Sentinel*, *New England Monthly*, *New York Times*, *Yankee Magazine*, Ted Sizer, Helen Martin Eccles, the Coalition of Essential Schools, and the staff at Thayer High School.

I thank my editors: Mary Lee Grisanti for her prudent cuts, Tonia Payne for often being a voice of calm in a sometimes stormy sea, and, most of all, Bernard Shir-Cliff for his unwavering commitment, level head, and insight.

I also thank Ernie Herbert for the initial contact, Ted Parent for his sound advice, the *Keene Sentinel* and particularly Tom Kearney for generous support, and Michael Moore for his sensitive photography. Thanks to the folks at the Fitzwilliam Inn for providing an idyllic writing environment and to Molly Symons for the same. Thanks to Linda LaPoint and Carol Howe at Thayer, Federal Express drivers Tim and Bill for their punctuality and for occasionally enduring my lack of it, Frank Sherman, Dotti Pierson for making me computer literate, and Kristie Pierson for maintaining sanity in a sometimes insane household.

And, finally, I am grateful to my friends and family: John Weigel and Milton White, good teachers, good people, good friends; Russ McCollom III who showed me the ropes of reporting lo those many years ago and offered sensitive editing suggestions; and my parents Lloyd and Sally Kammeraad for believing in me. Lastly and most importantly, I thank my husband, William, my best friend, my sounding board, who endured me, supported me, and always kept me clear on what was important. And to Abigail, who was born in the midst of it all.

1
Graduation 1987

A YOUNG GIRL IN A powder-pink dress that might have been her older sister's prom gown clutched a small stack of programs in the crook of her arm, thrusting one at everybody within range. Behind her, cars streamed into the parking lot, some festooned with balloons and signs. "Congrats Terri!" one read. The lot filled quickly. After that, cars pulled off onto the lawn in front of the elementary school. A baseball throw away sat Thayer High School, where most of the hubbub was taking place.

Several hundred folding chairs in tidy rows lined the lawn facing a stage and podium. Overhead, Old Glory hung languidly; occasionally, as a hot breeze seized it, it snapped loudly enough to cut through the din of the crowd below. Clusters of people milled about, talking, laughing, wielding cameras and video recorders like kids with toy guns.

Through the large windows of the high school, girls and boys gawked at the crowd below. Some preened, others adjusted their mortar boards, giggling nervously. Above the ruddy brick building, the sky was an ocean blue with a few clouds stirred in like dollops of cream.

On the lawn near the stage, a paltry band—lacking several members who were marching in the processional— struck up a labored version of "Pomp and Circumstance." A pretty black girl, all the more striking because she was one

1

of only five or six blacks to be seen, led the procession, marking time to her methodical step-touch with a ribboned baton. Behind her, capped and gowned seniors flowed out of the high school in orderly waves of peach and black.

Like all graduations, this one had its share of minor dramas:

Katrina was there but she wasn't marching with her chums. She'd dropped out of school three months earlier. The ceremonies hadn't even started and she was already crying.

Sixteen-month-old Elizabeth Racine pulled playfully on her grandmother's ear, oblivious that her mother, Terri, senior class president, was graduating.

Ernie Royce, who'd graduated from Thayer decades earlier, potbellied, rumple-haired, wore a work shirt and no bottom front teeth. He proudly paraded his twelve-year-old son clad in a starched, blindingly white uniform and crisp white cap. A shiny medal pinned to his chest proclaimed him the Best Young Cadet from a private academy. Ernie Royce had nothing against public schools in general, but he refused to send his son to the public schools in Winchester. Ernie talked affably and loudly, fracturing rules of grammar. His son answered nearly every inquiry, "Yes, sir," "Yes, ma'am." When a woman suggested that he needn't address her as ma'am, he replied succinctly, "It's proper, ma'am."

But there was more going on here. Tensions not typically associated with small-town high school graduations.

"I absolutely refuse to shake his hand," one of the graduating seniors whispered to her friend. "Board chairman or not, that man's *not* going to touch my hand."

"I wouldn't care if he was President of the United States," her friend hissed. "He tried to ruin our education. I'm not giving him the satisfaction of shaking my hand either."

Others were whispering about the salutatorian.

"I heard she's going to give a speech slamming the principal."

"My brother said he'd tackle her right there on the stage if she did. . . . I think he would, too."

Standing on the flat roof of the school, two men manned a large television camera. Their dark silhouettes loomed ominously over the crowd—they looked like snipers. Even Jim Harrison, the police chief, did a double take. A man in blue jeans and blazer, obviously too slick-looking to be a local, shouted directions to the camera crew as they moved in and out of the school with a businesslike air that reeked of the big city.

There were more like them—outsiders. They were easy to spot; they moved more quickly, more purposefully than everyone else. They carried notebooks, tape recorders, cameras. They scratched quick notes, pressed microphones in people's faces, shot pictures with big-nosed cameras. Local newspaper and radio reporters were there, but this wasn't a purely local affair—CBS's "West 57th" had a crew there, so did the *Washington Post*, the *Boston Globe*, and National Public Radio.

They were all there for the same reason. News was being made in the quiet, back-road town of Winchester, New Hampshire. It had been happening for well over a year. At the root of it all was one man—Dennis Littky.

2
Winchester

WINCHESTER SITS ON A CROSSROAD, as close to Massachusetts on one side as Vermont on the other. Main Street, the major artery through town, runs along the Ashuelot River, whose waters once supplied power for the town's now defunct lumber industry, provided fish for many of Winchester's dinner tables, and carried away its raw sewage. It's a town, like the state, built on granite, one of nature's hardest substances, and, like the rocky substrate, it has its share of cracks, fissures, and—occasionally—earthquakes.

The pickup trucks, station wagons, jacked-up clunkers, and aging sedans that carry mothers to Kulick's Market, husbands to the shearling tannery, or kids to the Monadnock Speedway all display the state's motto: Live Free or Die. In Winchester, that slogan is taken seriously. It's a hard-lot town run by a handful of powerful landholders. Those who work for their living work hard—mostly as farmers and mill hands. Those who don't or can't are a drain on an already poor town. Over the years, Winchester has become the major repository for the county's welfare load. Property is cheap, zoning laws lax; trailer parks grow like suckers out of tree trunks. A town of only 3,700 people, Winchester carries one of the highest welfare populations in the state. More than one in five Winchester residents lives below the poverty level, and the unemployment is double

4

that of the state as a whole. The *New Hampshire Times*, a statewide newspaper, once called the town "a little piece of Appalachia."

Swollen hills and a few modestly sized mountains rim Winchester; a couple of these glacial remains push up inside the town lines. They are the foothills of Mount Monadnock, a 3,165-foot-high mountain that juts into the clouds northeast of town. Red maple, silver birch, evergreen, sweet gum, and scarlet oak trees abound along the river banks, rimming the farmland, covering the mountains and hills. In winter, when the trees are stripped of leaves, the mountains around Winchester resemble the backs of porcupines bristling at the presence of an intruder. The seasons ride hard through Winchester. When the deep snows of winter melt, draining down the mountainsides, the town suffocates under a layer of mud until spring passes through; then the mud dries. Summer turns the town lush and green and bucolic. This natural beauty was alluring enough to place Winchester in the running for the site of Dartmouth College a couple of centuries ago.

To understand Winchester politics, it helps to know a few things about the state as a whole. New Hampshire, as any school kid can tell you, was one of the thirteen original colonies. Natives never forget their lineage and are masters at the art of the subtle reminder. They take the political process very seriously.

Most of the state's people live in knot-sized towns, communities whose populations barely reach into the thousands. One person's vote does make a difference—it is not unheard-of for a political race to end in a tie. Annual town meetings draw whole families to trim white clapboard town halls to conduct the community's business: voters decide how much money must be raised to run the town, which roads need to be repaired, how many police cruisers or fire trucks need to be replaced, if a new back hoe should be purchased.

On issues of a more cataclysmic nature, town meetings have served as an effective weapon against assault from some of the dimmer prospects of the nuclear age. In 1986, communities the state over passed referenda at town meetings opposing the burial of high-level radioactive waste anywhere in the state. That year the federal government designated New Hampshire one of a handful of states being considered for the disposal of nuclear waste: federal officials figured granite would make a good, cheap natural lining for their nuclear dump. Residents lost no time rising to the threat. A strong grassroots effort battled the government's plan, bombarding it with geological, emotional, historical, and environmental arguments. Later that year, the Nuclear Regulatory Commission took New Hampshire off the list of proposed sites.

As the nation's first primary state, New Hampshire has traditionally played a prominent role in deciding the political fate of the country. It is with an inviolable—though perhaps not unwarranted—smugness that New Hampshire residents will remind the rest of the country that no presidential candidate since 1952 has reached the highest office in the land without first winning in the New Hampshire primary. Direct participation in government and the power of the vote are lessons natives learn early.

Reputations and towns are odd things. Once a town gets one, it's hard to shake it. People seem to expect things in Winchester to go wrong. When they do, folks nod their heads: "It's Winchester, after all."

Of course, Winchester has its good points as well as its bad. Not everything there goes wrong. But it's a poor town, and in poor communities bad things seem to happen more often—or at least more conspicuously—than in well-maintained, wealthy neighborhoods.

Crimes prosecuted in Cheshire County always seem to have a link to Winchester. Either the crime took place there, the victim or the perpetrator lives there, or some thread leads to Winchester. It's been that way for a long time.

Deserved or not, the town has a bad reputation. People who say they're from Winchester get looked at: "What? Down on yer luck?" But a lot of folks in Winchester insist they wouldn't live anywhere else. It's home. They can walk to church. They know the postman, the librarian, the grocer, the hardware store owner by name. They walk on the old wood-covered sidewalks that still line storefronts along Main Street and exchange hellos all along the way. Don's Barber Shop is the clearinghouse for local scuttlebutt, located right next to Pisgah Diner, another caldron for hot, meaty gossip. The concrete and steel bridge over Mirey Brook, an ambling thread of water running under Route 10 and connecting with the Ashuelot River, is a favorite fishing spot. During the long winters, the major recreational activity is basketball—playing it and watching it. The people of Winchester flock to the game like evangelicals to prayer meetings. Kids start playing organized basketball as soon as they can bounce the ball. The fans have been regularly rewarded for their support of local basketball by trips to state and regional tournaments.

Every Saturday, once the weather warms, people come from miles around to hawk their wares in the open-air flea market next to the community center. Almost as reliably, octogenarians occupy the plank porch of the community home, rocking and watching the traffic. For many, neighbors are like family. If a neighbor falls sick or hard times hit, freshly baked pies, casseroles, ruby-skinned tomatoes, shucked corn in bushel baskets appear at the doorstep.

The town itself has been on an economic downturn since World War II. Major plant closings in the 1960s and '70s, including three of the town's largest employers, left a lot of residents without jobs. Today, there is no movie theater, no motel, no bar, no department store. But, in the halcyon years before the war, W. L. Goodnow's Department Store sold the first transistor radios, passenger trains made regular stops shuffling folks to and from Keene, mills flourished, backyard gardens were as common as front porches. Hefty private endowments gave rise to sturdy, ornate municipal buildings, such as the Conant Library, still an architectural showpiece. Everywhere, it seemed, was prosperity.

Winchester House, the town's only hotel, thrived under a string of names and owners. The cavernous wood structure rivaled in size its neighbor, the town hall. A long wooden porch rimmed the entire building, the third floor surmounted by a stately cupola. Though the building survived the storm of economic downturn, it was the worse for wear. Eventually it became an eyesore, though it provided a certain succor for local inhabitants. A man could go there after his shift, get wicked drunk, and swing his fists. Sometimes patrons spilled onto the streets, shouting and causing a ruckus. More than once a misplaced punch or a wobble-footed drunk broke through the huge plate-glass window at F. J. Amarosa Jr. & Son's Hardware on Main Street. But those days are over. For years the hotel lay derelict. One day it burned to the ground.

To the outside world, or, more realistically, the rest of the state, Winchester seems like a rogue elephant, a political rapscallion. It's a town that has rejected federal and state aid over concern that it would compromise the town's independence. "If you take their money, the next thing they'll do is tell you how to spend it." In Concord, the state capital, Winchester has a reputation for rabble rousing, a community inclined to put itself above the law or get around it.

As the area outside Winchester developed, so too did the regional newspapers. Heretofore passed over by the fourth estate, Winchester suddenly became its darling, a trump card for reporters in search of a hot story. Winchester has always resented the probing eyes of the outside world and did not take kindly to newspaper reporters who gathered altogether too much of the town's dirty laundry to air in public.

The following story is often told at the *Keene Sentinel*, the area's major news organization, located twenty miles to the north. The first time a reporter was sent to the town to cover the weekly selectmen's meeting during the late 1960s, the young reporter drove up in his green MGB sports car, nattily clad in prep-school toggery, strode into the town hall, sat down close to the selectmen who were conducting the town's business, and opened his reporter's notebook. The room, a flurry of talk and activity, turned stone quiet. The reporter apologized for the interruption, introduced himself, then urged the town officials to continue with their business. Silence. The reporter urged again. One of the selectmen spoke up: "Why don't you just go out that door, get in your car, drive back to Keene, and don't come back."

Thayer High School and Winchester Elementary School sit at the end of a shady residential street. The grade school is a one-story, concrete-block, flat-topped building that houses the town's four hundred or so grade schoolers. The high school, built in 1922, is two and a half stories, making it one of the tallest buildings in Winchester. It's a big red-brick box—plain but not austere, softened by the tidy row of houses in front of the parking lot and the expansive field, woods, and mountains in back and beyond.

3

Arrival 1978

A BRIDE AND GROOM EMERGED from the United Church of Winchester. For a moment, only the wedding party was clustered on the church steps like a fresh nosegay. Then a medley of young and old people spilled out of the church—large women wrapped in long dresses, men in pastel leisure suits, children in shoes that looked too small.

A Ryder truck, pulling an aging yellow Karmann Ghia, edged past the town hall, turned off Main Street toward the church, and slowed almost to a stop in front of Winchester House, still functioning though long past its prime as an inn. A man with a rust-colored beard and wire-rimmed glasses was driving. Next to him sat an attractive woman wearing blue jeans, a bandanna over her hair. When the truck rolled to a stop, the golden retriever at the woman's feet picked up its head. Another golden next to the woman hooked both its front legs over the open window and barked once. A man in a station wagon pulled up behind the truck. He was the other man's good friend. He too sported Levis and a beard. A golden retriever was lying half on the front seat, half on him.

"Pretty amazing scene," the man said to the woman. The woman nodded. "Not a bad way to begin life as a mountain man."

That was the thirty-fifth birthday of the man in the truck. His untrimmed beard was dappled with gray; a spray of laugh lines shot out from the corners of his eyes like paper fans. He wore a flannel lumberman's shirt, sleeves rolled up, jeans, running shoes, and a baseball cap with the letter *D* sewn above the visor. He lifted the hat, running his hand over the top of his head, where there was little hair.

Dennis Littky was not from Winchester. That much was obvious. He didn't talk New Hampshire—his accent was plain, Midwestern, the way people talk on television, only Dennis talked much faster, as though he were in a hurry. He constantly peppered his speech with outdated expressions like "Cool," "Hey, man, it was really wild," and "What's his consciousness?" He had a way of walking that made it look as though he were having a genuinely good time, something like the pace of a person humming "Put on a Happy Face."

If the finer details of Dennis's comportment escaped the viewer, the startling yellow Karmann Ghia didn't. Nobody in Winchester drove a sports car, even a rusty one. Too many dirt roads, too many hills. Winter, which lasted nearly half the year, could dump enough snow in one helping to swallow a car like that. Spring would choke it with mud. Besides, there weren't many folks in town who'd spend money on a toy like that. If they had money to burn, more than likely they'd buy a good sturdy American car, a Cadillac or a four-wheel-drive pickup with all the bells and whistles.

Dennis had stumbled on Winchester by chance. He'd happened by about four years earlier on his way to vacation in Maine. A member of his staff had a mother with a mountain cabin in southern New Hampshire; did he want to stay there one night on his way to Maine? He did. He never got to Maine. Dennis wrote a poem to the elderly woman who owned the mountaintop cabin and left it on the kitchen table. About a year later, the mother of his teacher friend decided to sell the cabin. She contacted her daughter to see if the fellow who'd written the poem wanted to buy it. He did.

Under the best of conditions, the road up Pudding Hill to Dennis's cabin was a challenge. Ruts were ankle-deep on average, shin-deep frequently. The dirt road did not step up the mountain gradually; it shot straight up, bending only to avoid a sheer drop-off or cliff. Mud season lingered, turning the road into a bone-jarring passage over rocks and ruts. Trying to climb Pudding Hill with a rental truck towing a sports car was more than going out of one's way to make life difficult. It was insane.

Before leaving his beach house overlooking Long Island Sound, Dennis had thrown a party, telling his friends they could take anything that wasn't packed in a box, a sort of pre-rummage sale giveaway. His assortment of giveaways included everything electrical, a hodgepodge of wide fluorescent ties, his only suit. By the end of the party, everything was gone, even the Lectric Shave Dennis had gotten for his bar mitzvah, the year he turned thirteen. He wanted only the essentials of his life in his cabin—his books, his files, a typewriter, a couch, a large Oriental rug, some odd pieces of furniture, his hat collection, his pipe collection, his "lady," and her three dogs.

Dennis, his girlfriend, Patricia, and his best friend spent the better portion of the day unloading the truck and car, cleaning out the cabin, hooking up the propane to the lights, the two-burner stove, and the refrigerator, making up the beds, and equipping the outhouse with the necessities—toilet paper and air freshener. His neighbors, Brooks and Cyndy Ryder, drove the mile to the cabin that afternoon with a basket of fresh vegetables from their garden. That night they danced and drank mugs full of beer at the annual Polish festival on the stage behind the VFW hall.

Through the summer, Dennis entertained a stream of friends at the cabin, twenty people in all. They came from

Long Island, Brooklyn, Detroit, and California and stayed a
few days, sometimes a week, until they got tired of the
cramped, primitive quarters, the outhouse, the mosquitoes,
the cabin mice, the leaky roof, and the absence of running
water, electricity, showers, and telephones.

"How long are you going to live like this?" they asked.

"I'm in no hurry," Dennis would say, then show them the
books and literature he and Patricia had collected about
Bali. "When the weather turns, that's where we're going."

Dennis sold his Karmann Ghia to his best friend in New
York and bought a jeep. He bought an out-of-tune piano for
$20. Frankie Amarosa, whose family ran the hardware
store, helped him dig a second outhouse, on which Dennis
painted the words "Think globally, act locally."

Frankie showed him how to cut down a tree without
killing himself, how to lay a new floor in his cabin, how to
rig up an outdoor shower. A plumber, Frankie devised a sort
of Rube Goldberg method for bathing. Water was collected
in rain barrels in the back of the cabin, mostly supplied by
the rain that ran off the roof. Dennis heated three or four
gallons of water on his stove, poured it into a bucket, and
hoisted it up a tall tree. A complex convergence of pipes and
faucets and—voilà!—a hot shower.

Dennis loved to show off his new contraption. "This is
my shower. And this," he'd say opening his arms in a
magnanimous gesture that took in the cabin, the trees, and
the better portion of his wooded world, "is my shower
curtain."

Toward the end of summer, Patricia called it quits. She
moved back to New York, taking her dogs with her. Dennis
was alone. And free. He could do anything. He had no
commitments, few responsibilities, no one to answer to. He
assembled the pile of information on Bali, neatly stacked it
away in his file cabinet. He would spend the winter at his
cabin.

For Dennis, the summer had felt no different from any other. As a student and then an educator, he was used to having his summers off, carousing with friends and then returning to school in September. But this September had arrived and he was still on vacation. "Vacation?" he thought to himself. "This isn't vacation. This is my *life*." Fewer out-of-town friends came to visit, until none came at all. They had returned to their jobs, their school-year routines.

Dennis spent more and more time at the hardware store, shooting the breeze with the Amarosa family, picking up advice on cabin living.

"Yep, I've decided to stay here through the winter," Dennis told the Amarosas.

"Are you planning on renting a room at Winchester House?" Frankie's dad, Mr. Amarosa, asked.

"No, no. I'm staying in my cabin," Dennis said.

"Am I invited to your funeral?" Frankie asked.

Mornings, Dennis worked around the cabin. Toward noon, he drove his jeep down the mountain, parked it in front of the hardware store, did a few minutes of warm-up exercises, then took off down Main Street at a jog. He developed a circuit that took him through the heart of downtown, then left up Warwick Road into the country, along a long stretch of land owned by farmer Elmer Johnson, left again to Route 119, then back into town, completing the first five miles. Then he'd run the route again. He was conditioning for a marathon that fall. Dennis's jogging garb included sweat pants, jogging shorts over the sweat pants, a T-shirt or sweatshirt with the hood pulled over his head, and sometimes a knit hat over that. When Mr. Amarosa saw him dressed like that, it nearly always prompted a lecture.

"Dennis, folks around here just don't dress that way. They don't go jogging either. Men here work up an honest sweat in the fields or the mill. They don't need to run around to do that."

While he was at it, Mr. Amarosa would usually get in a jab about Dennis's beard.

"Why don't you shave it off, Dennis? It doesn't do anything for you. If you ask me, you're hiding behind it."

"C'mon, Frank, I'd get cold without my beard," Dennis would joke. Then on a more serious note, he'd shrug, saying, "Hey man, this is me. This isn't a costume. This is what I feel comfortable in."

After jogging, he'd typically order a pizza at Deano's Pizzeria, then take it next door to the hardware store, where he'd sit and eat lunch with the Amarosas. The back room was actually an oversized closet with filing cabinets, a wooden desk, and shelves to the ceiling, heaped with stock, paperwork, family pictures. Sitting back there, Dennis felt like an insider. Occasionally, he pitched in at the store if something needed to be unloaded, stacked, or moved. But more often than not, he'd just talk or listen.

Dennis was at the hardware store one day that summer when he heard Frankie say he had a plumbing job to do in neighboring Richmond at the Seekircher's.

"Walt and Louise Seekircher?" Dennis asked excitedly.

"Yeah, how'd you know?"

"I can't believe it," Dennis said. "I'd forgotten they had a summer place in southern New Hampshire. They're people I knew from my job on Long Island."

Within a minute, Frankie had supplied Dennis with a hat and a work jacket. The two of them piled into his truck—a pickup with a storage top over the truck bed that read, on both sides, Amarosa's Plumbing, Heating, Cooling. Just before reaching the house, Dennis and Frankie switched seats, and Dennis drove the last bit into the Seekircher's driveway. Just as they'd hoped, Walt and Louise were there to greet them. Dennis got out of the cab, carrying a tool box.

"Excuse me, is this the Seekircher residence?" he said.
The couple did a double take.

"Yes," they stammered, trying to place the bearded man who was so far from the context in which they knew him. Then it snapped clear. "Dennis? Is that you?"

Dennis roared with laughter.

"It *is* you! I recognize that laugh anywhere!"

He and the Seekirchers talked and reminisced, hovering near Frankie as he did the plumbing repairs.

"Did you know what an *amazing principal* Dr. Littky was?" the Seekirchers gushed. "He built that middle school from scratch and turned it into a model of great education. Educators came from all over the place to see it. We sure were sorry to see him go."

As the errant plumbers headed back to town, Frankie turned to his friend. "*Doctor* Littky?" he said. "I had no idea you were some hotshot principal from Long Island."

"I'm not anymore. I'm *Dennis* Littky from Winchester. I'm just cuttin' wood like everybody else."

As the summer days shortened, Dennis worried more and more about making the cabin livable for the winter. He didn't know, except in a vague, ephemeral sort of way, what that meant. He knew he had to insulate the cabin and obtain some firewood. He had the jeep, but figured he might get a snowmobile too. Frankie, all too aware of his friend's ignorance about the ways of the wild, often drove up to the cabin to lend a hand. Frankie's father just shook his head and said, "How can you *look* so much like a mountain man, but know so little about being one?"

With his great shock of beard, plaid flannel shirts, down vests, jeans, hiking boots, and leather hats, Dennis could have passed any Hollywood screening test for a mountain man. Unaided, however, he likely would have perished that first winter.

One day, a man drove up the road to the cabin. He introduced himself to Dennis as Frankie's father-in-law.

"Frankie said you could use some help. I wasn't doing anything. Thought maybe I'd give you a hand."

He made the rounds of the small rough-hewn home, rubbing his chin, punching on walls, climbing up on the roof. He kept making comments about what needed to be done to "the camp."

"Hey, man," Dennis protested. "It's not a camp, it's my *castle.*"

"You need a new roof for the camp, no doubt about it," Frankie's father-in-law said. "Probably won't last the winter. If it doesn't, you won't." Then he spouted off a list of materials Dennis would need to do the job—flashing, shingles, tar, nails—a list Dennis ran through his mind several times so that he would be sure to remember.

The net result of the visit was a flurry of hammering, ripping, and cursing. New roof, insulation, sealed cracks. Dennis, who was more adept at handling a pencil than a hammer, more comfortable leading than following, tried his best to keep pace with his woodsmen friends.

Still, even with all this progress, Dennis woke up with a knot in his stomach. Some said winter could happen in New England well before Thanksgiving; it could hit very hard. Several made a point to tell Dennis about the man with a cabin at the base of Pudding Hill, within shouting distance of Dennis's home, who returned one winter only to discover his cabin missing. He finally found it—so the story goes—when he realized that underneath the snow where he stood was the roof of his house.

Dennis became obsessed with the approach of winter. From his front door, he'd draw deeply on his pipe, watching the sun-saturated valley chill under long shadows, darkness soaking up the light earlier and earlier. Alone, in the cool ink of night, he would worry. Up there, he was utterly isolated: no telephone, no electricity, no running water, no ready companion except the families of mice that shared his cabin. Lying on his bed in the dark, he listened to the mice nosing the kitchen for their dinner, night birds (he wasn't sure what kinds) calling in the distance. He could hear the wind whip up the hillside, feel it cut through the chinks in the cabin. Sometimes he heard high-pitched screams and howls from the woods. Fascinated by the sounds, Dennis would rouse himself from bed to stand on his deck and drink in the nighttime noises. Were the animals mating or just throwing a party? he wondered. He'd read about wild dogs. They were a strange breed, something that looked like a cross between a dog and a fox, and they roamed the woods, rarely seen.

Dennis listened, watching as the bats swooped past the cabin, then hovered overhead.

4
The Mountain Man

IN HIS CABIN, IT WAS as though he were stranded on some uncharted atoll. But he was no castaway. He'd planned this, dreamed of making it happen. He'd walked away from a lot to get here; this cabin was where he wanted to be.

He'd driven his jeep past Thayer High School the other day, deliberately going out of his way. The parking lot was full of cars but devoid of people. The only sound was his engine winding down as he shifted. Behind those doors, he knew, was a beehive of activity. He didn't know the faces or the names, but the bustle was something he knew about. Most of his life had been spent in buildings like this.

This mountain man stuff was his latest challenge. He'd been out of his element before, but this challenge was a kind he'd never experienced. A suburban boy, a city boy, Dennis was definitely out of his element in the woods. In the past, he'd always battled familiar elements on known turf— school. A decade earlier he'd taken on principalship of a brand new middle school at the age of twenty-seven. That had been a risk. He'd done it without flinching, and he'd done it successfully. It'd been a risk to walk away from the University of Michigan, with his Ph.D. unfinished, to take a job as program director at Ocean Hill-Brownsville Demonstration School District, a black and Puerto Rican community in Brooklyn, New York.

"You want action?" one of the educators involved with the district had said. "Then get your ass down here. You want to sit in the ivory tower, stay home."

The challenge had been irresistible.

His mother hadn't liked his talk of "the action"—she knew what men meant when they used that phrase. She'd been chilled to the bone by the vision of her only son lying dead in the middle of all that action. One day she stormed into his cramped apartment in Ann Arbor, flanked by his father, one of his sisters, an aunt, an uncle, and a grandmother—waving copies of *Time* magazine under his nose.

"Black vs. Jew," the headline screamed. "Confrontation at Ocean Hill-Brownsville." There had been several shootings, stabbings, and fires in the school district.

His mother was firm. "I'm not leaving your place, Denny, not until you tell me you won't go. You're only twenty-four! I won't lose a son this way. I won't!"

Born July 19, 1944, Dennis grew up in a tidy, red-brick house on a corner lot of one of Detroit's working class neighborhoods, the son of a podiatrist. Despite Detroit's sullied reputation, the Littky family led a fairly cloistered and secure life in their protected patch of the Motor City. Dennis was the second and middle child of a strong-willed mother and a mild-mannered father. The Littkys were exceptional in their neighborhood because they were Jewish, one of only a few Jewish families in that area. This condition had no bearing, good or bad, on the young Dennis—it was simply the case.

Dennis attended a small school in his neighborhood through the eighth grade, where he was a good athlete, a top student, a jokester, very popular, and vice president of his eighth grade class. High school was a different story entirely. Some four thousand students flooded the building from several of the swankiest communities in the city.

When Dennis was a student there, the school was aggressively competitive. It registered some of the highest achievement scores in the state and consistently sent an impressive majority of its graduates to college. Dennis Littky was not among the highest achievers at the school, but he managed to hold his own. The only area in which he excelled was baseball, exercising a fast arm and a loud mouth.

He entered the University of Michigan in 1962. His older sister, who also attended U of M, had passed along the lore of the campus—*the* Jewish fraternity to belong to was Zeta Beta Tau. Dennis felt out of his league in the company of the "cool, rich guys" who dominated the fraternity, but persisted in his determination to be accepted into its ranks. To his amazement, he was.

The fraternity served an enormous and important role during his years in college. Socially insecure, Dennis had fallen in with some of the coolest dudes on campus, automatically gaining an identity he craved and entrée into elite circles. Unlike most of his fraternity brothers, Dennis had to work to help pay his way through school. He waited tables and washed dishes at the fraternity house to earn money. Dennis was proud of himself for being un-wealthy but still cool.

His first year in school was an academic disaster. A combination of gang housing, bad study habits, and chronic carousing conspired to set Dennis off on a bad track. Following a tip from a veteran student, he'd scheduled his classes in such a way that he'd be forced to stay on campus all day, thus giving him structured time to study between classes. The plan backfired. Instead of studying between classes, he loafed around, then returned to his dorm in time for dinner and partying with his chums. He didn't start studying, typically, until close to midnight. The next day he'd force himself out of bed to attend his 8 A.M. class. The net effect of all this was infectious mononucleosis. It kept him in bed, perpetually tired, for months. In the meantime, his grades slipped ever lower until, with a 1.9 grade point average his first semester, he was placed on academic probation. The following semester, he managed to pull up his grades enough to stay in school and declare himself a psychology major. His choice of psychology was more default than plan. He balked at the notion that anyone could determine his life's work at the young age of eighteen. The one thing he did know was that he wanted variety; he didn't want his work to look the same every day.

By the time he entered his third year, Dennis was still waffling about what to pursue. Still, he signed himself into psychology courses. Then, on a whim, two weeks into the semester, he declared a new major—advertising—and entered the journalism department, where he was required to complete a series of newspaper courses. The first day in a newswriting class, Littky, already two weeks behind in the course work before he'd even started, was listening to the professor, enthralled by a story he was telling about a bank robbery. Then the professor shouted, "Begin!" Suddenly, from out of nowhere, typewriters appeared on all the desks in the class, save for his. It was some minutes before Littky discovered the typewriter attached under his desk and figured out how to pull it out. All around him, students were typing away furiously on what he concluded was a news story about the bank robbery the professor had been talking about. Littky began hunting and pecking on the typewriter. Just as he finished typing his name and the title of the news story, the teacher shouted out, "Time!" In one great wave, the students yanked their stories out of their typewriters and handed them in. Littky pulled his out, crumpled it up, and returned to his psychology classes the next day.

That year, one of Dennis's classes sent him and his classmates to an area mental hospital, where they worked directly with patients. Suddenly, as though someone had found his "on" button, he reeled with energy and enthusiasm. School, which had been a passive medium, changed for him. He was *involved*—thinking, creating. He devised a recreation program to help in the recovery of severely ill mental patients. Dennis, the mediocre student, suddenly became the star pupil.

He entered graduate school at U of M in a combined clinical psychology/education major, where he developed an introductory psychology course for undergraduates. Those who signed up for his class received a room number, time and days of the week the class would meet, but no instructor's name. At the first class, Dennis arrived wearing chinos, boots, and a crewneck sweater and sat in the back of the room chatting nervously with the students, many of whom were experiencing their first college class.

Clean-shaven, with neatly trimmed hair, and consummately boyish in his appearance, Dennis looked as much like a freshman as the real ones sitting around him. In walked a handsome, stern-faced man with a close-cropped beard, wearing a dark blue three-piece suit and carrying a briefcase and an armload of books. The class quieted down. Without smiling, the man turned to the board and wrote his name—Mr. Wolfe.

"Class," Mr. Wolfe barked, "there will be surprise quizzes in this course—a lot of them. The only one you'll know about will be tomorrow."

Dennis raised his hand. "Mr. Wolfe, now that we are in college, do we still need surprise quizzes?"

"Young man, my graduate students need surprise quizzes." Mr. Wolfe set his jaw. "I work on a bell-shaped curve—the same number will get A's as fail in this course and most of you will earn grades somewhere in between. That's the law in this class."

Dennis raised his hand.

"Is this important, young man?"

"Don't you think it's kind of discouraging to know that a set number of us will fail regardless of how hard we try?"

"That's life."

"What if we all work hard, do well, and deserve A's?"

"A bell-shaped curve doesn't work that way."

"I know, that's exactly my complaint."

By now, students had turned in their seats, stunned by the aggressive fellow in the back of the room.

Mr. Wolfe continued his labored description of the course.

Dennis's hand shot up.

"What is it this time?" Mr. Wolfe snapped.

"I thought this course was supposed to get us out into the world and actually work with mental patients."

Mr. Wolfe slammed his books on the desk, packed his briefcase, and turned on his heel. "Young man, if you think you can do a better job, then get up here." He stormed out of the room.

"I'm gettin' out of this class," one student said, and got up to leave. Others followed his lead.

"Hang on a second," Dennis said. "Wasn't I speaking for all of you?"

"Yeah, I guess you were," a thin, bespectacled freshman said.

"That teacher seems real unfair," another student said.

The discussion continued. Finally, Dennis stood up, walked to the front of the room, and said, "Hi. I'm Dennis Littky. Your teacher."

He definitely had their attention.

"The guy out in the hall—that's my roommate." Wolfe came back in the room, smiling this time. The students applauded.

The first unit of the class was aimed at learning through formal education, exploring different ways people learn.

Littky's antics were intended to confront those issues head-on, engaging the students, getting them involved in the class.

By the time Dennis's mother was demanding that he keep clear of the educational imbroglio in Brooklyn, Dennis had been a teaching fellow for three years, earned the University of Michigan's distinguished teaching award, and completed all his course work for a Ph.D. in education and psychology. Two weeks later he was married to his graduate school sweetheart and was living in New York, sporting the great shock of beard that would become his trademark. Though the U of M campus roiled with long-haired, antiwar protestors, Dennis had never joined the fray. It was on his mother's advice that he grew a beard; she hoped it would make him look older.

Ocean Hill–Brownsville was in the middle of the most conspicuous display of public school reform in the nation, and Dennis intended to be a part of it. This was educational change—he'd read about it, learned the mechanisms of it, and now he wanted to be part of it. It was an experimental school district set up to explore decentralization. A three-month teachers' strike had just ended. Dennis was determined to make a contribution, and he sure as hell wanted it to be somewhere that would make a difference. Ocean Hill–Brownsville was looking for someone to head Project Giant Step, a reading program for kindergartners through eighth graders. The object of the program was to teach reading skills by involving parents and providing concrete incentives for the children.

At his job interview, he'd been dumbstruck by the hostility of the place. It had the flavor of despair. There was a palpable ache to the need for change.

It was his training in the psychology of behavior modification that landed him the job. But the incident that convinced him he wanted it happened right after his initial interview. As he left the building, he saw a school bus pass by. From wheel to wheel, black children were dangling from the *outside* of the bus, laughing, shrieking, swearing.

"This is wild!" Dennis had exclaimed, bug-eyed. He'd never seen anything like that—it struck him as other-worldly, exciting, tantalizing. This was the place he wanted to be. A couple of weeks later he packed everything he had into two suitcases and moved to New York with his new wife.

The Brooklyn schools had problems on top of problems. They'd been besieged by hot-shot academics from all over the country—most of them white. These "educators" looked at the schools as laboratories, typically confining their experiments to one or two days. One gaggle would no sooner leave than another would show up, ready to test yet another pet theory. Then they'd move out to make room for the next batch.

On Dennis's first day in one of the elementary schools, the principal, the PTA president, and a parent threw him out. They told him never to come back. They didn't know who he was, why he was there, or anything about him, and they didn't care to. When he tried to tell them he was supposed to work with them full-time they didn't hear him or didn't believe him. He was from a university, wasn't he? He was *white*, wasn't he? That was enough—they told him to get lost.

Littky persevered. The unit administrator of Ocean Hill–Brownsville was a tough, taciturn black man by the name of Rhody McCoy, an innovator who put the needs of children before all else. McCoy, Littky's boss, warmed to him almost immediately. Littky regarded McCoy as his mentor.

Shortly after Littky arrived, McCoy told him the New York City Board of Education was giving him trouble about

Project Giant Step. He said the project was in jeopardy; it might be stopped and the money returned to the state. Even so, Littky continued to work, quickly realizing that his knowledge of the principles of behavior modification and ability to coordinate programs were not all it would take to make things work at Ocean Hill–Brownsville. Meanwhile, McCoy was being harassed by members of the community for fraternizing with "that honky with the red beard." After three months, Littky, all but impoverished, had still received no paycheck.

"Not only was I learning about unknown forces and hidden factors which were influencing my program, but I was now able to use this knowledge to further my chances of conducting a successful project," Littky would write in his dissertation, printed in 1970. After five months working at the school, Littky managed to gain some allies. He gathered enough information about the community and the school to implement his experimental reading program. The program used behavior modification techniques to influence children to learn to read. For example, students were rewarded with points for answering questions correctly, then were able to use their points to "buy" free time to play games, model clay, draw, or build models. When possible, children who broke the rules were ignored, while those obeying the rules were rewarded with points. If a discipline problem continued, the child was told to close his or her book, silently count to sixty, then open the book and begin again. Or children were divided into groups and rewarded with points for good behavior. The members of the group would handle disturbances in their own ranks in order to keep earning points.

In the end, the experiment proved fruitful, turning nonreaders into happy, competent learners.

Littky worked well with the students, staff, and school board of the Ocean Hill–Brownsville experimental district.

For the most part, he'd known what he was doing. When he didn't, he took risks and managed to improvise effectively, which was nearly as good. But his feelings toward the all-white New York City Board of Education were of a different stripe. He was more at odds with them than he'd ever been in the black community. The local board worked *with* McCoy and his staff. The city board, which had power over the local districts, seemed to Littky to be more effective at obstructing rather than helping education.

But under any circumstances, the experimental district was time tagged. When the experiment ended in the summer of 1970 and the Ocean Hill–Brownsville Schools were absorbed into another larger district, Littky moved on. In the midst of it all, he'd completed his dissertation and earned his doctorate.

He began teaching at Stony Brook, one of the state universities of New York, training teachers. After less than a year in that position, it occurred to him that training teachers was a futile task if they were immediately absorbed in an environment that didn't allow them to exercise the concepts that he wanted to pass along. So he went into the schools and started working with practicing teachers, who would then take on some of Littky's students as student teachers. Very quickly he learned that even these efforts were stymied by administrators who were resistant to change. After Littky had been working three months with a handful of teachers at a Long Island school developing a paperback reading program, the principal at the last minute reinstated into the reading program the traditional basal readers—the "Dick, Jane, and Sally" approach to reading, which Littky found limiting and, more often than not, counterproductive.

Littky had been working actively with teachers in the Shoreham school when the head of the Shoreham School District asked Littky to write up a job description for the principal of a new multimillion-dollar middle school that would merge the Shoreham and Wading River school districts on Long Island. Littky drafted a profile of the kind of person who ought to run this new school. The principal would have to be someone who could successfully coordinate curriculum with the "open-concept" plan of the building. The building was designed with three wings—spokes—anchored to a central hub that housed the library and the fine arts areas. The walls between classrooms were moveable. The open structure of the building practically demanded an innovative educational structure.

Starting a school from scratch, unencumbered by preset routine, old ideas, and bad habits was an extraordinary opportunity, Littky figured. The possibilities of building a school that integrated academic subjects and brought learning to life for students were exhilarating.

Littky decided he'd be perfect for the job.

He submitted his application and, after a series of rigorous interviews, was voted in unanimously by the school board in the spring of 1972. He began work immediately, handpicking his staff. With attractive salaries and prospects for a new school that was open to innovative methods of teaching, Littky attracted a young, energetic, promising staff. As Littky put it, he'd attracted "the best and brightest in the field."

Littky threw himself into his job with unwavering commitment and energy. He went at it with his full body, talking fast, acting fast, making decisions, doling out responsibility. He lived his life in and through the school. It was all-absorbing, all-encompassing. His three-year marriage foundered from neglect. Soon he and his wife amicably agreed to divorce. For Littky, it was the beginning of a pattern. He would have many more intense relationships with women, all of which would end after a few years when Dennis's attention flagged in favor of work. He would persist in his unwillingness to make an enduring commitment that included marriage and children.

For Littky, forming the school was like building his own home. He even picked out the curtains. Long before the students tumbled in, he collected his staff for a week-long planning session and then spent the rest of the summer preparing. The staff, for the most part, worked with the same feverish energy. Many of the teachers had worked under the yoke of traditional teaching systems, where the people and methodologies were all but impervious to change. Their efforts to open the learning process had been met with wrath by administrations that called one husband-wife teaching team "detrimental to kids." They resisted the mind-set that treated students as a category instead of as individuals who learn in many different ways and at different rates. They were, on the whole, people who had been frustrated in their previous jobs and wanted desperately to make a change that would allow them to do some "real teaching."

Littky wanted people who were inclined toward complete devotion to their work. Ross Burkhardt, a social studies teacher who'd come to Shoreham with his wife, Diane, also a social studies teacher, kept a copious log of his transition from a traditional high school to the very atypical middle school under Dennis Littky. Through hundreds and hundreds of pages and several volumes, Ross recorded, reflected on, and analyzed his professional development in the new school. His devotion to Littky was unwavering.

Ross, like many of Littky's teachers, had been a superstar to the students at his previous school and a pain in the ass to his administrators. At meetings, he'd learned to steel himself to the resistance he encountered when he tried to communicate his ideas about education. Then, suddenly, at Shoreham he found himself surrounded by open-minded individuals who seemed as eager to receive his ideas as spout their own. And to top it off, he had a principal who harnessed, encouraged, and activated these ideas, and who looked and acted more like a friend or camp counselor than the stiff, besuited administrators Ross had become so accustomed to.

The week of the first staff workshop, when many of the faculty members were meeting for the first time, Ross wrote:

I found it perplexingly easy to communicate ideas, something I wasn't used to among so large a group of teachers. At one point I turned to Randi and said, "It's really difficult to communicate easily." I'm used to having to try harder to get my ideas across. Normally I expect my listener (providing he is even listening) to be hostile, uninterested, stupid, unable to understand, unsympathetic, and lacking in education. With this group, I found them to be interested and quick to grasp what I was trying to say. I floundered at first, because I was overstating my ideas, but then it dawned on me that these people, by virtue of common and similar experiences, dug what I was saying right away.

... The week long workshop began on Monday morning the 26th at 7 A.M. with 22 people grouped around a large table in the cluster. The nervousness expressed in smiles and chatter was predictable. Dennis quieted us down and started telling/sharing his vision of a school for kids. He touched upon several points: "A school for kids—they should take a more important role in making decisions— kids should work with us—kids ought to know more about the education process—the arts—usually seen as specials— should be integrated—kids as consumers vs. producers—we want producers—kids traditionally consume; give them real roles and let them produce—flexibility." He spoke of advisory groups that each of us will have, with 15 kids in a group. It will be like a homeroom but the function will be counselling, advising, keeping tabs on those kids (and their parents), creating at least one stable and permanent nonchoice fixture as a constant throughout the year. Dennis also spoke of the importance of involving the community as a part of the school. Getting kids out into the community was one aspect of it, but there were other things he mentioned also. We talked about the political climate of the community and how a first name basis that Dennis had with kids had drawn a lot of fire, so he had decided that that battle at this point is not politically worth it, and there will be no first name thing next year. Okay, I understand, even though I wish that kids would have the choice to use our first names or not, as they pleased. . . . Somewhere on that first day the board elections were mentioned, and at present all five of the board members favor the open concept and support Dennis. There is a conservative running, according to the story we got, and he might win, but that would still make it a 4–1 voting majority with a multi-million dollar open-concept school under construction and probably ready for occupancy in September '73. So even if a swing occurred on the board, the building is there, and the program must reflect the realities of the building.

Indeed, Ross's concern about the conservative element proved prescient. A tight cadre of self-proclaimed conservatives came down hard on the open system of education and on the existing board's hiring a man who wasn't properly certified to be a principal. They also didn't like Littky's style, complaining that he was too radical. At a meeting just before the election, several candidates aired their complaints to a packed audience. The calm of the incumbent members, all of whom supported Littky and the brand of education he was pushing, didn't prepare the audience for the caustic personal attack on Littky from the malcontents. One called him "an unqualified person" and swore that he'd not subject his kids to Littky's experimentations.

Though Littky was in the process of completing course work for certification, the board that hired him had not made that fact public. At the meeting, the opposition candidates spent considerable energy ripping up the turf at Littky's expense. Dennis appealed to the moderator to give him a chance to respond to the tirade, but the moderator refused. Littky, wearing a $2 sport coat he'd picked up at a mission store and a wide multicolored tie, sat quietly and ate the criticism. When he asked again for a chance to comment, the moderator said, "Absolutely not. This is a meeting for the board candidates. However, after this meeting is adjourned, anyone wishing to hear you speak can do so." Someone called immediately for an adjournment. People began to stalk out of the room. Littky strode to the front of the room and pleaded with the audience to stay, admonishing those who had the nerve to criticize but not the decency to stay and listen to another side. He appealed to the critics to give the middle school a chance.

"With his voice trembling at times, at times nearly breaking with emotion, he spelled out his amazing credentials and qualifications," Ross wrote. "Then he talked about the staff of the middle school, and outlined the amount of hours we have all been putting in since last June. He urged anyone interested to come to the meeting next Tuesday night to have their questions answered. It was Dennis baring his soul, stripping himself naked in front of the wolves and saying, 'Here I am.'"

When Littky finished, a loud ovation erupted.

Though none of the opposition candidates won seats on the board, the criticism continued. Littky understood that until the move to the new building was completed and the staff had worked together long enough to hone their new ideas, the criticism would persist. But he also believed that once the school was running in line with his vision, no one could miss seeing the magic of the place.

Toward the end of the first semester, Ross's wife, Diane, made an observation that reflected the view of many. "Shoreham is a school based on rationality," she said. By that she meant there were no blanket rules for anyone. If a teacher asked students to do something, the teacher could expect it to be done. If a kid blurted out, "No, forget it," the teacher might force the student to undertake the task anyway. But if the kid approached the teacher and explained rationally why he or she didn't want to do it, generally the student got his or her way, provided an alternative could be found. Ross, echoing the sentiment, wrote: "The teachers at Shoreham seem to listen to kids more and recognize that not every kid fits into a peg hole, and that if a kid has a legitimate gripe, the kid deserves a fair shake. That is what I call a rational school. And I love it."

If it was possible for a school to bear the imprint of a single man, Shoreham–Wading River Middle School was Dennis Littky's. The school was personal. It took a student body of some six hundred and divided it into three smaller middle schools. Each wing housed about two hundred students, each with its own staff. During his tenure as principal, two hundred people visited the school each year. They came to study the programs, to see how they worked. There were three television programs, a short movie, sixty conference presentations, and more published articles than Dennis could remember. One of the compliments was from prominent psychologist Leonard Krasner in a book about learning environments, which described Littky's Long Island school as possibly "the most innovative use of designed environments in a school setting since Dewey's lab school." Being linked with a giant like John Dewey was the highest praise he'd ever received. But the students gave the most telling endorsement of the school possible: it was hard to keep them away. Overall, the most severe criticism the school suffered was from parents who said their children were rarely home. It was, above all things, a place of learning, a place of joy. By the end of Littky's sixth year at Shoreham, many of his most vicious detractors had become his most outspoken supporters.

It was the middle school, his life on Long Island, the accolades and attention that he left behind when he came to his cabin on Pudding Hill. In Winchester, he was no longer the wunderkind principal of a fancy school, the firebrand educator, the master of change. Now he was just Dennis, the mountain man.

Nights grew cooler; the sun sank below the horizon earlier each day. Together, chill nights and short days made a quickening rhythm that marked the headlong pace toward winter. A lush green canopy had shielded the cabin from the summer sun; now the leaves had thinned, turned amber and brittle. All around him, the woods were getting ready. There was movement everywhere: scurrying, furry beasts darted here and there, carrying food to their winter stores. The wind rasped and rattled the dry leaves.

Getting ready for winter became his passion: How many cords of wood would he need? How many nails to finish shingling the roof? How many days to insulate the cabin?

The dawn woke him, drew him from his bed, set him to work. Nightfall signaled the end of day and carried him to sleep.

The mountain became his timekeeper, his taskmaster. It stirred him, calmed him, made him work. The mountain's brooding quiet became his quiet; its drama became his drama. His moods shifted from high to low with the ease of the wind. With the added hours of night, he slept long and comfortably, ten, sometimes twelve, hours at a stretch. Sleep was not the escape it had been before, no longer the six-hour respite from interminably hard days spent outside himself. Things were different now. Sleep was the soft underbelly of awakeness.

The day was cold, clear—a perfect New England autumn. Dennis teetered on the cabin roof, nailing down the last shingles. He'd fallen into a rhythm—place a shingle, pick up a nail and pound it home with two whacks, place another shingle. His shirt sleeves were rolled up over his elbows; a light sweat stained the rim of his Detroit Tigers cap.

He was nearly done. Along the front of the cabin was a stack of firewood almost as high as the eaves. The insulation was in, the floor finished. He'd hung two doors and built a new kitchen counter.

Dennis looked out over the valley. He could see more than seventy miles, all the way to Vermont and Massachusetts. The sun had begun its plunge toward the horizon. He hardly ever missed a sunset. Here on the peak of the roof, the view was somehow more beautiful. Long before it was his, the cabin was called the House of the Golden Windows. Light from the setting sun sprayed off the windows, sending golden rays shooting back. Shadows collided with the light to produce an earthbound aurora on the trees and leaves below. The sky soaked up gold and amber from the sun. Cirrus clouds rode high, like flaxen, wind-ruffled hair. The view made him gasp. He spread his arms. He was clearheaded, strong, happier than he could remember.

Any day it could snow. He was ready.

5
First Winter

THE SNOW CAME DOWN STEADILY. As night wore on and the mercury dropped, the big flakes froze into a slick glaze. By morning Dennis's corner of New England lay covered in a thick blanket of white.

Dawn streamed through his window—diffused, penetrating. Dennis woke up.

Yeah! It had happened!

Let's see—jeep and chains: ready. Cross-country skis: waxed. Snowmobile: gassed up. Snowshoes: inspected, hung over the fireplace. Right. So what to do? Ski? Bushwack? There were countless options—he couldn't make up his mind. He went back to bed.

An hour later he threw open the door and walked onto the front porch. The snow crunched happily with each footfall. Everything was white. The evergreens sagged, aching under their new weight. Snow was stacked in line-like heaps on the bare branches of the trees. The down-slope of Pudding Hill looked like a charcoal sketch—a twisting tangle of gray trunks and white limbs, as though an artist had taken a sketch pad and hastily penciled in a smattering of trees.

The snow-covered valley beyond seemed bigger than the day before. Scattered houses were marked by fingers of smoke rising from chimney tops; mountain ranges marched into the distance like the white-gray backs of tremendous hibernating beasts. Everything was snow-white, sky-blue or shadow-gray.

The day before, this same scene had been a hodgepodge of browns—rust, brindle, ocher, umber—the air harsh, windswept, ominous. All day Dennis had felt anxious, tentative. He had split a waist-high stack of wood, more than he needed for a week. He had driven into town, stocked up on propane, filled water jugs.

Now, from where he stood on the porch, his world appeared soft, blunt. All the sharp lines, the autumn decay, had disappeared under a clean unsullied blanket, everything rounded and quiet.

"Amazing," Dennis said reverently.

He took a deep breath. The cold air that came into him carried a kind of ecstasy. It was the kind of thing he had to share with somebody.

He spun on his heels, stepping into the cabin. He crossed the room in two steps and grabbed a microphone. He twisted a dial with one hand and drove the mike button home with the other.

"Breaker, breaker! One-nine breaker!" He held the mike at arm's length and boomed. "Breaker! Come on back to the Mountain on this wild white mornin'."

A female voice crackled with static and laughter from the speaker.

"Whoa! Hello, Mountain! Drop yer gain a notch or two, will ya? Lordy, you'll wake the dead! And good mornin' back atcha. It's a beaut, for true."

"What a storm! It's *bee-you-tee-ful!*"

"I hear ya, Mountain."

"Who've I got here?" Dennis said. "Is that you, Vanna?"

"Right on, Mountain."

"Isn't it . . . wild?" The word was inadequate.

"One of God's gifts, Mountain."

"True, true. Say, hold on a minute, Vanna. I want to peek outside." He pushed open a window and peered out.

Dazzled again by the view, he clicked the button. "I can make out the river and the trailer park and . . . there! Yeah, I gotcha, Vanna! You got that blue housecoat on again, don't ya?"

"Aw, go on, Mountain—you're full of it."

"What gave me away?"

"It's two miles from your window to mine, Mountain. I can't even make out your cabin from down here."

"So I got good eyes."

"My bathrobe's pink."

"So I'm color-blind."

"So what am I drinking?"

"Coffee, what else?"

"It's orange juice."

"I *said* I was color-blind."

"You're a riot, Mountain."

"That's my charm."

"So I've heard you say."

Dennis studied the view while a woman in another trailer broke in to say good morning and swap some gossip with Vanna. After a few minutes, the friends turned to practical matters. For people who couldn't afford telephones, and many thereabouts couldn't, the CB provided a vital link with the outside world.

Sure-Shot Shirley, Vanna's sister, broke in to join the coffee klatch. Dennis smiled and eavesdropped. As he listened, he fed some logs into the stove. He heard the friendly morning banter and ate alone, but he wasn't alone. He might never meet the people behind those voices, but they were a family to him, of sorts.

Since coming to Pudding Hill, Dennis had kept a journal. He'd already filled one spiral notebook with his thoughts and was starting on a new one.

Sunday, Jan. 7, 1979. Evening.

I am beginning to understand what being alone really

means—There are different levels of being alone—I feel I am venturing on a very deep level because of my circumstances—Man can depend on all kinds of things for support and communication & connections to the world.

The usual support systems are gone—No job—the biggest for me—No best friend—which became very important over the last couple of years—

No one thing that I am focused around—merely living—No intensity. No easy access out of the cabin—an adventure or catastrophe each time—

Cold—which is not only physical but psychological—
No TV—

No hangouts where there are familiar faces—

But then why do I think it is so important—neither being with somebody or being alone is necessarily better—each can be amazing—each can be bad—(it is easier to be bad with someone)

I realize I need a little yes or good or do that to tip me over the edge—I have been working hard to do it myself—No where near as successful as I would like—I keep waiting for the time—

The being alone teaches me that I can be anything I want.

Oh I respect excellence so much—anybody good at anything—it is clean & beautiful.

It warmed up, then got cold again. The net effect was ice. Dennis, now a practiced winter driver, was cavalier about his forays outdoors. He no longer minced up and down the mountain—he attacked it. Chains gave him the added traction and confidence to drive into town nearly every day. On the way, he'd check to see if the white sheet was flying at the Ryders'. They had worked out a code. If someone phoned for Dennis, one of the Ryders tied a white sheet to a tree to signal him. If the sheet was up, he would stop, use the phone, and shoot the breeze with the family. Then he would continue to the post office to check on his mail and to the hardware store for supplies and conversation.

At times, it took him several hours to scale Pudding Hill, but time was one thing he had a lot of. The drive became his daily challenge. His point of glory. His new life made it possible for him to do things he'd never had time to do before.

> For all my life I have worked mostly with my brain—it is time to work with my hands—it is time to further develop my soul—it is time to have no structure in my life—it is time to read—it is time to listen to my body & soul & do what I wish.

In March, Dennis traveled with a busload of fans to Plymouth, where the Thayer High School boys were to compete in the state basketball tournament. He'd become a strong supporter of the local team. He knew most of the boys and was looking forward to the match.

Winchester was a basketball town. The people thereabouts positively loved the game. On weekends in the winter, Dennis could usually find a pickup game at the high school gym. The activity drew boys who played on the high school team, the coach, and some "old timers" like himself who were just after a good workout and some fun.

But Dennis was nervous as he approached the bus. That surprised him. As was his habit with most appointments, he'd arrived early, one of the first to climb aboard. He sat and smiled at the basketball fans as they first straggled, then streamed, into the bus. He recognized some of them but didn't actually know any of them. They gave him curious looks, or no look at all. One by one, the seats filled. Nobody sat beside him. He shifted uncomfortably in his seat.

Moments before the bus roared off, a man dashed across the parking lot and clambered on board. He was the last person standing. He looked for a seat—the last one was next to Dennis. Resigned, he sat down.

Vaguely, Dennis felt punctured.

That night he sat puffing a pipe, watching the sun set. He rubbed the black briar root—it was one of his favorite pipes. Rhody McCoy, head of the Ocean Hill–Brownsville School District during the turbulent sixties, had given it to him. Bulldog tough, McCoy had been his mentor. Dennis admired his strength, his willingness to go to the mat to make schools work for children. It was still a point of pride for Dennis to recall McCoy's words when he handed him the pipe: "To help you remember—Black Is Beautiful."

Smoking this pipe and watching the sun set should have calmed him. But this night, it wasn't working. He gave up on the sun and started pacing. He grabbed a stray twig and snapped it into matchsticks. He did his chores mechanically—logs stacked in the fireplace, dishes washed and put away, pipe cleaned. He stoked his shower with water and washed quickly. His winter shower was a scaled-down version of the Rube Goldberg outdoor model: a bucket hung from a hook driven into the transom of the doorway between the stoveroom and the kitchen. Dennis heated water on the stove and poured it into the bucket, then stood shivering in a metal washtub. He scrubbed himself, dried off, dressed, and began to pace.

His eyes lighted on the big thank-you album that lay on his desk. His friends—students and colleagues alike—had put it together when he left the principal's job on Long Island. He felt a rush of nostalgia and grabbed the album. Pages flicked like rustling leaves.

The twenty-pound scrapbook was held between large leather-bound covers. On the front, the art teacher had drilled two half-dollar-sized holes, then inset behind glass a pencil drawing of a set of eyes—Dennis's—and connected the holes with a line to look like glasses. A beard made of copper enamel completed the illustration.

Dennis ran his hand over the cover, a gesture he'd performed a hundred times before. He flipped through the pages, stared at the snapshots of familiar faces and the friendly letters of farewell—all of them happy. The writers told Dennis what he'd meant to them personally and professionally. There were testimonials from parents, students, and educators.

One caught his eye. It was written by an eighth grader: "How you live, what your outlook is, and how you treat us is really great!"

On another page: "The most satisfying and rewarding years of my professional life were spent working with you during the birth pangs of the Middle School." —Ken Gorman, director of Elementary Education.

Another page: "I love coming to work . . . you offer me a home."

He laughed when he read the sentiments of one sixth grader who, on the first day of school, had mistaken Dennis for the janitor. "I learned one thing," the sixth-grader wrote. "Don't think people are smart because of what they wear. Dr. Littky is very smart, even with jeans on."

They were all like that.

He reached to the corner of the desk, taking up one of the several thick journals Ross Burkhardt had put together. The hundreds of pages Ross wrote during the years he taught under Littky at Shoreham-Wading River Middle School served as a welcome and useful tool for Dennis. Ross made carbon copies of every page and each week gave the new entries to Dennis, hoping they might be helpful.

He read one of Ross's moments of prose and smiled fondly.

Dennis is a genius, a bewhiskered jolly little giant of a man, 27 years old, full of hell and energy, capable of handling divergent personalities, calm, and gentle, shooting baskets every day after the meetings, talking calmly with people about their problems as they perceive them or as he perceives them, urging, prodding, suggesting, joking, supplying the supportive glue for the entire operation, giving us all free rein to do as we please and then working to fit it into the master plan for the super school. Energy flows from him, and he stimulates you to do more, to do it yourself, to get it done. He is in it up to his elbows and doing a fantastic job of getting the school started.

Dennis nodded to himself.

Those were good days.

Everything had turned out perfectly at Shoreham. He had given it his best. He'd left at the right time.

He roamed the inside of his cabin with his eyes: shelves thick with books, poster of Mao Tse-tung as a young man, head-shot of Einstein, banjo on the fireplace mantle. He paused when he got to the $20 piano he'd picked up at the flea market. Books, running shoes, and files cluttered the instrument; a layer of dust covered all of that.

Dennis concentrated on his daily regime. The winter passed. He ran, ate well, wrote, read, meditated, split wood, visited the Ryders and the Amarosas. He worked on a series of six articles about education for the *Keene Sentinel*. The paper had agreed to print the pieces on the editorial pages over a period of weeks. The articles explored ways community members could get involved in their schools to make them better places for learning.

One of the articles carried this line: "The list of ways to get involved is endless. What is important is that you begin. Someone must take the first step."

6
The Star

DENNIS BEGAN HIS SECOND SUMMER an honest-to-God, card-carrying mountain man. The work, the silence, and the solitude were now routine. A little of the magic had washed away.

During the cold months, he'd gotten to know the Ryders and the Amarosas better. By spring, he began to feel a part of the community. He collected tidbits of gossip like a seamstress saving scraps of cloth for a quilt.

Cyndy Ryder, the tiny, bespectacled, silver-haired school-marm of a woman, was a school-board member and active in the PTA. She liked to talk about how things were going. Mostly, they weren't going well.

"Everything's in a state of flux," Cyndy told Dennis over tea one morning. "The old-timers are quitting. A new, younger membership is taking over. I'm hopeful that will help make a difference. But things at school only seem to be changing for the worse."

"What do you mean?"

"Everything seems out of control. Kids are destructive, disrespectful—there's no leadership to speak of."

"I see that every time I go into town," Dennis said. "I've never been inside the high school, except the gym. But I see kids hanging out downtown. They slouch against the stores and blow cigarette smoke at folks. I see a little girl there all the time. She couldn't be more than ten or eleven. It was after midnight when I drove by the other night—there she was smokin' and talkin' to some guys."

"Honest, Dennis, the school's a joke all over the region. They say, 'Can't spell? You must've gone to Thayer!' Some joke!"

"You're not laughing, Cyndy."

"That's because I'm so close to tears. I wish I knew what to do, but the problem seems so *big*—too big for me. We're in trouble, Dennis—real trouble. If there's anything you can do to help us out . . . well, I'm a friend in need and I'm asking for your help."

"Well . . ."

"I know you feel like you'd be butting in, but that's not how *I* see it."

Dennis's resolve not to get involved couldn't stand up under the plain pain of Cyndy's worry.

"Okay," he said. "Let's see what we can come up with."

They fell into a pattern. Tea and conversation, snippets of advice from one friend to another. Cyndy took his ideas back to the PTA and found them well received. More tea, more conversation, more advice. Dennis felt himself being pulled closer to the town. The more he learned from Cyndy, the more he cared. Old fires were being rekindled.

One day Cyndy asked him to come to the next PTA meeting. "You're full of good ideas. I keep passing them along, but somehow I think they'd have more impact if you presented them yourself."

Dennis hesitated.

Cyndy continued quickly. "The next meeting's on Tuesday night. At the Ashuelot Library."

Dennis had gotten lost on the way. The PTA meeting was in progress when he arrived. Of the fifteen people present, he was the only man.

"So much for not standing out," Dennis thought.

Cyndy Ryder interrupted the meeting to introduce her friend. She gave the group a quick rundown of his credentials.

"I invited him to the meeting because I think he's got some good ideas."

Agitated, Dennis nodded to the women and took a seat. He gave his attention to the young, energetic woman who was running the meeting. Her name was Cindy Nelson and she was the PTA's new president. She had plenty of raw energy bottled up in her diminutive frame. She wanted change. She *demanded* it. But she just wasn't sure how to go about making it happen.

"The rumors I hear coming out of the school are appalling," she said. "Most of them are true, I'm afraid. We need to get *into* the school, make some changes. The problem is, we're really limited by our budget."

Dennis listened. For a long while he said nothing. Then he raised his hand. Cindy nodded at him.

"The community is your best resource," he said. "If you can get the community involved, get people in this town to think as they should be thinking—that this school is *their* responsibility—then you can accomplish what you want. Communication is the key to start."

After the meeting, he waited to talk directly to the president. He tossed out some suggestions on how to organize meetings. "Break people up into small groups," he told her. "You'll get a lot more done that way . . ."

In the weeks that followed, Dennis gave Cindy solid suggestions on how to organize meetings, develop ideas, solve problems, and improve communication between the people at the school and the people in town.

In September, he convinced the PTA to put up $280 to start a community newspaper. He knew next to nothing about the newspaper business, but that didn't bother him much. "After all, I've *read* enough newspapers in my day,"

he said. "It can't be all that tough to put one out." His
energy was infectious. Members of the PTA agreed to help,
saying they'd try to corral others to join in the effort.

Cindy Nelson called her friend Marcia Ammann and
asked her to come to the organizational meeting. Marcia
was a Winchester native who'd just quit her job as director
of a nursery school she'd founded three years earlier. Her
two sons had been the reason she'd started the school, but
the boys were in elementary school now and Marcia had
decided it was time to do something else. All summer she'd
mulled over the idea of starting a community newspaper or
a community theater. When Cindy's call came, she still
hadn't decided which one. The call was fortuitous.

"By the way," Cindy said, "do you know Dennis Littky?
He's the one who's organizing this."

Marcia confessed she didn't.

"Oh, you will!" Cindy said.

On a rainy, windswept night in early October, a handful
of townspeople gathered in a classroom at the Winchester
Elementary School. Marcia was late. As she walked into the
squat building, she could *hear* the meeting—boisterous
laughter rippled from a room down the hall. She picked up
her pace, a curious smile spreading across her face.

She stepped into the room and looked around. A man
she'd never seen before was talking loudly, gesturing, and
laughing. Who was this guy? And why was a stranger
running a meeting in *her* town? His face was an explosion
of whiskers, his whole head a riot of fur. He wore a long-
sleeved undershirt, faded blue jeans, hiking boots. He
looked like one of those hippies she'd seen so often sprawled
on the lawns of downtown Brattleboro, Vermont.

"Oh, God," she thought. "They've crossed the river."

Dennis taped wide sheets of blank newsprint on the chalk

board. At the top of one he scrawled, THE RETURN OF THE WINCHESTER STAR. Under that he wrote the word IDEAS. He held the thick magic marker in one hand and gesticulated wildly with the other. He spoke to the group.

"Communication in this town is bad," he said. "I hear all sorts of stories about the sorry condition of the high school, but nobody really seems to know what's going on there. Where's the community spirit? There are beautiful, fascinating people in this town—why don't we celebrate them? There are good things going on here, but who would know? Winchester is scoffed at, laughed at—even by folks who live here. Why?

"The only reliable source of information in this town is the *Keene Sentinel*, and they seem to report only the bad stuff. There was a paper in town here once called the *Winchester Star*. We can revive the *Star*; we can get communication flowing again. Let's give people something to sing about, something to help make them feel good about themselves!"

The townspeople were swayed by his words. Even Marcia suspended her first impression and nodded her head in approval.

"It's going to take a lot of work to get this paper going," Dennis said. "But one thing I can guarantee is that we're *going* to do it—and we're going to have some fun in the process. This is your paper, you can do anything you like with it!"

Someone called out, "Are we going to sell the paper?"

"The original *Winchester Star* of the late 1800s was a for-profit paper," Dennis said. "But our *Star* won't be about money. This time, it'll be distributed free to every household in town. We don't want to leave anybody out. I think the money the PTA gave us will be enough to cover the first issue. After that, we'll have to figure something else out."

He looked around, spreading his arms before him.

"So," he said, "what do you want to see in your paper?"

"Sports stories about the high school," one man shouted out.

"Great!" Dennis scribbled SPORTS on the newsprint.

Another voice rang out. "Minutes of meetings. You know, selectmen's meetings, school board, planning commission."

Dennis wrote MEETING COVERAGE.

Another hand shot up. "What about a calendar listing all the meetings and events coming up?"

"Excellent!" Dennis scribbled away.

"How about a recipe section?" Cyndy Ryder suggested.

The ideas came out quicker. Dennis wrote furiously. School lunch listings, crossword puzzles, births, weddings, obits, ambulance news, letters to the editor.

When the ideas ran dry, Dennis spoke up. "Okay," he said. "Now we need volunteers. Who can do photography?"

Marcia Ammann's hand shot up. "Ted, my brother, is a good photographer. I'll see if I can get him to help."

"Typists?" Dennis asked.

Marcia's hand shot up again. "I can type, and my sister is lightning fast. Let me see if I can convince her to help."

A woman raised her hand. "I've got a manual typewriter at home we could use."

"I've got a portable electric," another said.

Dennis nodded and held up a hand. "I think we'll be able to use the elementary school for some meetings and layout sessions, but we really need a more permanent place where people can come and go throughout the day."

Marcia smiled. "I suppose we could use my garage. There's a stove we could put in there for heat, and there's a lot of countertop space. . . ."

The group applauded. Marcia blushed.

"All *right!*" exclaimed Dennis. "I'll be over tomorrow." Dennis continued to scribble on the newsprint, marking down categories and leaving space for names—reporters, proofreaders, typists, layout people, and so on.

He turned and looked around. "So tell me," he said, "has anyone here ever put out a newspaper before?"

"I used to deliver newspapers as a kid," one man offered.

"Great. You're in charge." Dennis laughed. "Well, it's true, my experience is limited to reading the newspaper. But I figure that's a pretty good start. I've ordered a book on how to put out a community newspaper, and that should help. I thought I'd go visit a couple newspapers and print shops in the area and see what I can pick up. My first stop's at the *Sentinel* on Monday. If anyone wants to come, I'll pick you up at the school parking lot at noon. I'm also going to check out some print shops to see if we can find someone who'll print it. Anyone want to help?"

"Oh, what the heck!" Marcia laughed.

By the time the meeting ended, several people were talking excitedly about story ideas for the first edition. Jobs had been assigned, among them the position of assistant editor to Marcia Ammann.

Marcia cornered her friend Marian Polaski.

"I can't believe we're finally going to have a community paper," she said. "And I'm going to be assistant editor. When I first walked into this meeting and saw who was running it, I was tempted to walk right back out."

"Yes, I know what you mean," her friend confided.

"I'm still not sure about him. I mean, there's something *foreign* about him. But he's got great energy—if he can get the paper to go, he's okay by me."

The next day, rolled newsprint under his arm, Dennis went to Marcia Ammann's house on Michigan Street in one of the oldest parts of town. Her house sat on a long hill overlooking Main Street and the small commons in front of the United Church of Winchester.

Though Dennis had warned Marcia he would stop by to look at the garage, he still felt a little uncomfortable. He didn't know her or her family. As he drove up to the house, he saw Marcia and a man, apparently her husband, unloading something from a truck. Dennis quickly parked his jeep and ran over to give Jim Ammann a hand carrying a new wood-burning stove into the house.

Jim, affable and low-key, warmed to Dennis immediately. So did the two Ammann boys.

"Here, let me show you the garage," Marcia said after the stove was set in place.

Though a little dark and cool, the garage seemed a good place to work. In the weeks that followed, the Ammann's house was host to an almost unending onslaught of workers. The cold, dark garage quickly gave way to the warmth and convenience of the Ammann living room. Dennis was there almost every day. He always came armed with a new device or gimmick to help with page layout. The book he ordered hadn't come yet, so the staff studied whatever newspapers were at hand, hoping to learn ways to put together a page.

Bottles of rubber cement, black matte construction paper, scissors, press type, and rulers littered Marcia's living room table. Less than a week after the organizational meeting, articles started to trickle in. Marian Polaski brought in a handwritten roster of the area's church news. Marcia lined up interviews with the high school principal and new guidance counselor.

Mostly it was hit or miss. The staff pasted up pages, ripped them apart, and tried again. A printer in Brattleboro agreed to print the paper and gave Dennis some tips on layout. For two days and nights before the *Star* was scheduled to go to press, about a dozen workers typed, cut, pasted, proofread, and retyped long into the night. At 2 A.M. on publication day, the weary staff finally "put the first edition to bed," as Dennis said—showing off the newspaper lingo he'd picked up.

"I think we should say something to these pages before we send them off," Dennis said, motioning to the staff. The crew, laughing, huddled ceremoniously around the stack, interlocking arms. Dennis stretched out a hand and closed his eyes. "The mission you are about to embark on, Pages, may be the most important mission of your lives."

"Do it with style!" Marcia chimed in.

"And may we all rest in peace," Marian added.

Tired, but happy, the staff lumbered off into the night.

With the pages neatly stacked in a large box, Dennis drove to Brattleboro early that morning, waiting most of the day for the first edition to roll off the presses. When the first copy landed in his hands, Dennis felt a rush of adrenaline. A little bleary-eyed, he opened the first copy of the paper.

The front page—dated October 27, 1979—was spare. The only photograph showed Vera Qualters receiving Winchester's Citizen of the Year award. The picture was rimmed with stars. An article in the upper right-hand corner told when the tax bills would be sent. There were seven man-on-the-street interviews airing residents' opinions on the new sewer system and a hand-drawn illustration by one of the staff members showing a group of people with stars for eyes. And just above the fold, in a box, was an announcement that a recent resignation had opened a spot on the Winchester School Board.

The following day the first edition of the revived *Star* thumped onto the front porches of all sixteen hundred houses in town. Staff members, the local Girl Scouts, and a father-son group piled the papers in wagons, bicycle baskets, cars, and trucks and made the rounds.

The response was immediate. Letters poured into the local post office; the Ammanns' phone started ringing off the hook. Residents called in dates of events, suggested tips for feature stories, and complimented the staff on its efforts. Every letter, every comment, every pat on the back was a boost to the fledgling staff.

"I've learned more about Winchester from reading the *Star* than I have by living here for the past seven years," one reader wrote.

The only complaints received were from folks perturbed because they hadn't gotten a copy of the paper. When such a call arrived, the nearest staff member would grab a paper and zip over to the complainer's door.

Nearly everybody, one way or another, got involved with the *Star*. Littky felt great. He was helping the town solve a problem; lines of communication were opening.

7
Hometown

HALLOWEEN NIGHT. The doorbell rang at the Ammann house. Marcia answered it, a basket of candy in her hands. A huge red-suited Santa Claus threw his arms around her, grabbed a fistful of candy, and bounded into the house hollering, "Ho! Ho! Ho!"

"Dennis, is that you?" Marcia said, trying to catch her breath.

"I'm making the rounds of all my favorite homes. I saved the best for last." He ripped open a candy bar and pushed the whole thing in his mouth.

"Oh, I bet you say that everywhere you go," Marcia laughed.

"You're right," he said. "But in this case it might be true." Marcia had known Dennis for only three weeks, yet somehow he made it seem like a lifetime. But she didn't kid herself—he was an enigma to her. She really didn't know much about him at all. He was single, in his late thirties, mountain man, former principal from New York, hippie. He said he was going to travel to Cuba next month—*Cuba*. She'd never met anyone who wanted to go to Cuba. Was he a communist? The other day she'd been talking to Dennis about a man in town she knew to be gay. Midway in the conversation she became unsure of herself. Was Dennis a homosexual? She didn't know. She certainly didn't feel comfortable asking. So what if he was a communist, or gay, or both? Did it matter? She didn't think so. Still, she hoped he wasn't.

In three weeks, he'd managed to turn her life, and her household, upside down. She loved it. She was doing exactly what she wanted—helping run her community's newspaper. It was exciting putting together the pages of the *Star* in her own house. She liked having staff members stop off with stories, help with layout, or run an idea past her. She liked the responsibility. She could feel the undertaking tightening the connection between her family and the community. That was important to her.

Dennis was at her house almost daily. He'd knock on the side door and bluster in without waiting for an answer, talking a mile a minute. He'd come armed with yet another device, book, or idea for the paper; sometimes, he'd come toting a pizza or a couple of hoagies. He'd traverse the kitchen, open the refrigerator, examine the contents, and help himself. Then he would get down to business. It all seemed somehow natural to Marcia. She'd light a cigarette and wait for him, then she'd hand him whatever had come in that day—articles, photos, news items.

In addition to plans for future editions of the *Star*, they spent a good deal of time talking about the role of the paper in the community and how the paper could best address community concerns. Marcia wanted it to help revive the tight-knit town she remembered as a child. Something was wrong in Winchester, but she couldn't quite put her finger on the root of the problem.

She worried out loud about the management of the town, the condition of the schools, and all the rumors that spilled out about each. She worried about her sons' education.

Her newspaper interview with the high school principal hadn't eased her worries. He was lax—almost cavalier—about the conditions at Thayer. He told her Winchester was a poor town; there was no money for the school; the kids had no respect—they didn't give a damn about anything and most of them turned into dropouts anyway.

The principal skipped through his list of complaints so quickly and automatically that Marcia figured it was part of his regular patter. He'd even advised her not to send her kids to Thayer. They'd be much better off *anywhere* else, he'd said.

Her walk through the school the day of the interview had angered her. She'd spent her high school years there in the sixties, and she felt a sentimental attachment to the place. Now the school seemed alien to her, filled with things she'd never expected to see—broken walls, graffiti, cigarette smoke, kids roaming the hallways and swearing like sailors.

"It's like a different school," she told Dennis one day. "There's an incredible anger in that building, a violence. Thayer was nothing like that when I was there. It's not the school I remember."

Marcia Ryll Ammann was a Winchester girl. Her great-grandparents made Winchester their home. So did her parents. Now she was raising her family there in a house right next door to the one in which she'd grown up. As a girl, from the front stoop, she often greeted Joe Dominick on his mail route and got a stick of gum or a ripe shiny apple in return. She jumped rope on her front lawn and walked down the hill to the home of Edith Atkins, the town librarian, for weekly piano lessons. After school and during summers, she helped Mrs. Atkins at the library.

One of Marcia's childhood best friends was the daughter of the then-high school principal, Paul McNamara—a crusty but good-natured man whose reputation as a tough disciplinarian didn't fool Marcia. She knew her friend's father in the comfort of his home long before she became a student in his school. Underneath all that gruffness, she knew, he was really a softy. Mr. McNamara regularly entertained the girls with school items he stored in his house over the summer. Once he brought home a tape recorder— the first Marcia had ever seen. Another time he brought home a human skeleton from the biology room.

She liked school; she was an exemplary student. In 1964, the year before she graduated, Marcia was chosen Community Ambassador to Holland and spent a summer studying there. She went off to Keene State College's teacher school a few years later with no plans to return to live in her hometown.

Her marriage to Jimmy Ammann sent a minor shock wave through Winchester. They were the first couple in the history of the town to have an ecumenical wedding—Catholic marrying Protestant. It was that kind of small town thinking that had made her want to live in a large and active city. Her first assignment student teaching at a large junior high in Concord, New Hampshire, however, was enough to tell her that bigger didn't mean better. She was overwhelmed by the numbers, the rows and rows of students seated in alphabetical order. She owned up to her misconceptions and applied for teaching positions at small country schools all over New England. When she went for an interview at a rural elementary school in Westminster, Vermont, she knew almost instantly she'd found the right place.

Most of Westminster's students came from the surrounding farms. They were up before dawn to complete their chores, then they hopped the bus to school, where they worked harder. Parents often came to spend a day at school to share in their children's education. Many times, when Marcia helped a confused fifth grader through a difficult assignment, his or her parents would invite her to dinner or send her a batch of home-baked cookies as their way of saying thanks. This home support and the strength of the school's leadership, Marcia soon realized, were the keys that made the school work so well.

Before the end of her second year, she and her husband were expecting their first child. The question of where they would raise their family became paramount, and Marcia found the idea of living in Winchester less repellent than it once had been. She knew the school system was good—she had firsthand knowledge of that. They bought the house next door to her parents' home, and Marcia settled into life in her old hometown. The first public event she and her husband attended was the retirement party of her former principal, Paul McNamara.

There was a romantic, mysterious side to Marcia. She placed as much stock in intuition as she did an assemblage of facts. She considered the eyes as reliable an insight about a person as his or her actions. Dennis Littky's eyes struck her as kind, gentle, and playful, which served to soften any suspicions she had about the mysterious mountain man.

At sixteen, she became fascinated by a woman, a friend of her grandmother's, who claimed to have psychic powers. Marcia had known the woman all her life but, until that year, was unaware of this side of her. The woman told Marcia she had a vision that Marcia's name would one day appear in a book. The woman claimed she could fortell the future by reading an ordinary deck of cards. Intrigued, Marcia urged the woman to teach her.

Finally, when Marcia was in college, her grandmother's friend sought her out. Marcia was the person to whom she wanted to give "her gift," as she called it.

"Don't ever take money for this," the woman cautioned her, "and don't ever take it too seriously."

So Marcia began reading cards. She fancied herself a gypsy, a strange image for one so plain and fair. She'd read anybody's cards, but mostly her friends. Call it a gift or call it coincidence, she wasn't sure which, but she knew for certain it was good, cheap entertainment. Two or three times a year, Marcia drove to Northfield, Massachusetts, to visit a professional card reader, who would read her cards.

Upon returning to live in Winchester, Marcia decided to forego her teaching career and stay home with her two sons. But when kids passed her house on their way to school, she felt a kind of longing. She missed teaching.

She compromised and opened a nursery school so she could do both—be with her kids and be in the classroom. But she was ready to shift gears when her boys entered grade school. So when a third-grade teacher asked her to fill in for her during a six-week maternity leave, Marcia jumped at the chance.

But now she saw something she hadn't expected—high school students hanging out in the parking lot, sitting on the front porch of Winchester House, leaning shirtless against the hoods of cars. She was almost certain it was booze they were drinking, pot they were smoking. She couldn't cross the parking lot or walk down the street without having a car rip past, inscribing zigzags or dough-nuts in the pavement.

For the first time, she questioned the decision that had landed her and her family back in Winchester.

Marcia sometimes talked about her misgivings with Dennis. During one such talk, the matter of the vacancy on the school board came up. In November the board would ap-point a member to serve out the five months that remained of the term.

"Why don't you apply?" Marcia said. "With your organi-zational skills and educational background, you'd be a definite asset."

Marian Polaski, Cyndy Ryder, and Cindy Nelson, all members of the board, were receptive to the idea and en-couraged Dennis to apply. His work on the *Star* had shown him he wasn't an outsider anymore. This was *his* town, too. He didn't hesitate—he applied for the job, and he got it.

In addition to his new duties with the school board, Dennis spent much of his time working on the newspaper. He figured budgets, solicited funds, thought up ideas for the cover, wrote feature stories, editorials, news items. He made sure all the categories were covered for each issue, carefully organizing a checklist of names and duties. He applied for a $5,000 grant to help the paper and got it. Now the paper could rent space downtown next to the hardware store and buy a fancy IBM electric typewriter and some darkroom equipment.

As the new school board member, he had pages and pages of financial information to absorb. The board had to work up a proposed budget, which it would then take to the town's budget committee—a corps of eleven tightfisted conservatives who weren't at all keen on tax increases. The budget committee, which was independent of the school board, inspected all the town's money matters. School board members needed to make sure they had their facts together, that they could justify any and all items in the budget.

On the frigid February day that the budget committee was to review the school board's budget, Dennis spent the better part of the morning in Marcia's living room, pacing the floor and rehearsing his facts and figures.

Marcia gave him some sage advice. "They're not real fond of tax hikes. Be prepared for a grilling."

Marcia didn't exaggerate. The committee was tough, the members snide in their criticisms. Several of the most outspoken members were also the town's biggest landholders and were especially testy on matters of property taxes.

Dennis was prepared, confident about his ability to state the crying need for the requested tax increase. Nevertheless, he found himself quavering under the grueling questions. He'd faced hostile audiences before, but these people were different. They seemed implacable.

In the end, the committee rejected the school board's budget. It had to be cut, they said. There would be no tax increase.

In the February issue of the *Star*, Dennis fired off a signed editorial headlined, "UNFORTUNATELY, WE ACT BY NOT ACTING":

> Unless individual citizens are involved in their government, self government will pass us all by.
> Who controls Winchester? Who controls the schools? Who sets the zoning laws? Who decides what or if industry may enter town? Should you be involved in helping to make some of these decisions? The next month and a half is a crucial time for Winchester. The town budget is being prepared. There are 3 openings on the Budget Committee for next year. There is a Selectman position open. There are 2 School Board positions to be filled. There are articles to be voted upon.
> There are meetings. Select one that may interest you. Attend. . . .
> It is ironic: we get 500 people to a basketball game and 5 to a School Board meeting.
> If you do not get involved, then a small few will make the day-to-day decisions for you and your children.
> "TO LOSE YOUR IDENTITY AS A CITIZEN OF DEMOCRACY IS BUT A STEP FROM LOSING YOUR IDENTITY AS A PERSON."
> Dennis Littky

The deadline for signing up to run for the three-year school board position was fast approaching. Marian Polaski, the plump, round-faced Irish woman, who'd married into her Polish name, chaired the board. She was impressed with Dennis and urged him to run. So did Cyndy, Cindy, and Marcia.

Dennis's money was holding out much better than anticipated. He had enough to carry him comfortably for another year, but after that he'd have to find employment. He'd gotten into the habit of half-heartedly scanning newspapers and magazines for jobs. He wasn't much interested in becoming a principal again—the only way he'd consider doing *that* would be if he started a school from scratch or served as principal in his hometown. He decided against running for the school board. He'd focus his attention on the *Star*.

Dennis got the paper another grant. This one helped fund a single-issue historical magazine celebrating the people of Winchester.

The one-hundred-page special issue of the *Star* was intended to tell Winchester's story through the eyes of its residents. The history began with the recollections of one of its oldest lifelong citizens, Ray Whipple (born 1882), and ended with the thoughts of young newlyweds.

It was a tremendous undertaking for the staff, and there was still all the work for the regular monthly newspaper to be done. Dennis recruited writers and workers anywhere he could find them. One letter to the editor particularly attracted his attention. It came from a Winchester woman who was upset at the *Star*'s handling of an article on education. Her writing impressed Dennis; he felt the fire in her words. He was less interested in what the letter said than *how* it had said it. The name at the bottom of the letter was Marilyn Nolan.

Dennis recruited her. Marilyn Nolan turned out to be a reliable, meticulous worker. She was eager to work on the special issue and planned to do a critical review of the history of education in Winchester.

Marilyn Nolan was a woman of excesses. Huge, a chain smoker, she read voraciously and regularly clipped articles about education, which she carefully filed away. Her passion was education, even though her own formal education had ended with high school, and she'd watched five of her six daughters drop out of school one by one. Her shelves at home were lined with dozens of books on the history of education in the United States.

Though her confidence was low, she had a knack for writing and loved to spend hours at the *Star*'s IBM Selectric typewriter. A woman of single-minded determination, she could be a valuable coworker or an implacable enemy.

8
Man of Many Hats

DENNIS LITTKY AND ED ZITTA each gathered a stack of newspapers from the back seat of the jeep. They'd spent most of the afternoon delivering the *Star* to homes and businesses around town. Ed, a former town selectman, covered town government for the *Star*. Dennis liked the florid-faced energy Ed brought to everything he did, including delivering newspapers. Both men were riding high that afternoon. Nearly every place they'd gone, someone had a good word to say about the paper. Ed, as though basking in the glow of a celebrity, proudly introduced Dennis as the paper's editor.

Big S Discount Co. sat off Winchester's Main Street at the end of a long unpaved driveway. Francis Gutoski owned the store and its contents, a mishmash of factory tail ends, discontinued goods, and buy-outs. The stock wasn't arranged in any particular order, just aisles and aisles of suntan oil, children's cowboy hats, beer, cigarettes, lip balm, and sundry other gewgaws. Gutoski, his prodigious gut bulging over the top of his belt like an ocean swell, threw another empty cigarette carton onto the growing mound of cartons behind him. In front of him was the latest edition of the *Winchester Star*. There were two other men in the store, one of whom was a town selectman, and they too had copies of the paper.

Dennis and Ed sauntered into the store with a stack of

Stars under their arms and smiles on their faces.

"Hey, man, how ya doin'?" Dennis sang out.

Ed was about to introduce Dennis when Gutoski snatched a paper from the top of the stack and pointed it at Dennis like a bayonet.

"So *you're* the person who publishes this."

"Well, yes," Dennis said.

"I never want to see this trash in my store again!" Gutoski barked, lifting the whole stack of papers off the counter and dumping them on the floor.

Dennis pulled at the brim of his hat, trying to recover from the man's unexpected vehemence. "Excuse me?" It was all he could say.

"I don't like what you print!" Gutoski roared.

Dennis picked up the papers and shambled out the door. Ed was right behind him. They climbed into the jeep and exchanged curious looks.

"Holy shit," Dennis said. "What was that all about?"

"I should have warned you," Ed said. "Bucky's letter about the deal the selectmen worked out with the owner of that abandoned factory—" (Bucky Jones, a Winchester town official, wrote a letter to the *Star* condemning the selectmen for granting a tax abatement to the factory owner. Jones said the deal was illegal. Dennis ran the letter on the front page of the *Star*.)

"Yeah—so?" Dennis said.

"Gutoski—he's the owner of the factory."

One day, Dennis was leafing through a *Smithsonian* magazine when he spied an article about White House fellowships, some of the most coveted and prestigious positions of their kind. Only those applicants who had demonstrated outstanding leadership skills would be considered.

"Maybe that's something I should do. I certainly have the credentials . . . ," he thought.

He fired off a letter asking for an application. When the

packet arrived, he filled out the thirty-page form. He labored over the essay questions and carefully compiled his credentials and accolades from his years in education. He sent the application to Boston, then sat back and hoped.

Several weeks later he was notified that he'd been selected as a regional finalist. The three-day interviews would be in the spring.

Marcia was one of the first he told of his plans. "Oh," she said. Her tone betrayed her. "It sounds like an incredible opportunity. It also sounds like you have a pretty good shot at getting appointed." On the one hand, she was happy for Dennis. On the other, it could mean he'd be leaving—she wasn't ready for that. The town needed him. For her, the only bright spot in Winchester was the *Star* and Dennis was the cause of that.

She and her husband had grown increasingly distressed at the state of things in town, particularly in the schools. When the high school called her in February to substitute for a junior-high math teacher who'd had open heart surgery, Marcia accepted. Even though math was not her strong suit, she looked at the assignment as an opportunity to see firsthand if the rumors were true.

They were. The first day, a big-shouldered, tough-looking boy threatened to make her "the next notch on the wall."

"See these lines here?" he had said, rubbing his hand along the wooden frame of the chalkboard. "Each of these marks stands for a substitute teacher we chewed up and spit out. I put the fifth mark here on Friday. You're going to be mark number six."

Within a week, the notch was on the wall. The Ammanns put their house up for sale. They wanted to get their boys out of Winchester and into another school system—the sooner the better. Dennis had been her last hope, but now even he was probably leaving.

The day before Dennis traveled to Washington for his White House interview, he drove to Keene to buy a new suit. Out of ten finalists in Boston, Dennis had been one of two to make the cut a few weeks earlier. He had appeared for the three days of interviews dressed in a freshly laundered button-down shirt and corduroys. He and the other candidates were invited to a large party at the lavish home of one of the politicos involved in the selection process. The invitation said "informal," so Dennis arrived wearing corduroys. No one shared his backwoods notions of informality. Everyone else wore three-piece suits and ties.

"Back where I come from," he said to whoever would listen, "what I'm wearing is a couple steps *up* from informal."

Somewhere in the back of his closet was a blazer; he figured that since the second phase of interviews in Washington was going to take the better part of a week, there might come a time when he'd want to change his clothes. The suit and blazer gave him options. Dennis boarded the flight carrying most of his things in the sturdy leather mailbag that had traveled with him as far as China and Africa. He carried the blazer and new suit in the black plastic bag they'd given him at the men's store in Keene.

The interviews were exhaustive and exhausting. A panel of six men and women fired questions at him. They wanted to know about his management style, his views on White House policy, his personal goals, and his opinions on this, that, and the other thing. Dennis was confident under the questioning. He was sure of his qualifications, but he wasn't so hell-bent on being selected that he didn't joke comfortably with the interviewers.

His Washington itinerary was densely packed—orientation, meetings, cocktail parties, dinners, interviews, and more interviews. The night the fellowships were to be announced, the candidates assembled in the White House

Gold Room, and Lady Bird Johnson, who had served as a member of the selection committee, delivered a speech. Then each candidate received a card indicating whether he or she had made the final selection. President Jimmy Carter waited in the next room to congratulate the winners. Support people were stationed all over the conference room to console those who had not been selected. As candidates unsealed their cards and read the results, some exulted, while others tried to hide their disappointment.

Dennis opened his card and stared blankly at the results. He smiled. He wasn't the slightest bit upset that he wasn't going to be a White House fellow, but he *was* dumbfounded that he hadn't been chosen. He asked the committee members why, and they told him he was well qualified but far too independent. They thought he'd have a hard time toeing the line.

Well, they were right about that.

His stint in the nation's capital wasn't a complete lesson in humility. On the basis of his interviews, the National Institute of Education, the research arm of the U.S. Department of Education, later offered him an administrative internship dishing out grant monies. His budget would be in the multimillions.

He was given a tour of the office building he'd work in. He walked up and down the rows and rows of desks occupied by starched, well-manicured bureaucrats. His job would be to read grant proposals from schools all over the country and decide which ones were worthy.

It came down to this: he realized he didn't want to hand out money to *other* people to run school projects; he wanted to run projects himself.

He told them thanks, but no thanks.

He returned to Winchester renewed, recharged, and exuberant. When Marcia first saw Dennis, her heart sank. He looked so happy and excited, she figured he'd taken the fellowship in educational leadership.

"You got it." She tried to sound excited.

"Heck, no!" he boomed. "I wasn't right for the job. The Washington scene just isn't for me. Everybody there looks and acts alike."

Marcia was so happy she threw her arms around him. For Marcia, the fact that Dennis had come so close to so important a position was reassuring. After all, the FBI had come out to investigate him. Certainly, if he were the communist or wild-eyed subversive that some in Winchester accused him of being, he wouldn't have come out of the official investigation so smoothly.

One fact remained unchanged—Dennis's money was running low. He knew he'd have to go back to work soon.

Every day he scanned newspapers and magazines looking for jobs that might catch his fancy. He let his imagination wander. *Anything* was possible. He talked to Marcia about opening a summer camp on Forest Lake, a good-sized lake on Winchester's northern side. He'd found a large piece of property for sale, and he thought it would make a dandy place for a high-powered educational camp that would teach survival skills, photography, mountain climbing, farming, and hobbies. He liked the schedule he could work out for himself—six months on, six months off; work intensely for half a year, hang loose for the other half.

Marcia prodded Dennis to think about becoming Winchester's town manager. She figured that since Dennis had done such a good job reviving the newspaper without experience, he could have the same success as town manager. Maybe he could bring new industry to town, maybe he could get everybody working together rather than against each other. The thought intrigued him.

The summer of 1980, Dennis decided to commit himself to Winchester—at least for a while. He put his name on the ballot for a seat on the state legislature.

Armed with fliers that pictured him in a Jeep-monogrammed cap with untrimmed beard, wire-rimmed glasses, and plaid work shirt, he ran for a two-year seat as Winchester's representative to the state house. His main goal was to recast the distribution of state education aid to help his town and other poor communities. Besides, it was a rare time in his life that he would have the time to try his hand at public office. Legislators got paid $100 per year, plus mileage.

That there were inequities in the distribution of state aid to New Hampshire public schools didn't surprise Dennis, but the degree of those inequities riled him. The state was ranked the lowest in the nation in terms of the money it gave its schools. That put Winchester near the bottom of the bottom in the aid it got for education.

The overwhelming share of schools' funds came from local tax dollars, which meant poor towns like Winchester were hit the hardest of all. Without a solid tax base from industries, Winchester's tax burden shifted to its struggling residents. That left the town with a paltry operating budget and its residents, many already financially strapped, with comparatively high tax bills.

The fact that Winchester residents were saddled with a tax burden that was breaking their backs angered Dennis. He wanted to change that.

Dennis was up against six candidates running for three seats—three of them incumbents. One of the incumbents was Elmer Johnson, a legislator for the past quarter century and a long-standing member of the town's budget committee.

In his campaign literature, Dennis wrote:

> To be honest, I haven't campaigned the way I would like to. It is hard for me to sell myself. It is not my style to say, "Hello, I'm Dennis Littky. Vote for me." I meet new people in town and I don't even tell them I'm running for Representative. I do think about telling them, but then think that

it would change my interaction with the person. It would seem as if I'm talking to them because of the election.

When someone makes a sly remark about a politician I say, "Hey, I'm one," but my friends in Winchester then say, "You are not like one." It is a compliment.

. . . Winchester has become my home. I love my cabin in the woods, the *Star* office in town, and the people I talk with and meet every day.

I moved here planning to stay a year. I am now on my third and feel it is just the beginning.

Dennis won his seat that November, capturing almost as many votes as veteran politician Elmer Johnson. Dennis joined the New Hampshire House of Representatives Education Committee and a subcommittee on special education. He immediately began work helping to redistribute state education aid to towns. But very quickly, he learned that in government, especially in a part-time legislature with more than four hundred representatives, the wheels of statecraft grind at only two speeds—dead slow or not at all. The big-city legislators had the most power, and it wasn't to their benefit to send money out of their districts. That, coupled with his status as a freshman legislator, gave Littky next to no clout. Dennis was used to turning ideas into action in no time flat. That's how he'd run the school on Long Island, that's how he'd revived the newspaper—and that's how he wanted to help education in the town of Winchester. The do-nothing, everything-needs-more-study attitudes of his fellow legislators frustrated him mightily.

The word at the *Star* was that Saunders, the high school principal, was on his way out. Even before the resignation was official, townspeople speculated about his successor. The men who gathered at Don's Barber Shop downtown knew a tough disciplinarian was in order. At the *Star*, staffers agreed—they wanted a strong disciplinarian too, but they also wanted somebody with new and creative ideas, somebody who would bring some of the old pride and joy back to the school.

Dennis held himself aloof from these discussions.

"Dennis," Marcia said, "you'd be perfect for the job."

Dennis hesitated. "I always said I wouldn't become a principal again unless I started a school from scratch or unless I was principal in my hometown," he said.

Dennis took long walks in the quiet evenings. The more he thought about becoming principal, the better it sounded.

"Well, *this* is my hometown now, isn't it?" he told himself. "The school needs someone with fresh ideas, someone who can make school into *the* place to be. I would be perfect for the job. I could do it!"

9
The School

IT WAS THE THIRD TIME that day Police Officer Jim Harrison, soon to be police chief, had been called to Thayer High School. This time a fight had broken out in the cafeteria. Two or three students were involved. As Harrison and his partner got out of the cruiser in front of the school, they braced themselves for the volley of insults and obscenities they knew would be hurled at them from the open windows. Against his will, the barbs hit Harrison deep, cutting to his core. He entered the school stone-faced.

The battered, broken building unnerved him. It always did. It made him sort of sad—the gouged walls, the ribald graffiti, the missing ceiling tiles, the stains, the chinks, the dirt, the students roaming the halls. It wasn't the school he'd known growing up in Winchester. Clouds of blue cigarette smoke rolled out of the girls' restroom. In the hallway, a teenage girl sat on the floor, legs straddling the waist of what was presumably a teenage boy. Harrison couldn't be sure—the hair was longer than the girl's and the face was buried deep into her neck, hidden from view. He *hoped* it was a boy.

This place didn't look like a school. He did his best to ignore it and headed toward the raucous voices rising up from the basement. Down the hall, two boys opened and slammed lockers, one after the other, kicking the ones that didn't open easily. They were oblivious to his approach.

73

Harrison reached out and grabbed one of the boys by the arm.

"Cut that out," he barked. The other boy stopped and stood still. Harrison and his partner shot sharp looks at both boys, then hurried toward the cafeteria. As the officers rounded the corner to the stairs, they heard two loud crashes behind them—as two metal lockers slammed shut.

In the cafeteria, the police officers found a crowd of students cheering on two teenage girls in a fight. Barb Eibell, Thayer's language teacher, tried feebly to stop the brawl. Harrison recognized one of the girls and caught her wrist before she could throw her next punch, aimed squarely for the other girl's chin.

"That's enough, Maggie," Harrison said. The girl struggled, but it didn't take long to stop the fight.

Harrison didn't know what or who had started the fight. It didn't matter. Both girls would get three-day suspensions. Afterwards, they might or might not come to school, depending on how bored they were, how angry they felt. Harrison knew he would be back the next day to break up yet another fight.

Barb Eibell, the teacher who'd tried to break up the fight, was in her second year at Thayer. She and her husband, Fred, had made a thorough survey of the United States while living in New Jersey. They were looking for the perfect place to live, the ideal environment in which to raise their two children. New England appeared to fill the bill— beautiful countryside, picture-perfect small towns with close-knit communities, and that quaint, homespun feeling they recognized from years of reading *Yankee Magazine*. They fell hard for southwestern New Hampshire—the lush green mountains got them.

Life in Winchester turned out to be nothing like what they'd hoped for. They were young, idealistic, filled with the roseate visions of the counterculture movement, attitudes they displayed with her gauze dress, his beard, and the van they drove. The vehicle was a rolling billboard, tattooed with bumper stickers heralding their opposition to nuclear power, endorsing the wonders of solar energy, and so on.

Winchester didn't warm to the Eibells; their education began almost immediately. They were looking for an old rambling farmhouse tucked into one of Winchester's secluded clearings, surrounded by a few lush acres they could call their own. They never saw a house that came *close* to their dream. Instead, they were shown a series of claustrophobic prefab crackerboxes on sandwich-sized plots of bulldozed land. Their dream house just wasn't available, they were told.

The Eibells bought a small, newly built ranch house on State Route 119, close to the school complex. It wasn't what they wanted, but they took it in stride, comforting themselves with their low mortgage and easy access to school.

Barb's first day teaching turned out to be a trauma that got worse as the days dragged by. She wasn't prepared for the adjustments she had to make to work at Thayer. In New Jersey she'd taught in a large, wealthy school district where she was just one teacher in a large department. Most of her students there were college-bound.

At Thayer, she *was* the language department—the whole department. She had no chairperson to make the decisions for her, no colleagues to lean on. She was on her own.

Instead of an urban high school of two thousand, she found herself in a poor, rural junior/senior high school of three hundred. Her first year at Thayer, only four of the thirty-two graduating seniors went on to college. More students dropped out than graduated.

She was thrown further off balance when the principal told her she'd be teaching English in addition to her language classes. Barb had taught only French and Spanish up until then. She felt ill-equipped to handle the load, but managed to come to school energetic and optimistic. She armed herself with flowering plants to brighten the window sills in her classroom, and she carried a cache of materials to help make the classroom *her* classroom—posters, scissors, colored pens, pictures, records, and other materials.

She knew students and teachers were always a little keyed up when they came back to school after summer vacation. She expected that, but there was something fundamentally different about the students at Thayer.

As the days passed, Barb felt less and less like a teacher and more like a custodian. Students walked in and out of her classes at will. Long after the tardy bell sounded, students sauntered in, talking loudly, ignoring her.

She didn't know who had an excused absence, who was skipping. She had students she saw once but never again. The principal's office didn't seem to know much of anything about the students. She got the idea the administration just didn't give a damn.

Things turned up missing from her desk drawers. She often found the language room's record player in the gym, volume turned up full blast.

She hated to admit it, but she was afraid of her homeroom. She had no rapport with the students who made up her class. The only direct contact she had with them was the first five minutes of every school day. They formed a knot in the back of the room, talking through the announcements, chewing gum, trying on each other's hats, shooting paper wads, leaning out the windows. It was great sport for them to drop erasers, chalk, pens, notebooks, textbooks, and anything else they could lay their hands on, out of her second-floor windows—even desks. After the first few days of school, her plants were destroyed.

She cleaned her personal belongings out of her drawers

and took them home. Her classroom turned bare and anonymous. That was exactly how she felt.

Barb struggled to keep pace in her English class. She found herself leaning on Valerie Cole, the honors English teacher who was somehow able to hold the attention of her students. Cole shared her curriculum and provided occasional, much-needed encouragement. Barb did her best to plow through the French and Spanish textbooks, dragging her students along with her as best she could. Quickly, she gave up any dreams she had of bringing the wonders of language to the children of Winchester. As long as she got them through the subjunctive case, the point that the textbook put as the finish line for first-year students, she figured she'd have done her job.

One frosty winter day, Barb punished a group of kids in her homeroom for swearing at her. She sent them to the office. When she left her house for school the next morning, she found a used condom frozen on the front windshield of her car.

It didn't take long for Barb to figure out what was wrong with these kids—they didn't give a damn. They really didn't care. They didn't care about school, they didn't care about their futures. Saddest of all, they didn't care about themselves.

Hostility hung in the air so thick she couldn't get away from it. When the school day ended, she'd drag herself home. She didn't find much comfort in her husband, who was unemployed and depressed. She'd spend what was left of her evenings dreading her return to school the next morning.

Fred had tried hard to find a social service job in the region but had come up empty-handed. Barb found herself getting more depressed than he was. She started missing school, taking sick days when she wasn't ill, just burned out. She was out for a total of fifteen days her first year.

Barb was the family's sole supporter. Her salary at Thayer was $11,000—*before* taxes. She felt like she was a rat in a trap: no way out. Day after day, the cycle continued. Before long, the Eibells ate through the small nest egg they'd squirreled away. More and more often, Barb came home to find Fred rocking back and forth in a dark room—not speaking, not aware of anything outside himself, rocking back and forth, back and forth.

For students like Karen Thompson, school was a lark, a place to hang out, a place for fun and games—all sorts of games. She was a tough kid.

Karen Thompson came from a family with roots sunk deep in Winchester's soil. Her father worked most of his life at a book bindery in Brattleboro, Vermont, just over the river from Winchester. Her mother was the produce manager at Kulick's Market in Winchester. Their effort to get her to take school seriously had played itself out, a bad song only they wanted to hear.

For Karen, the classroom portion of school was a joke, a system to beat—far more energy went into disrupting or skipping class than into actual learning. Though Karen rarely drank in school, she knew that virtually any time of the day she could slip into the girls' locker room and find liquor. Cigarettes, vodka, and joints were always on hand. Girls stood at the back door of the locker room smoking "Charlie joints," cigar-sized marijuana cigarettes named for the dealer who sold them.

Karen was part of a knot of eight sophomore girls who cut a savage swath through the school. The other students, girls and boys alike, got out of the Group's way. Students crossed to the other side of the hall or took the other staircase just to avoid them.

They were an angry, coarse clique that held court whenever and wherever they chose. Their system of justice was enforced with shouts, fists, fingernails—whatever worked the fastest. Often they used their blossoming sexuality as a potent weapon in their grabs for power or attention. When their partners overlapped, the girls settled their differences when and where the mood struck them.

It was easy for the Group to hold on to its power throughout the school day. They'd scheduled almost all their classes together, always looking for a teacher who was known to be lax, an easy grader, or easily chewed up. They took as few courses as they could—no more than they needed to fulfill the state requirements—and padded the rest of the day with study halls. They were aided by the "arena" scheduling process, in which swarms of students mobbed the cafeteria to sign up for classes of their own choosing.

The most popular class at Thayer was study hall. It was held in the cafeteria, located in the high school's concrete block basement. Many students scheduled two, sometimes three, study halls in a row. On the way to the cafeteria, students stopped at their lockers to drop off their books. Except for a handful of students who huddled by themselves at a back table, nobody studied there.

At each study hall, a hundred or so students swarmed into the cafeteria, filling the room with the smell of orange peel, meat sandwiches, and teenage sweat. They didn't talk, they shouted, as though competing to see who could be the loudest.

They used pens, pencils, forks, and knives to gnaw through the tabletops. They etched obscenities, bored holes through chair seats. As the weeks passed, the vandalized tables and chairs were chipped and hacked until they were a set of gaping holes, some big enough to drop a student through. So much ink and graphite built up that elbows and shirt sleeves were filthy by the end of the day.

The pressed-fiber tiles of the suspended ceiling served as targets for spit wads and soggy heaps of toilet paper. The gobs turned brittle when they dried. Paper airplanes were an art form. Fork flipping was high sport. If a fork was hit with just the right force off the edge of a table or hand, it would flip up toward the ceiling and stick tines-first into the food-splattered tiles.

Teachers faced study hall duty with the same enthusiasm with which they would have faced the Inquisition. It was far preferable to teach an added course than to supervise study hall.

Yet Thayer was not completely devoid of discipline. Often students passing by Principal Saunders's office would hear him shoving a student up against the wall. Saunders, a former army man, liked to exercise his ancient and honored right to force law and order onto the adolescent bodies of the disobedient. He was a big, athletic man, fond of yelling—as though the volume in and of itself made him think he must be doing some good. Discipline, when it happened at Thayer, came hard. But it was a random occurrence—exacting one day, nonexistent the next.

It was a bad situation, bad for everyone. Behavior that most everyone considered deviant had become commonplace at Thayer. Hell, it was expected.

The teachers were exasperated and demoralized. They gave up trying to enforce rules and took refuge in their classrooms, doing their best to maintain what little order they could. The teachers' lounge became the sanctuary, the infirmary where teachers huddled together, gnashed their teeth, and chain-smoked. They bitched about this, that, and the other thing. *Nothing* was right. *Nothing* worked.

10
The Interview

SEVENTEEN EDUCATORS APPLIED FOR THE
$22,000-a-year job as principal of Thayer Junior/Senior
High School. Five were offered interviews.

Dennis Littky was one.

He dug back in his closet and pulled out the $2 green and
gray herringbone blazer he'd picked up at a mission store a
dozen years ago. A little crumpled and smelling of smoke,
like nearly everything in the cabin, it still had lots of wear
left in it.

The mirror on the wall next to his bed was old; everything it reflected had a foggy glow, dark and out of focus.
He put on the jacket and studied his image. He shifted his
shoulders, then tried smiling at himself in the mirror. He
looked like something out of his own history.

Becoming principal had become his major occupation.
He thought about it all the time. For the most part, he
avoided visiting Thayer because he didn't want to interfere
with the outgoing principal. But he let his mind wander
over how he'd run things and what changes he'd make.

One day he had happened by the high school's main
office and found the secretaries sending out 270 failure
notices to students. Dennis was momentarily speechless.

"How many students are there here?" he asked.

"About 320," she said.

January 26, 1981
Dear Dr. Sundstrom and the Board of Education,

I am very interested in the job of principal of Thayer Jr./ Sr. High School. Living in the town and working with the community thru the PTA, the School Board, the *Winchester Star*, gives me a great advantage or head start. I not only understand the school and the needs of students and the community, but also my present situation gives me the flexibility to consult with the teachers and Dr. Saunders before the end of the school year. Hopefully, this will lead to a few months of planning and organizing before school re-opens in the Fall.

In order to improve the education for our children, the community must not only support the schools, but be actively involved. Accomplishing this task will be a priority of mine.

I will try to help every student excel in at least one area in the school. Each student must feel good about himself/ herself. An emphasis will be on learning to read and to communicate one's feelings and thoughts. Students must be able to make positive decisions about life after high school. Students may spend some of their time working out in the community either as a tutor, helper, or intern with various residents. A priority is to provide enough options in the school to prevent drop outs to the work world or to the private school.

An overall goal is to have the students and the community be proud of their school. I feel my background as an educational and community leader prepares me well for the task.

I know the long hours and hard work that the school will demand. I am ready to use my skill, knowledge, and time to help Thayer become the best school in the State. I hope the Board will work with me towards this exciting endeavor. I am looking forward to a personal interview.
Thank you,
Dennis Littky

In his mind, the possibility that he might not get the job

was remote, hardly worth thinking about. His résumé was impressive—doctorate in psychology and education; distinguished teaching award from the University of Michigan; assistant professor at State University of New York at Stony Brook; director of an experimental teacher-training program in New York; established a model middle school on Long Island and served as its principal for six years; founder and editor of the *Star*; former school board member; state legislator.

The glowing recommendations that accompanied his application included some of the biggest names in education. Added to that were the contributions he'd made to Winchester during the past two years. Added to that was the fact that he was willing to take a substantial cut in pay. His last job had paid $42,000. The principal's job at Thayer would pay him about what he had earned in his first job out of college.

Most of the applicants, he knew, would be educators who'd never before worked as principals—the low pay and the size of the school almost ensured that. And besides, he reminded himself, he enjoyed no small advantage by virtue of the fact that he'd worked closely with three of the five school board members—Cyndy Ryder, Cindy Nelson, and Marian Polaski were active staffers on the *Star*. He'd served on the school board and PTA with them. They'd seen him in action; they knew he meant what he said about transforming the school into the best in the state.

In his own estimation, he was the ideal candidate.

Dennis took the herringbone jacket from his desk chair, where it'd hung cockeyed since the day before, and hung it back in the closet. His interview was that afternoon. He picked up a stack of papers and books and placed them neatly in his leather backpack. He refolded the school board's letter and slipped it into his shirt pocket.

He glanced at his watch and headed out the door with Chester, his golden retriever, at his heels. He wore a down jacket, corduroy pants, button-down shirt, and baseball cap—the same outfit he usually wore when he went to the state house or an important school board meeting. Cindy, Marian, and Cyndy were his friends. They were used to seeing him in shirt sleeves, joking and working. The thought of putting on a suit to meet with people he knew so well made him feel uncomfortable, even a little hypocritical, so he didn't do it.

He left the cabin more than an hour before his interview was scheduled to take place. He wanted to leave plenty of time just in case he got stuck going down the mountain or encountered some other unforeseen delay. As a result, he arrived at the high school long before his appointment. Two men in tailored three-piece business suits, balancing briefcases on their knees, sat in chairs just outside the room where the board was meeting. Dennis introduced himself.

"You guys candidates too?" he asked.

They nodded. They didn't appear the least bit interested in talking to him. Dennis took off his baseball cap.

He had only a few minutes of sitting in him. He got up and paced. A few minutes later he went outside to let Chester run. He watched the dog cavort and sniff for a few minutes, then called him back and ushered him into the jeep. He went back into the school and waited.

Finally, it was his turn. He entered the conference room and greeted the board members, calling several of them by their first names. Marian Polaski, board chairperson, spoke first.

"Hello, Dennis," she said frostily. "Please sit down."

Her formal tone and the cool stares he got from the other board members instantly put him on edge. Marian sorted some papers. She read the first question from one of the papers in front of her. Dennis tried to adjust to the mood.

He was puzzled and answered perfunctorily. A few of the board members scribbled notes as he talked. Marian read the next question. "What is your stand on a dress code?"

Dennis looked around the room. "Do you mean for me or the kids?"

One of the board members narrowed his eyes. "It seems in your case we mean both."

"Well, folks, what you see is what you get!"

Dennis's response, delivered in an upbeat, musical tone, clearly did not amuse the board.

He retrenched. "Most of you know me already and know this is how I dress. Coming here in a suit just seemed somehow pretentious. I just don't feel right in a suit. I don't feel like me. I live in a cabin, and whether I'm working there or in school, I want to be comfortable. If I become principal, this is the kind of thing I'll wear. A good principal moves around a lot. That's what I intend to do at Thayer."

Marian asked the next question: "A lot of students already know you in town as Dennis. What would you have them call you in school?"

Dennis tried to muffle his sigh. "*I* don't really care if kids call me Dennis, but I know a lot of parents would. So, rather than make an issue of it, I would make it very clear that students must call me Mr. Littky, Dr. Littky, or Doc."

Once Dennis got past those questions, the issues of dress and name left his mind. He didn't want to dwell on them; he wanted to talk education. Soon he was seized by the energy of his own ideas and began firing out his plans, philosophies, and goals. He spoke in short, staccato sentences, gesturing wildly at times.

"It's not enough just to change the school. We've got to change the community's perception of it. Parents have to be involved. Teachers need to feel in control. We've got to change the negativism inside *and* outside the building.

School must be a place where students, teachers, and parents want to be."

They seemed to listen to him—but had they *heard*? He didn't know.

On the night the board planned to pick a principal and offer the job, Dennis told Marian Polaski that he could be contacted at Marcia Ammann's house.

Marcia had bought champagne and munchies to celebrate the announcement. Marian was to call between 7 and 8 P.M. to let them know the board's decision. After that, Dennis and Marcia planned to call the *Star* staff for an impromptu celebration. Chester sensed the excitement in the air and gnawed at Dennis's heels. At eight o'clock, Marcia assembled a tray of cheese and crackers. She chattered nervously, smoked several cigarettes. Dennis picked at a piece of cheese with the edge of a cracker. The telephone stubbornly refused to ring.

Two hours passed. Finally Marcia called the Polaskis'.

"Hi, Pete, this is Marcia. Is Marian still at the meeting?"

"No, Marcia. She's been back for a while. Let me go get her."

Marcia held her breath. Marian picked up the phone.

"Well?" Marcia asked.

"I'm sorry, I can't tell you anything."

"Did you reach a decision?"

"I can't even tell you that, Marcia."

When Marcia hung up the phone, she looked at Dennis and shrugged her shoulders.

"She didn't tell me anything. She said she couldn't."

"It just means they haven't come to a decision yet," Dennis said.

Marcia wasn't so sure, but she didn't tell Dennis that. She knew that Dennis's "What you see is what you get" comment had irritated several board members. Dennis left a few minutes later. The champagne was in the refrigerator, still corked.

The five school board members had deliberated long and hard that night. When they finally reached their decision, Dennis wasn't their choice. They offered the job to one of the men in the three-piece suits. The man told the board the next morning that he'd thought it over and he didn't want the job.

Dennis Littky was second in line.

The assistant superintendent called Marian to give her the news. When she heard, she cried, just as she had the night before when she learned he hadn't gotten the job.

Marian tracked down Dennis at the *Star* office. "Hello, Mr. Principal!" she caroled.

"Hi, Boss!" Dennis called out, then crossed the room in three steps and hugged her, picking his short chubby friend off her feet.

"So how come you waited until this morning to tell me?" Marian studied Dennis closely.

"Dennis, you weren't the board's first choice. The man we offered the position to turned us down this morning."

This was a possibility that had never occurred to Dennis. For whatever reason, he had just figured they'd postponed making the decision.

"You were my first choice, Dennis," Marian said. "I want you to know that. I think you'll make an outstanding principal. As far as the other board members go—I don't feel at liberty to tell you how they voted. And I'm sorry about the stiff, formal manner of the interview. We didn't want to show any favoritism. We wanted to treat your interview in the same manner as we did all the candidates."

When Marian left the office, Dennis reeled—elated that he was going to be the principal, crestfallen that he hadn't been the board's first choice.

Later that day, Cindy Nelson came to the office and asked to speak to him alone.

"Dennis, I want you to hear this from me. I want to explain myself to you. I didn't vote for you. This last week has been torture for me. I went back and forth about supporting you or not. Your credentials are amazing. Your leadership ability—well, you know what an incredible leader I think you are. But, in good conscience, I just couldn't vote for you."

Dennis's mind raced. Cindy was the person he'd worked most closely with on the PTA. He'd spent hours and hours offering suggestions and helping her organize meetings. She'd seen him in action on the *Star*. She knew he'd been a good school board member during the five months he served. *Why?* Why hadn't she voted for him? He waited for her to answer on her own.

"Dennis, as good as you are, and as much as I, personally, wanted to see you in the job, I just don't think you're right for this town. You're a couple of decades ahead of Winchester. Your ideas *sound* great—but I just think you're too much too fast. I know this town; I know what they think of people like you. I'm afraid of the rejection you're going to suffer. I've already heard talk . . ."

She stopped. Her eyes were tear-rimmed. Her voice was half-choked.

"This was the most difficult decision I think I've ever had to make. The man I voted for was very well qualified. I think he would have made an excellent principal. I know the same is true for you. I just think you'd do better at a different school in a different town."

When Marcia Ammann heard Dennis got the job, her own reaction surprised her. She'd wanted Dennis to be principal so desperately, for so many reasons: it meant he'd stay in Winchester; it meant there was hope for the school again; it meant the Ammanns could take their home off the market. Now there was something to stay for.

But when it was confirmed that Dennis had the job, Marcia felt a creeping unease. Other considerations occurred to her. She wondered why she hadn't thought of them before.

She was afraid for Dennis. The kids were tough as nails, the staff members too. She'd seen him accomplish some absolutely amazing things before, but winning the confidence of these hard kids and their hard teachers would take a miracle. And there were bigger worries.

Dennis had enemies. She'd heard talk from the men at the barber shop. They thought Dennis was a "commie subversive." They said he was a "womanizer," a "dirty hippie." They thought he had some kind of master plan to take over the town and that she, Marian, Cyndy, Cindy, Winnie Amarosa, and all the other *Star* staffers had been duped, maybe even brainwashed.

The *Keene Sentinel* ran a long article that day about Littky's appointment. The story outlined his credentials, listed the education awards he'd received and the accolades from nationally known educators. The picture in the paper was the same one Dennis had used on his campaign literature for state representative—woolly beard, plaid work shirt, Jeep cap, wire-rimmed glasses.

An assembly was held in the gymnasium a few days later to introduce Littky to the students. Dr. Saunders, the outgoing principal, gave a brief introduction, then sat down. He let Dennis carry the ball.

The five members of the Winchester School Board sat next to the podium, along with the assistant superintendent and principal. Dennis walked confidently to the podium, carrying a few sheets of paper with him. His voice boomed when he spoke. He kept things upbeat, excited, and strong. He never looked at his notes. His attention was on the rows of students in front of him.

His voice rang out: "Many of you already know me," he said. "I recognize several faces out there. I've played basket-

ball with some of you, gone jogging with some and talked
with several of you hangin' out on Main Street. Most of you
know me as Dennis. That was fine then, but as of July 1, I'll
be your principal. From here on, I'm 'Dr. Littky,' 'Doc,' or
'Mr. Littky.'

"You'll probably be seeing a lot of me during the next
several weeks before summer vacation. I'm going to try to
stay out of Dr. Saunders's way, but I'd like to get to know as
many of you as possible and see how things operate here.

"I'm really looking forward to being your principal."

Marian Polaski studied Dennis. His voice was strong and
confident, but from her place behind the podium she could
see Dennis's legs shaking. She smiled softly, endeared.

Karen Thompson studied the new principal with a mix-
ture of curiosity, bemusement, and awe. He was so different
from any principal she'd ever seen—he seemed nice, in a
crazy sort of way. Maybe he'd let kids get away with more
stuff, she thought. Maybe he'd be cool with kids. Maybe next
year would be different—*better*.

When Dennis finished his speech, a handful of students
stood and applauded. In a slow, lackluster way, the rest
followed. Littky felt great.

11
The First Step

IT WAS MONTHS BEFORE JULY 1, when Littky would take over as principal and start drawing pay, but he was spending more than eight hours a day observing, planning, and pounding the pavement for the school. He talked about the school with anyone he came across.

Without exception, every parent Littky talked to was deeply discouraged. Several were embarrassed to tell outsiders where they lived and where their children went to school. Many longed for Thayer to return to the way it was when they were students there.

Dennis talked to every Thayer student he knew.

"Who are the leaders in school?" he asked. "Are there any gangs? Which teachers do you think are the best? Which are the worst? If you could change anything in school, what would it be?"

He listened and learned.

Littky was in school the day students got their report cards. Kids ran up and down the halls congratulating each other on how many F's they'd gotten. The scene rattled him.

In May, Littky invited all the teachers to meet with him at the community center for juice, soda, conversation, and a briefing on goals and programs he had in mind. He billed it as "a chance to get to know your new principal."

Littky stood near the door and greeted the teachers as

they arrived. He'd had private talks with several of them, and he called those teachers by their first names. He did his best to make everyone feel comfortable and important. Then he got things going.

"The individual conferences I've had so far have been extremely valuable. A couple of things keep coming up—like study halls and discipline. I think I'm going to eliminate study halls completely. None of the students seem to use them for their intended purpose, and I haven't talked to a teacher yet who wouldn't prefer doing six months of hard labor to a day of supervising study hall."

Several teachers laughed.

"I think you all recognize the school is in tough shape, physically and educationally. I give you all a lot of credit for hanging in there as well as you have; a lesser group wouldn't have survived. With your help, I expect to make a lot of changes throughout the school—to the building, the curriculum, the structure of the day."

The teachers were attentive.

"I believe in creating environments, both physical and educational. An environment built on respect will go a long way toward reducing the discipline problem. The real task is trying to find out what kind of environments will work best for the kids at Thayer—and that's where I depend on you. I can't do anything unless you work with me. I need your ideas, your insights, your grievances. You're the ones who've worked in the school over the past months and years, and you're the ones who've got the best grasp of what's working and what needs to be changed.

"I have a strong faith in the kids in this town. I know a number of students already from my activities in town, and they're *good* kids. A lot of Thayer students may think it's cool to be bad. I believe we can change that. Nobody really wants to fail. If kids are given the chance to succeed, most will—but we've got to provide the right environment, we've got to work together to make school an exciting, rewarding place to be. We've got to make kids feel good about themselves. Only then can we really get them to be active learners.

"This summer I plan to meet individually with all of you. I'll ask you about your goals, your dreams, what's worked for you as a teacher, what hasn't. I'll ask you what you think most needs changing at Thayer—so be ready to answer.

"The biggest project for the summer will be to set up students' schedules. I plan to do that personally."

Several teachers looked up, amazed.

"I've stopped the practice of arena scheduling for a lot of reasons, but mostly because I just don't think it's a good way to make sure that the kids are getting into the classes they ought to be in. A student's curriculum is far too important to leave up to a random process.

"I want to build a curriculum around the *needs* of the kids. I can't know what those needs are until I get to know the kids better. I've put together a questionnaire for students, asking them about their interests, plans after graduation, and so on. I've gotten clearance from Dr. Saunders to pass it out during school next week. This information will help me set up a preliminary schedule, but during the summer I plan to meet individually with each student in the high school, so I'll be making adjustments in the schedule regularly.

"Your suggestions about new courses are encouraged. I can use any help I can get . . ."

A hand shot up. Littky nodded to the art teacher. "I can come in any morning during the week to help with scheduling."

"Good!"

Another teacher raised her hand. "I'm not sure what my summer schedule will be," she said, "but I think I can spare a few afternoons a week."

"Great!" Littky wrote down their names. "I'll be meeting

with everybody again in June, on the day after the last day of school. I know that's usually a time for cleaning out your rooms and saying good-bye for the summer, but I really need that day to organize for the start of school in the fall. So be prepared to work.

"I'll be out of town for the next several weeks, but after that I plan to be at the school every day. So any time you can give to the school would be a big help. This is *your* school. Without you it can't work.

"We have one of the smallest budgets of all school districts in New Hampshire, but that doesn't mean we can't be the best school in the state. We may never have the highest SAT scores or the most impressive list of colleges our graduates have gone to, but we will be the most appropriate school around. Thayer will be tailor-made to fit the needs of its kids. Most of all, I want to give them options. I want them to know there's more out there than factory work and farming. If that's what they decide they want, that's fine—I just want them to make an *informed* decision.

"Since we're not a money-rich school, we're going to have to be creative. This town is rich in resources; we only need to find out who and what they are. I want to hear your thoughts. No idea is too outrageous, too farfetched to consider. Start thinking and dreaming about your vision of what a good school is all about.

"Beyond us, we also need to learn from the community and the kids what they want from school. Then let's pull it all together and formulate a united vision. From there, everything else will follow."

When the meeting ended, a few stayed behind to talk about their ideas and about the problems they saw plaguing the school.

"We feel like we've been ripped off," one teacher said to Dennis. "The teachers get blamed for everything that goes wrong at this school, and all we're trying to do is keep our heads above water."

There were murmurs of agreement.

Littky nodded. *"That's* what we're going to change," he said.

The day after school ended, teachers were required by contract to show up for an end-of-the-year workshop. Littky didn't want to pass up the opportunity to use the time productively. He needed to work with them, needed it bad, but when the day came he was uneasy about it. It'd been a tough year for them all, and the last thing they wanted to think about was *next* year.

When the teachers were all together, Dr. Saunders made a brief farewell speech and handed the meeting over to Littky, who apologized for making them stay and work, then got down to business. He spoke quickly, precisely.

"A lot of what we're going to do today is look at ideas I've worked out based on what you've told me, as well as what I've gathered from students, administration, and the community. Please speak out if you disagree with any of these ideas.

"My strategy is to state how I feel, the direction I want to move—I'll provide the guidelines, then I'll allow each of you to develop those guidelines in whatever way seems best for you. My goal is to make the school appropriate for the kids. The school must change, and a lot of those changes will be instituted this summer. Unfortunately, that means more direction from me than I'd like. I'd prefer to involve everyone much more actively in the initial changes, but I just don't see how it's possible in the few months before school starts.

"The biggest complaint I've heard from you, besides discipline and study halls, is being required to teach junior high. As high school teachers, most of you have said you don't like having to shift gears to teach a junior high class. I've adjusted the schedule in a way that will eliminate that.

"Two major changes will take place: first of all, I'm

separating the seventh and eighth graders from the high school. The transition from elementary school to junior high is difficult enough for kids without tossing them into the same building with high schoolers. Those kids are too young to be mingling in the halls with the older kids, so I've designated part of the building the junior high wing. Class change will also occur at different times.

"As far as the teaching staff is concerned, I'd like one teacher from every content area to volunteer to teach seventh and eighth grades exclusively. That way, you can work together as a group to integrate the curriculum in a way that will emphasize each of your specialties. You'll have *no* responsibilities to the high school. The idea is to give the junior high its own identity."

A hand went up. "Dr. Littky, I think I'd be interested in teaching junior high."

Another hand went up. "I'd like to think about it some more, but I'm definitely interested."

Littky nodded and smiled. "Later we'll be meeting in small groups for discussions. All those interested in teaching junior high will form one group. I'd like you to make your decision during the next several weeks if possible.

"The next important topic is the academic advisory system, which pertains to all students and faculty, and the high school schedule.

"The student questionnaire was a big help to me. Many of the kids don't know what they need. Most of the juniors and seniors who responded had no idea what they wanted to do after graduation. We had seventy students drop classes last year. Last semester 270 failure notices were sent home. There's something wrong with that, and it's not just the kids. We need to work more closely with each student in setting up their schedules, starting with the seventh grade.

"One guidance counselor can't handle 325 kids alone, and that's where your role as an adviser comes in. I had our counselor, Phil Hamm, separate the kids into groups of seventeen by grade. Each of you will be responsible for a group. If you want to trade students with another teacher, that's fine with me. Your role will be to make sure each student in your advisory group develops a schedule according to his or her needs and abilities. You'll keep tabs on how your students are doing, record their grades, and evaluate their progress. If a child is having problems, it's your role to bring it to my attention and work with me and the student in solving it.

"Advisory will replace homeroom for the first ten minutes of every school day. In addition, you'll meet once a month individually with each member of your group to talk about how he's doing in school—his goals, his concerns, his classes—or anything else.

"When the first report cards come out ten weeks into the semester, I'd like you to set up conferences with parents and students. You'll provide parents with their direct link to school. I want their first contact with us to be personal and positive—failure notices aren't the way to help parents feel good about what's going on in school.

"The advisory program will start out slowly, but with time I want you to build on it. The idea behind advisory is to give every student *somebody*—a staff member—who they can go to with any problems or questions they have about school. Since you'll have them as a group for up to four years, you'll be the consistent staff member in their school lives."

The sky was darkening as Littky left the school that day. His jeep was alone in the parking lot. As he walked down the sidewalk, a Winchester police cruiser pulled up. A cop got out of the car.

"Hi, officer," Littky shouted out. "Am I double-parked or something?"

The cop stood by his cruiser. He didn't speak. Littky shifted his pack of books and papers from his right shoulder to his left and kept walking. He stopped when he got to the cruiser. He reached out his hand.

"Hi, I'm Dennis Littky, the new principal."

"Yeah, I know," the officer said slowly. "I'm Jim Harrison, the police chief."

"Hey, man, nice to meet you in person. I've heard your name often enough."

"I figured I ought to introduce myself. Winchester police tend to spend a lot of time here when school's in session."

"Well I hope that won't be the case so much next year."

"We'll see." There was a long silence. Harrison looked him over. "Say . . . Mr. Littky . . ."

"Call me Dennis."

"I'd like to offer you a suggestion. Shave off your beard and wear a tie to school."

Littky thought for a moment before replying. "Thanks for the advice," he said. He turned and walked to his jeep. Harrison was still standing next to his cruiser when Littky left the parking lot.

Summer vacation had only just begun, but Karen Thompson was bored. When the postman walked up to the house to deliver the mail, Karen was there to greet him. She sorted through the stack of letters and cards, excited when she saw her name on one of the envelopes. The return address was Thayer High School. That didn't excite her. She tore it open.

Please come to Thayer High School on July 14 at 1 P.M. to schedule your classes for next fall. You will be meeting with your new principal, Dr. Littky. If you can't make the scheduled time, please call the office as soon as possible to reschedule. Parents are welcome to attend. I'm looking forward to meeting with you.
Sincerely, Dennis Littky

Karen had never before received a letter from her principal. She reread the message, eager to show her father when he got home from the paper mill.

Val Cole was openly suspicious of Littky. She'd never really talked to the man, and she'd missed the meeting at the conference center because of a dentist appointment to have a tooth pulled. It was the first time in her life she was actually glad she was getting a tooth yanked. The few times she'd seen Littky in school chatting with students or walking the hall with Dr. Saunders, she'd passed him by without saying a word. When she was introduced to him, she confined herself to a polite response and walked away from the hippie principal as quickly as she could manage. Her summer meeting with him would be her first direct encounter.

When she walked into the office, Val saw Littky talking on the phone, feet propped up on his desk. He wore white carpenter pants, a green T-shirt from the Newfane Banjo Festival, a painter's cap, and Birkenstock sandals. Val scowled, annoyed by Littky's brazen casualness. She overlooked her own attire—jeans, T-shirt, and sneakers.

Littky motioned Val into his office and hung up the phone.

"Val," he shook her hand, "good to see you again." He took a box of books off a chair. "I know it looks like I've moved the library into my office, but actually this is only about half my books. There's another dozen boxes or so still up at my cabin."

Val sat down, unengaged by Littky's casual conversation. He looked her straight in the eye.

"So," he said. "I understand you didn't want me to get the job."

Val's heart sunk. Her mind raced—who told him *that*? For a moment she said nothing. Then she returned his steady stare.

"You're right." The bald truth made her feel better.

"Mind saying why?"

"Well, if the truth be told, I'm a little put off by your looks—you just don't fit my image of a principal. I think we need a strong disciplinarian to get this school back on its feet, and you just don't look like you're cut out to do the job."

Littky nodded. "I don't disagree with you that we need strong discipline. I'm tough when I need to be, but for the most part I think discipline problems can be controlled if the kids respect the school and the teachers, and if they want to be here."

Val laughed. "Good luck," she said.

Littky didn't return her cynicism.

"I need you to work with me," he said. "Cyndy Ryder's girls tell me you're one of the best teachers in the school. I'm counting on you to help me plan for next year."

No wonder he got the job, Val thought. He's a politician all the way.

Her lack of enthusiasm showed in her voice. "Oh yes, of course. I'm willing to work with you. I'll do what I can to help you get the school back together."

Littky ignored her halfheartedness.

"So," he said, "tell me about the school."

Against her will, Val felt herself responding to something in Littky's manner. Maybe it was the sincere ring in his voice, his direct manner. She dropped her guard some. The more she talked, the more forthright she became. Before she knew it, she was spilling out stories about life at Thayer. She detailed its strengths and weaknesses, and even allowed herself to speak critically of a fellow teacher. She said she didn't want any of her six children to get anywhere near this teacher.

"The kids don't learn *anything* in his class. They sit around day after day playing these silly board games and gossiping. My oldest son had him. He was supposed to hand in a thirty-five-page paper on Greek gods. He did, but on the last dozen pages or so the margins got wider and wider until he only had about three words per line on the last several pages to bring it up to the requisite number. I read the paper and I can honestly say I wouldn't have given him an F for it. *This* guy gave him a B-minus.

"What really galls me is that there wasn't a single comment on the entire paper. I'm sure he didn't even read it."

Right after her conference with Littky, Val headed to Barb Eibell's house. Barb wasn't scheduled to meet with him until the following week, but she was anxious about it.

"Well, how'd it go?" Barb asked.

"A lot better than I expected, almost too good."

"What does that mean?"

"He knew I didn't want him for the job. Phyllis Ryder must have told him."

"You mean he actually confronted you?"

"He wasn't confrontational about it at all. He just said it. Then somehow I started telling him *everything*. I don't even remember exactly how it happened. I just started talking and couldn't stop. I even told him about Mr. C. and my son's thirty-five-page paper."

"Wow."

"I feel terrible about it now. How incredibly unprofessional. I broke one of the cardinal rules—'Thou shalt never criticize a fellow teacher.' "

"Yeah," Barb agreed.

"I guess it was because I trusted him. Or maybe it's just that I *wanted* to trust him. He's got all these ideas and plans. And he wants me to work on ideas right away. We actually talked about teaching technique and curriculum. I told him about the section I taught on the Bible a couple of semesters ago. I told him how I just added the section on the spur of the moment to fill in the last month of school even though I knew next to nothing about the Bible. When I told him how I thought that worked to my advantage he looked really interested, even kind of excited.

"So I kept on. I told how I went to the library and took out everything there on the Bible and pored over it—we'd just finished reading *Moby Dick*, and there I stumbled on Ahab, Peleg, Bildad, and Jonah. I thought it was all so incredibly interesting. But I realized I couldn't spend three hours reading each night preparing for one or two days of lectures. I had other classes to prepare for as well. So I told Dennis how I met that Monday morning with my senior seminar class and confessed my ignorance about the literature of the Bible. But I explained why I thought learning about it would be a worthwhile pursuit and suggested we might tackle this problem together and that this class might now contain sixteen students and no teacher.

"You should have seen Dennis's face. It was all lit up like a little kid's. He was so excited, he kept saying, 'That's great! That's great! That's the kind of teaching I'm talking about!'

"I'm still not sure what's so great about confessing ignorance—but he's right, it was one of the most rewarding classes I've ever taught. Everything about it was fresh and warm, and the kids were excited and engaged. Several of them already knew about Ahab because they'd read about him in Sunday school, and they drew connections that I'd overlooked."

Barb's husband, Fred, came in from the next room.

"I don't know," he said. "He sounds great on one hand, but trouble on the other. It's tough working for a fanatic. They expect too much. They eat, sleep, and live for their job, and expect you to do the same."

At the end of June, Littky attended the annual New Hampshire Principals Conference in Bretton Woods. Conferences were not his favorite pastime. Rarely, if ever, did he come away from one of these things enlightened. More often than not his colleagues' passiveness and lack of imagination left him angry and frustrated. He wouldn't know anybody; nobody would know him. That always made him anxious. Besides, it meant losing two days he could put to better use getting ready for school.

Still, if the conference could put him in touch with people who might be of some help to the school, his time wouldn't be wasted.

That evening, cocktails and dinner were served at the formal dining room in the Mount Washington Hotel. Dennis donned a fresh shirt and corduroys and walked to the dining room, scanning the sea of suits and ties for friendly faces.

A man stepped up behind him. "I'm sorry, sir. I'm afraid you can't go in there."

Dennis wheeled around and stared. Before he could open his mouth, the maître d' took hold of his elbow and directed him away from the dining room.

"The house rules require that you wear a jacket and tie."

Finally grasping the situation, Dennis let out a laugh that rose straight up from his belly. But the maître d' wasn't laughing. "You'll have to put on a jacket and tie if you want to enter the dining room."

"I'd be happy to," Dennis said. "But all I've got in my room are a couple more shirts like this and another pair of corduroys, only they're not in nearly as good a shape as these."

There was a flurry of hushed conversation between the maître d' and another hotel worker, who returned a few moments later with a jacket and rep tie. Dennis put them on and walked into the dining room. The jacket sleeves came up well above his wrist bones. He had to walk with his shoulders hunched up to keep from ripping the jacket. He felt ridiculous.

But when he returned to Winchester, Littky was on an energy high. The several hours' drive back to town gave him time to think about school.

When he got to the cabin, he was bubbling with ideas. He opened his journal.

Everything—*everything* revolves around the schedule. It's by far the most important structure in the school. That's why it's so crucial that I get it right, or at least on target.

The problem is that I have to set up the schedule as soon as possible—and I know only vaguely what needs to be scheduled. Still, I've got to let teachers know what they'll be teaching so they can use the summer to prepare. Also, my plan to meet individually with all 250 high school students, to *personally* schedule their classes—that's going to take a huge chunk of time to organize and carry out. And, yet, how can I start setting up individual schedules if I don't know what classes are going to be offered? And I won't know what classes are going to be offered until I meet with the students.

Littky met with guidance counselor Phil Hamm to develop the schedule. Phil had turned out to be a good resource. During the previous school year, Phil and the assistant principal had found themselves managing the day-to-day business of the school. Dr. Saunders's flagging interest in the school had been worsened by his wife's lingering death from cancer. Phil was a guidance counselor; running a school was far outside his training, but he'd done his best. In addition, he dealt with the steady flow of students who were habitually kicked out of class for misbehaving—sometimes thirty-five kids a day were sent to him for discipline. Three or four days of every month, Hamm appeared in court to testify on behalf of students who were victims of physical and sexual abuse at home.

For Littky, Phil provided a straight-talking, essential shortcut. He spoke freely about teachers, students, classes, and daily school operations, supplying Littky with information that would have taken him months to gather on his own.

For three days they worked out a schedule, anxiously preparing for the first of the high school student conferences. All study halls had been eliminated, but that posed a problem. It meant students would have to be in one class or another *every* period of the day—and there simply weren't enough teachers to go around. When he looked at schedules from the previous year, Littky discovered that most students had taken only two or three classes, then padded the rest of their day with study halls.

"No wonder things were out of control," he said. "Those kids must have been bored as hell."

But study halls accomplished one thing. With so few class periods, there were enough teachers to cover the courses that were offered.

Littky and Phil Hamm grappled with the problem for several hours, then came up with a solution, albeit an imperfect one.

"Let's cut the class periods down from seven to five," Littky said. "We still don't have enough teachers, but let's try to make it work." They hammered out a general schedule, doing their best to match teachers and classes.

Four days into the process, Littky got a call from the bus company. Cheshire Transportation bused Winchester students to and from school, and a company official had phoned to ask what hours Thayer would be operating on in the fall. It had never occurred to Littky that the local district could control the length of the school day through something as simple as the bus schedule.

He told the man he'd call him back, hung up, and contacted the state department of education to find out the minimum number of hours students had to be in school daily. If he could control when students came to school, he could restructure the school day completely. The answer from the state was heartening—five and a half hours. By shortening the day and lengthening the class periods from fifty minutes to an hour there would be almost enough teachers for a full schedule of class periods and enough classes to handle all the students. Using outside resources and volunteers, he could fill in any holes that remained.

Dennis phoned Assistant Superintendent Roger Sundstrom.

"Roger," he said, "I want to cut the school day back to five one-hour periods."

"What was that?" Sundstrom asked.

"I want to shorten the day for students by an hour. They would come to school at 8:50 A.M. and leave at 2:20, but every student would be required to take five classes, with no study halls—it's like gaining two or three teachers."

"I don't know, Dennis," Sundstrom said reluctantly. "That sounds a little extreme. The state requires . . ."

"I just talked to the state," Littky said quickly. "The minimum is five and a half. I could use the hour in the morning to meet with teachers, maybe have a regular breakfast meeting every Monday. The other days could be used by teachers for individual student conferences, private meetings with me, or class preparation. I really need the time with the staff to set goals, work on curriculum, and get this school in order. Study halls have got to go—they almost ruined the school last year. This is the only way to do it."

Sundstrom dug his heels in. "I don't know Dennis. You'd have to get the okay from the board on that. Ultimately, it's their decision."

"Yeah, I know. I think I can manage that."

An issue that kept coming up was the need to make the schedule relevant to the students. "I don't want them to be in class just to be in a class," Littky said time and again. "I want their learning to be relevant and compelling. There are just too many kids who don't do well in a rigidly structured classroom environment. I want to offer them alternatives, some variety, something that makes learning come alive."

"The Cheshire Vocational Center does a pretty good job at that," Phil Hamm suggested. "It's got all the latest equipment." The center was located at Keene High School, offering all thirty-two communities in the region a wide range of occupational training from construction to child care.

"But look how far Winchester is from Keene," Littky protested. "It takes an hour out of the school day just shuffling them there and back. I agree the center is extremely well-equipped and works well for some of our students. But there's no reason why we can't provide some of it right here in Winchester."

"We'll *never* have the money to match what they've got at the center. That's a multimillion-dollar facility," Phil countered. "We have a hard time coming up with enough cash to outfit our shop with hammers and nails."

"That's just not true," Littky said. "We've already got it."

"What do you mean?"

"Just what I said—we've got it all right here in the community. There isn't a piece of machinery at the center that Ronnie Bedaw doesn't have in his garage. There isn't a single piece of beauty equipment they've got there that isn't at the Village Beauty Salon. Not only that, the beauty shop and Ronnie can provide the kids something the vocational center can't—real world experience. We wouldn't be *simulating* the work place, we'd actually be in it. It'd be something like an apprenticeship.

"The center is great for some of our students, but it's not flexible enough for others. Each apprenticeship could be custom-designed to suit a particular kid. Why try to re-create the world under one roof, when you can go out into your own community and see how the world works in a much more immediate way? Not only that, it would hardly cost the school anything."

"You're right!" Phil said. "All we need is someone to coordinate the thing."

"I've been working on that for a couple of days. The budget says we've got $10,500 to hire a new English teacher. While it's true we could use another English instructor, I've come up with a plan that'll make better use of that money. I want to hire three part-time people instead—one to run the apprenticeship program, one to act as a community coordinator, and one to run a building program. I'm still debating about the third job, bringing in a carpenter who would teach kids building skills. That could also help the school in a lot of ways. The kids would be learning and building structures that could be used by the school, maybe help expand our classroom space. God knows we need more of that."

"What are the chances of getting the three jobs past the school board?"

"Pretty good, I think. I've already started talking to several of them about what I have in mind, so they're getting used to the idea. Besides, one of Cindy Nelson's main concerns is providing good vocational education for our kids. It'd be a little tough for her to look at a proposal like the apprenticeship program and turn it down. Besides, I'll tell them up front I need their support for these things or I won't be able to do my job."

"Let's hope you convince them," Phil said. "By the way, your carpenter idea reminded me of something. I saw an ad in the newspaper this morning that I thought might interest you."

Phil handed Littky the article he'd clipped. The headline read, "TAKE THIS DOME!" and described a thirty-eight-foot geodesic dome that Marlboro College in Vermont wanted removed. The college used the dome as a campus center, coffee shop, and bookstore. A new building was to replace it. The ad asked for bids to remove the dome from the campus.

"That's perfect!" Littky said. "We could get a carpenter to oversee the project, then have some kids dismantle the thing and rebuild it here behind the school. We could use the building for additional classroom space—which we're desperate for anyway."

"A friend of mine is a fantastic carpenter—he just finished building his own house, and you should see it. He's always wanted to teach high school; I know he studied at a teacher's college for a while but just never finished. I think he might be interested."

By the end of the day, Littky had reached officials at Marlboro College and explained his plan to use the dome as an educational project. Littky's catch: he wanted the dome for free. Marlboro officials considered the proposal and agreed to give it to Thayer High if he could guarantee removal by August 21.

"No problem," Dennis said. He hung up and turned to Phil. "Can you get me in contact with your carpenter friend right now? Tell him I'd like to meet with him to talk about a teaching job."

Phil Hamm's friend impressed Littky. Though Dennis hadn't secured approval from the board for the position, he felt confident he'd get the backing he needed. If not, he'd fund it some other way.

12
Pegasus

BARB EIBELL'S CONFERENCE WITH LITTKY began like a fast dance. The things he said left her breathless and sweaty.

"As far as I'm concerned, foreign languages are taught all wrong just about everywhere in the country," Littky said. "Schools do a frighteningly good job of poisoning kids against learning and loving language.

"Barb, I really think what you ought to do is just throw out your books—dump 'em! Get rid of 'em—then go and teach your kids."

"Throw out my *books*?" Barb said.

"All of 'em. The fact is, memorizing the subjunctive case and studying declensions has about as much value to these kids as a broken record. It's just not possible to learn a language with any kind of competency when class meets for only an hour a day."

"Slow down," Barb said. "What are you saying?"

Littky smiled. "I got a call from an agency a few days ago asking if Thayer High was interested in taking a foreign exchange student. I told them I'd leave it up to the language teacher. But this is just the kind of relevancy I'm talking about—get some kid from Spain or Mexico to come here, give our kids someone to talk to, a way to *use* this new language they're learning.

"Most of our kids have never been outside of New En-

110

gland, let alone to a foreign country. How do they really know such things exist? I mean, think about it. Maybe on some abstract, intellectual level they know there are other lands and cultures, but do they know this in any kind of relevant or meaningful way? I doubt it. A foreign student who speaks little or no English would be ideal. That would help our kids understand there are other worlds out there besides their own, worlds they've never even dreamed of."

"What's involved with this foreign exchange program?" Littky shoved a piece of paper toward her.

"Here's the phone number," he said. "Find out."

Barb felt drained but exhilarated. It took a few moments to sink in—not only was she going to arrange for a foreign student to come live in Winchester for a year, she was to find out how Thayer students could be sent to foreign countries. She clutched the telephone number in her fist. Then a thought occurred to her.

"But how can we afford it?" she asked.

"Fund-raisers," Littky said. "All you need to do is think up some ways to make money—then do it."

"'All I need to do . . . ,'" she repeated to herself. "'All I need to do . . .'"

"I don't get it," Barb said to her husband when she got home. "A few days ago we were talking about moving away; now all of a sudden I'm thinking about foreign students and fund-raisers. He told me to throw out my books! He said it'd be the best thing I could do for my classes!"

"He's probably right," Fred said.

"Not only that, he wants me to teach French and Spanish to the eighth grade—the *entire* eighth grade."

"You mean he wants to make it a mandatory course?"

"Yes. That means I'll mostly be teaching students who don't want to be there. I told him conditions were tough enough without trying to teach a bunch of kids who couldn't care less about language—"

"What'd he say?" Fred asked.

"He said that's my job—my *challenge*, as he put it—to make them care. That's easy to say, but not so easy to do. I just don't know if I can keep up with him. He's really demanding a lot."

"What do you mean? This is the kind of teaching you've always craved. Now it's here, looking you right in the face, and you want to run away from it?"

The next day she called Littky.

"Dennis, are you definitely going through with the mandatory eighth-grade language class?"

"It's already in the schedule," Dennis said.

"Then I'd like to meet with you, if I could, about how to approach it."

"Great!" Littky said. "I've got appointments booked solid up 'til five; can you come after that?"

"Today?"

"Of course."

Barb marveled at his energy. She'd seen him jog past her house early that morning while she still was hugging a steaming coffee cup and staring blankly at the fog-en-shrouded cemetery across the way. His whole day was crammed with appointments, and he was still willing—no, *eager*—to meet with her to talk over her problems. If he brought that kind of energy to every meeting . . . Barb was just a little daunted.

When she arrived, Littky was hanging a plant in front of one of his office windows. He was still wearing his running shorts, T-shirt, and jogging shoes.

He stepped off the chair and smiled at the plant.

"It's life," he said, as if that explained something.

Barb glanced around the office. It was a veritable jungle of vegetation.

Littky beamed. "I grew them in the greenhouse at my cabin. I'm thinking about getting some students together for a building class and making a greenhouse right here at the school. The science and home economics classes could use it for study."

Once again, Barb was caught up in Littky's boundless enthusiasm.

"Language shouldn't be restricted to the small group of college-bound students," he told Barb. "Eighth grade is a good time to give all students a general exposure to new languages and cultures."

Barb found herself growing more and more excited about teaching the eighth graders. It really would be a challenge to do the job in one year. Since she knew most of the students weren't likely to go any farther with the language, that meant packing in as much as she could about Spain and France. She found herself saying "Spain" and "France" instead of "Spanish" and "French." With so short a time, language proficiency was out of the question. Even if she spent all her time on her traditional "Language I" format, what good would it do? Language I was supposed to be followed by Language II and so on. This was a whole new ball game. She had to get at the essentials. What would give them the clearest picture of those countries, a picture that would stick with them?

"How am I going to do it, Dennis?" she asked. "How am I going to make it relevant?"

He thought a moment. "If you only had one day to teach French and Spanish to your students, what would you do?"

Barb thought hard. "I guess I'd bring in a native speaker so the students could hear the sound of the language. I'd teach them basic phrases they could use if they ever went to the country, maybe set up a marketplace or cafe simulation so the kids could act out situations and learn about some of the culture."

"There you go, you've got it! That's your curriculum."

Barb was stunned.

"Just like that?" she said, unbelieving.

"Just like that."

Littky hired a new head custodian—Jim Burns, a hard worker, willing to take on repair of the dilapidated school as a sort of "ultimate challenge." The building's sorry shape seemed to energize him. He and Littky walked the halls and inspected classrooms, making a roster of needed repairs. When they were done, they organized them in order of priority, and the custodian went to work.

"I want the school to *look* different," Littky told him. "I want these kids to walk through that door on the first day of school and know immediately that things have changed."

The floors would be sanded down and refinished, stained or missing ceiling tiles replaced. Broken windows would be fixed and the walls painted.

"The colors should be upbeat and bright," Littky said.

"Gotcha, boss," Jim said with a smile.

Littky shook his head in amazement. "Look at these walls! Blue, brown, mustard yellow. They must've bought whatever color was on sale at the time!"

"Pretty ugly," the custodian agreed. "It's going to be a job cleaning those walls before we can paint."

Everything was dirty, nearly every inch covered with pencil and pen marks, smeared hand prints, or dirty words.

Dennis commandeered a few workers from CETA, the federally funded job training program. Most of them were Thayer High students pulling CETA duty as summer jobs.

Work began immediately—bathrooms first. Sinks had been broken off the walls. Graffiti was everywhere. Stall doors broken, trash cans bent. There was plenty to do.

Jim armed the kids with paint scrapers, buckets, sponges, and mops. They scraped the walls and floors, scoured the sinks and urinals, and helped Jim reattach them to the walls. With buckets of paint, the crew started covering over the graffiti. One CETA worker wiped his paintbrush over a string of obscenities scrawled across a section of the wall.

"Shit," he said. "I think *I* wrote this."

Bathrooms done, Jim set his crew to work pounding out dents in the lockers, fixing the latches, and painting over the army green with bright, cheery blues and oranges.

During lulls, Littky fixed up the main office. He'd ripped up the old, threadbare carpet and found a hardwood floor underneath. Jim and his crew refinished it, repainted the walls and the pressed-tin ceiling. Littky brought in some old chairs from his childhood home in Detroit; Evelyn, the secretary, recovered them. A large area rug and a copy machine were donated and put in place. Littky's girlfriend, a graduate student studying counseling at Antioch New England in Keene, had been living with Littky for several months. She made the curtains for the row of tall windows in the office. Plants they had grown at his cabin forested the area.

The entire project cost less than $100.

The day Karen Thompson walked to school to meet with Dr. Littky about her schedule, Jim and his work crew were putting up new ceiling tiles in the hallway.

"Not bad," she said.

"Gee, thanks," a crew worker shouted back.

She hesitated before going into the office. Littky's door was open. She heard laughter inside. A ninth grader left the office smiling.

"Karen, are you there?" Littky called out to her.

Karen walked in and sat down.

"Nice to meet you, Karen. Actually, I've known who you are for a while."

"How's that?" Karen said.

"You run with a pretty tough group of girls—it's hard to miss you in the school."

"Is that what I'm here to talk about?"

"Yes, in part. I've watched you enough to know that you're a natural leader and that you've generally got pretty good judgment. I want you to help me. This school is your school—if it looks bad, you look bad. If it looks good, you look good. I think you could make a difference at Thayer. I think you could help make it into a pretty cool place to be, a place you and your friends would want to come to. I think the other girls listen to you. I need you to help me out."

"In what way?" Karen asked skeptically.

"When it comes up, I think you'll know," Littky said with a half-smile. "Maybe you'd also like to help work up the discipline code for the school. I want students to help decide what rules to have and how to enforce them."

"You're going to let *kids* decide what the rules should be?" Karen asked, incredulous.

"If you have to live by the rules, it's only fair that you help decide what they should be."

"That's pretty cool," Karen said.

It was basic strategy for Littky—co-opt the leaders, the troublemakers, and get them working on his side for the good of the school.

"Now," he said, "let's take a look at your courses for next year. There are a couple of changes for everyone. First of all, the school day will be shorter, but you'll be in classes all day. No more study halls."

"Why not?" Karen said.

"Because nobody studied."

"That's true."

Dennis examined her past schedules and marked down the requirements she needed to graduate.

"Do you have any plans following graduation?" he said.

"I hadn't really thought about it."

"Are you thinking about college or anything?"

"No. Not really."

"What kinds of things are you interested in?"

"I dunno."

"Maybe you'd be interested in an apprenticeship. It's a new program—a little like work-study, only more emphasis on 'study.' You won't get paid, but you will get credit for your work. It'd give you a chance to explore jobs that interest you. What kind of work do you like?"

Karen thought for a moment. "Working with children."

"How'd you like to work with kids at the nursery school or elementary school?"

"That'd be great."

"Okay, hang on a second. Let me call the principal over at the elementary school." On the spot, Littky explained to the principal what he had in mind.

"The question isn't how many I can take," the principal told him. "The question is, how many can you spare?"

Littky hung up the phone and turned back to Karen. "How'd you like to work with second graders?"

"Just like that?" Karen said, wide-eyed.

"Just like that," Littky said with a smile.

Dennis met with students daily, making constant adjustments to the schedule as he gathered more information.

"I think scheduling is one of the most creative processes," he told Marcia Ammann one day. "I think, how can I get to this kid? What's another way to teach him? Then, all of a sudden, I get an idea and the kid likes it, starts getting excited, adds to it, and we're off! It gets me so high!"

That's how the Life After Thayer class got started. Senior after senior sat down in Littky's office and looked at him blankly when he asked them what they planned to do after graduation. A few were considering college, a few thought of enlisting in the army, but the overwhelming share of students shrugged their shoulders when asked about their plans. They said they'd get a job "somewhere."

Littky hit on the idea while talking with Phil Hamm one day.

"We need to do something to prepare these kids for life on the outside," he said. "We need to provide them with basic living skills and let them know what their options are. In a lot of cases, this is the last formal education they'll get. If we only come up with one class that's really tailored to the students' needs—this had better be it."

Phil thought a moment. "Kind of a life skills class?"

"Exactly," Littky said. "They could learn how to write a résumé, balance their checkbooks, make a household budget. We could examine housing and apartment costs, what it costs to own a car, buy gas, take someone out on a date, buy groceries, raise a kid. We could talk about how to look for jobs or the right college. We could ask the students what kinds of things they wanted to learn about, and then go out and do it."

"We could also deal with controversial issues that might have an impact on their daily lives," Phil said. "We could look at their attitudes and how they might affect their futures."

"We're not here to tell them what their values should be," Littky cautioned, "only that they can examine them intelligently. We need to teach them critical thinking skills so they at least know *why* they think what they think. I'd like the classes to be sort of like a rap session with a defined topic each week. We can divide up the fifty seniors among three teachers—every senior will take it, five days a week, grading simply pass or fail."

Then there were the nearly dozen juniors who said they were interested in farming. There was nothing in the curriculum to answer their particular need.

"I could've just shook my head when those kids told me what interested them," Littky told Marcia one day. " 'Sorry, we don't have anything like that for you. How about another English course instead?' But I couldn't do it. A program like that could make the difference for these kids. You should've seen the way they responded when I told them that they could design the program, they could decide what they wanted to learn. I told them they could build a barn. Before I finished my sentence, one kid blurted out, 'Yeah, and stock it with cows and chickens. And meet with local farmers who could show us how to do it.' And *this* was a kid that Phil Hamm said was ready to drop out of school last year."

"But who will teach them?" Marcia said.

"The kid suggested it—local farmers. We've got experts right out our back door—literally. I think they'd be willing to help out if we asked. Also, I think I might be able to hire a part-time carpenter. There's money in the budget to hire a new English teacher—I'm going to ask the board to let me use that money to hire three part-time people instead. We need a carpentry instructor, and someone to run the apprenticeship program." He looked deeply into Marcia's eyes. "And we need someone to work to get the community involved in the school."

Marcia grinned. "Is this where *I* come in?"

"You'd be perfect for the job," Littky said. "You understand me and the school. You know just about everybody in town, and everybody respects you. If anyone's going to succeed in changing the community's perceptions of this school, if anyone's going to help the community get excited and involved in what's going on here—it's you."

"The position isn't even official yet," Marcia said.

"It will be. One way or another, I'll get it funded."

Marcia had known all along she'd be involved in the school. She had to be. Not long ago, the sorry state of the school made her want to leave town. Now she had a shot at helping to make it into the kind of place she'd dreamed of for her kids. "We can make this school work," she said. "It's going to happen—I can feel it."

Littky nodded. "That's the spirit."

Littky had first met Judy Knox when she joined the *Star* staff. An aggressive, hardworking go-getter, her organizational skills and energy had impressed Dennis. Now he had his eyes on making her director of the apprenticeship program. Judy had endured a lifelong battle with crippling arthritis. Only recently, after a series of painful operations, was she finally able to walk independently. The ordeal had made her a formidable fighter.

Littky wanted a strong, independent person for the job, someone who didn't need much direction and who could take an idea and run with it. Judy fit the bill perfectly.

The year before, Judy had organized a series of community coffees starting the week Littky was named principal. He was desperate to discover community attitudes toward the school. He wanted to meet residents from all parts of town, all backgrounds, and he wanted to meet them on their own terms. Typically, their only contact with the high school principal was when there was some kind of problem.

That had to be changed. Littky also wanted to do everything he could to dispel his mystique as the strange, bearded mountain man turned principal. He figured the best way to do that was for people to meet him in person.

Dennis wanted the people in his town to know and like him. He wanted them to feel comfortable talking about school. He wanted them to know that they could make a difference at Thayer, that they could play an important role in making the school successful.

The coffees were set up a little like Tupperware parties. Judy would convince someone to hold one at home; the host or hostess was responsible for getting neighborhood people to attend. Judy told Littky where and when the coffee was to be and he'd show up, often with a school board member or two in tow.

He was asked to some of the largest and most elegant homes in town, and to some of the poorest. Always there were fresh pastries, home-baked cakes, coffee and tea. For the first half of the visit he'd mingle with the group, introducing himself, chatting and trying to make people feel comfortable. Then Judy would formally introduce him, and he'd talk about some of the changes in progress at the school, encouraging parents to voice their concerns and complaints. The invitation was all they needed. One after another, parents opened up about their concerns.

"I don't know what's going on at school."

"Everything that comes out of that building is bad news."

"It seems like more kids drop out than graduate."

"Why can't they read better?"

"I think my kid skips more than he's in school, but he won't talk to me and the school doesn't keep accurate records. When I call the office, they don't know whether he's been there all day or not."

Littky detailed the changes he had in mind, encouraging the parents to offer suggestions. Then he launched into his pitch with the fervor of a salesman.

"The only way Thayer High is going to succeed is if *you* help—and I mean every single one of you. The school has one of the smallest budgets in the state, but we can't let that get in our way. Anything you can offer the school, it doesn't matter what it is, *anything* you can offer will make a difference. I won't leave here until everybody offers something. I don't care what it is—time, money, talent, materials— *something*."

The formula worked. Offers poured in. Some said they were willing to drive students to early morning meetings or out-of-town events; one woman volunteered to give weaving demonstrations in her home; a Spanish-speaking woman offered to help the language teacher; another volunteered to organize a junior high cheerleading squad.

One day a stack of lumber was delivered to the school; a pottery kiln arrived on another. Every gathering resulted in more volunteers, more materials, and more good will.

Dennis also tapped into the CB community. One coffee meeting was held at a trailer park in town in a half-sized camper so small that the hostess sent her kids and the family dog out to play in the car. The aroma of fresh-baked brownies permeated the air as she filled cups with coffee.

"I never thought I'd have a principal over to my place," she said nervously. Guests moved around in the cramped space, looking for a place to set their cups. Littky's laugh filled the trailer as he moved from guest to guest, introducing himself, pumping hands, taking bites of brownie.

"So you're Mountain," one woman said. "I talked to you a couple times on the CB. Ya know, you look about like I thought you would."

"Nice to meet you in person," Littky said, shaking her hand.

He held his hand out to another woman. "Hi, I'm Dennis Littky."

"Yeah. I know," she said. "I came here to talk to you."

"What can I do for you?"

"It's about my son, Nick Collins. He dropped out of school this year. He's only sixteen."

"Any idea why?"

"He won't talk to me about it. Every time I try to get him to go back to school, he walks away from me. He thinks it's a waste of time. He won't listen to me."

"Does he have a job?"

"No—that's just it. He's got *nothing*. I know he hates school. I know he had a terrible time there. A lot of his friends dropped out, too. He's a real good artist, though. Draws all the time. He looks at something, draws it, and it looks exactly like the real thing."

"Do you think you could get him to come to school and talk to me?"

"I don't know. I could try."

"Tell him to come see me tomorrow afternoon. I'll be at school all day."

The next day a scraggly-haired teenager appeared in Littky's office.

"Look, I'm only here to get my mother off my back." The kid slouched in the chair.

"That's cool, Nick. Now I'm going to get on your back," Littky said. "First off. The state says you're old enough to drop out. You're entitled to make that decision. So, ultimately, you can do what you want. But it's my job to make sure you get the best education you can—to prepare you for life after Thayer. So you're not leaving this office until I give you a run for your money! Okay?"

"I guess," Nick said, a little unsure of himself.

"Good. So tell me, now that you've quit school, what are you doing with your time?"

"Well . . . nothin' really. I don't have a job yet. I'm sorta looking around for one."

"Any luck?"

"Nope."

"What do you want to do?"

"Earn some money so I can get out on my own."

"Does it matter how you earn money?"

"Nah—not as long as I make a lot of it."

"Do you have any skills?"

"Not really."

"Your mother tells me you're a good artist. I talked to the art teacher, and she says you're one of the best students she's ever had."

"So?" Nick scoffed. "You don't make money *drawing*."

"How about if I paid you to do some art work in the school?"

"C'mon," he said. His eyes narrowed.

"I'm serious. If I got you a job painting in the school, would you take it?"

Nick hesitated.

Littky waved a hand. "I don't mean just painting walls. I mean doing art on them. You know, painting murals."

"Really?"

"Sure. You can paint what you like, as long as you clear it with me first. If I could get you the job, would you do it?"

Nick nodded vigorously. He sat forward in the chair and grinned. "Yeah. I'd do it."

"Hang on a sec," he said. "Let me make a couple of phone calls and see if I can get some money to pay you."

Littky hunted through his Rolodex. He remembered a woman who was in charge of vocational education for the region. He found the number and dialed.

"Hello," he said. "Yeah. This is Dennis Littky down at Thayer High School in Winchester. Listen, I've got a kid here who just dropped out of school, but who wants to work here this summer painting murals. Is there any place we could get some money to pay him?"

He listened intently, nodding silently and smiling. He winked at Nick and hung up the phone.

"Bingo!" he said. "We just found enough money to keep you painting for the whole summer!"

Nick's jaw dropped open. "You kiddin'?" he said.

Littky smiled. "Here, let me show you the wall I had in mind." He jumped up and headed for the door. Nick bounced to his feet and followed Littky downstairs.

"I'll bet you can guess where we're going," Littky said.

"To the cafeteria?"

"Yep."

Nick snorted. "The grossest room in the building."

"Exactly."

It was quite a sight. Dried paperwads still clung to the

ceiling. The lunch tables had been washed, but they were still pockmarked with holes and gouges.

"There's your canvas," Littky said. He pointed to the far wall, covered with dirt and graffiti.

"Needs a few coats of fresh paint before you can do your mural—but the wall's all yours."

Nick hesitated. Then his eyes lit up, and he turned to Littky.

"It's *mine*? I can do *anything* I want?"

"Sure, within reason. No naked women or profanity. Beyond that—anything you want."

"Wow."

"Why don't you start tomorrow choosing your design? We'll provide the paint and everything else you need. You bring your talent and your ideas."

"Tomorrow?" Nick looked at the wall, then at Littky, then back to the wall. "Can I, ah . . . start today?"

Littky grinned. "Of course," he said.

Nick worked on ideas for days. He scoured books, his record collection, his imagination. Finally, from one of his album covers, he chose a white Pegasus, wings swooping back as it took flight.

"That's what I want to do," he told Dennis. "I figure first I'll paint the wall white, then use an opaque projector to get the drawing to scale."

Littky liked it. Pegasus was the favorite steed of the Muses and the bearer of poets into their flights of genius. There was poetry in the idea—a mythical creature taking flight. Nice metaphor for what was going on at Thayer.

Nick came to school every day. He spent hour after hour scrubbing and painting the walls to prepare a surface. He outlined the Pegasus. He came early and stayed late. Gradually, bit by bit, the great life-sized steed took form.

Word spread about what was going on in the cafeteria;

spectators passed by the windows to witness the creation.
Marian Polaski, school board chairperson, was often there
and entered a pool on how long the mural would survive
after school started. Marian's bet was five days.

Val Cole also heard about the Pegasus. She started riding
her bicycle to school with one or two of her kids to watch
progress. "It really is pretty," she marveled.

Nick was spurred on by his sudden celebrity status; he
worked all the more meticulously. People were applauding
his talents in a way they never had before. Littky was elated.
It was working just as he'd hoped. For the first time in his
life, Nick was coming to school because he wanted to be
there. Now he had a stake in the school on the most essential level, and he knew it.

"Hey, Doc," Nick said to Littky one day. "I've been
thinkin' about coming back to school."

Nick's announcement seemed to set off several others.
One by one, eleven other boys and girls called Littky or
stopped by his office to ask if they could come back.

"Heard things were changing. Thought maybe I'd come
back and give it another shot," one boy said.

A girl walked in carrying her baby. "If I'm going to give
my child an education, I figure maybe I need one first."

Another boy told Dennis he was spending weekends in
jail. With that on his record and no high school diploma,
he couldn't get close to a job. One had been kicked out of his
house and was living with friends "here and there." A
sixteen-year-old girl was living with her boyfriend.

In most cases, Littky knew that sticking those students
back in a classroom for five hours of academics spelled
failure. He took care of their requirements first—math,
science, English. Then he talked with each of them at
length, trying to sort out their interests. Several boys said
they liked working on cars and motors, so he signed them

up for apprenticeships at Ronnie Bedaw's auto shop. A girl said she liked working with hair, so he signed her up for an apprenticeship at the Village Beauty Salon.

Littky scheduled Nick for two hours of independent art classes under the art teacher's supervision. As soon as Nick completed the Pegasus, he planned to finish off the cafeteria with a colorful geometric that would cut across the other walls. He was also working on ideas for a mural in the front lobby and another in the gymnasium that he would be able to do as part of his independent study. The rest of his school day would be spent meeting graduation requirements.

As far as Littky was concerned, as long as the kids were learning something constructive, something that might give them a better shot at life, he couldn't care less whether or not they learned to sit obediently in a classroom or how to take a test. If the school could get them reading competently enough to follow an instruction manual, or give them enough math so they could handle whatever the job required, then he'd feel that the school had succeeded. It was a hell of a lot better than just giving up on them.

While Nick's work progressed, Jim and his gang of CETA workers started ripping the tops off the lunch tables. They cut new table tops and bolted them into place. They went to work on the windows, replacing the broken panes of glass. Then they washed them until they squeaked.

Littky watched; he approved. The more students involved in the refurbishing, the better, he thought. They'll take pride in their efforts and will work to take care of the place.

Littky had been in touch with the school board members all along, keeping them apprised of his plans. Approval from the board was crucial—without it he'd be stalemated.

"Dennis, I just think you're moving too fast," Marian Polaski said, repeating a line she'd delivered so often. She was one of Littky's biggest fans, but Marian nonetheless operated with a keen community conscience. She regularly found herself in the position of defending Littky—mostly his looks and manner—to her neighbors and friends.

"Why don't we just make a few of the changes you propose and gradually phase in the others if you still think they're needed—so people can get used to the idea."

Littky was adamant. "I'm telling you, Marian, if we don't make changes right away, we're going to have problems."

Early in August the school board met. Littky had prepared his agenda carefully and sent a lengthy letter to the board outlining his proposals, including shortening the school day; lengthening class periods; dropping study halls; approving the money for the apprenticeship, carpenter, and community coordinator positions; and putting the dome on school property. Just before the meeting, he took the board on a tour of the high school. He eagerly pointed out the physical improvements, saving the bright soaring Pegasus for last. The board was visibly impressed.

The meeting opened to an almost-empty house. Marcia Ammann and Judy Knox were there. So was Phil Hamm. Littky spoke about each proposal in turn. He took a lot of the stiffness out of the meeting by pacing the floor and talking to the board like a coach on a winning streak. If he were desperate to convince a cautious board of the merits of his plans, he didn't show it.

The board considered proposal after proposal. None of the votes were unanimous, but he got the okays he needed.

13
School Begins

A HANDFUL OF STUDENTS DROVE to school in pickup trucks. They carried wrecking bars, sledge hammers, and picks. Even at 7:30 A.M., it was plain that this August day would be a hot one.

Littky greeted the students as they arrived. He shouted orders and instructions, telling them how they were going to spend the next three or four days.

The students had signed up for the new building and farm program—nine boys and one girl. When school started in September, their first project would be to reassemble the dome behind the school and figure out how to heat the place. Littky wanted to involve the whole school in deciding how the dome would be used. Beaman Lumber and the local garbageman had offered the use of their trucks to haul the dome to Winchester.

Inside the school, Judy Knox and Marcia Ammann walked up and down the halls looking for a patch of unused space where they could set up their offices. The best they found was an oversized closet off the library. There was room for one desk, a file cabinet and three chairs—just barely. Through a drill hole, they pushed wires for a phone and electricity.

Knox and Ammann were scheduled to work thirty hours a week. Knox would earn $1,500, supplemented by a $2,500 state grant. Ammann would be paid $4,000. Carpenter

John Belcher-Timme would make $5,000 for three days per week of carpentry instruction.

The apprenticeship program, which Knox and Littky had planned to build up gradually, had taken off faster than expected. Instead of the dozen students they'd planned, nearly fifty signed up for the program. Littky had said, "We want to start out small, so we can do it well." But so many students expressed an interest, there was no choice but to do it big. As the numbers mounted, Judy Knox turned to Littky. "How are we going to do it?" Littky answered, "I'm the generalist. That's for you to figure out."

The elementary and nursery schools took every student who wanted to work there, then asked for more. The *Star* took on six apprentices. Ronnie Bedaw took in three kids at his garage. The hospital, the nursing home, Gary's Power Equipment, and the beauty shop took on some more. It was working out better than Littky had expected.

One day, Littky hit on the idea of a school newsletter to keep the community informed about what was going on at Thayer. He made some phone calls. Agway, an oil company in Keene, agreed to pay the entire cost of the newsletter in exchange for a one-by-two-inch ad on the front page.

Judy Knox plugged in a couple of apprentices to work with Marcia Ammann on running the newsletter. Marcia made plans to profile students, describe new programs, and run a calendar of school events.

Littky saw the newsletter as one more tool to help change the negative opinion people in Winchester had of the school.

"The fact is," he said, "it doesn't matter how good the school is if people keep thinking it stinks. It's not enough to change the reality—we've got to change perceptions, too.

"One of the things I did at my Long Island school that really worked was to set up a neighborhood communications network. One person from every neighborhood in the district acted as the spokesperson for the neighborhood. That person attended meetings at school and was kept informed of school happenings. Their job was to get in touch with families in their neighborhood and spread the news. They also collected questions and concerns from their people and passed them along to the school administration."

Marcia pulled a book from Littky's library that described a similar program of neighborhood spokespeople called Key Communicators. She dashed to the *Star* and found the list of twenty-one neighborhoods she'd pulled together for the newspaper's delivery route and started making phone calls. She wanted a good mix of people: some who supported what was going on, some who were skeptical. The response surprised her. By the end of the week, she'd signed up volunteers from every neighborhood in town and set a date for the first meeting in early September.

A week before the first day of school, Dennis got up with the sun and fired the jeep down the mountain to school. He toted bags of groceries, papers, books. Once everything was brought in, he set off at a run, placing squares of paper in Marcia and Judy's office, under Mrs. Hall's globe, on top of a dictionary in Mrs. Cole's classroom, propped on a video display terminal in the new computer lab. It was the first day of a two-day teacher workshop.

Marcia and Judy arrived at eight o'clock, nearly colliding with Dennis as he dashed downstairs to start cooking breakfast. In a flurry of activity, he got them flipping eggs, pouring orange juice, and making toast. Dennis grabbed a stack of information packets and ran back upstairs to the main entrance, just in time to greet Barb Eibell and Val Cole as they came through the door.

"G'morning," Littky sang out. "Welcome to Thayer High

School. Here's your first assignment." He handed Val and Barb packets and each a small piece of paper with a message:

"We have no bells, we'll use the clocks. Where would you put your office if you were Judy Knox?" Barb rubbed her chin, stumped.

"An apple a day keeps the doctor away. But an Apple for a teacher is a pretty nice feature. If you had such a creature, where would it be?"

"I get it!" Val said. "You're talking about our new Apple Computers." She set off down the hall toward the computer lab.

Littky handed a clue to every teacher. Pretty soon, they were criss-crossing the building following their clues. Everyone's last message was, "Now that you've toured, you probably want to eat. Go to our flying Pegasus, where you'll find a breakfast treat."

The home economics room was in the basement, adjacent to the cafeteria. A cluster of teachers, holding plates loaded with food, crowded around Nick's Pegasus.

"It's fantastic."

"I knew he was a good artist, but I didn't know he was this good."

"Beautiful! I just hope it survives."

"Welcome, everybody!" Littky boomed. "I hope my little scavenger hunt got you through the building so you could see some of what's been going on this summer.

"There are a lot of new faces here this morning—far more than the twenty-five faculty members you were probably expecting. I've invited everyone who'll be working with us in some way—some of the new faces are volunteers, some are handling new programs. If you read the letter I sent you, you know what I'm talking about."

There were a pair of interns from Antioch University, an instructor from Keene State College to teach computers, a woman to teach pottery, the director of community education from the New Hampshire Department of Education to help develop community resources, an assistant librarian, a woman who was writing her doctoral dissertation on the school, and more. All of them were volunteers.

"Why all the people?" Littky asked. "Because we're an expanding community. There are those of us who'll be here every day from eight to three, forming the strength and nucleus of the school. But we can't do it ourselves; twenty-five teachers for 350 kids just isn't enough. If education here is to work, the community and the school must be one— we've got to be open to using all the resources we have.

"All the changes we've made this summer were done with a single idea in mind—to build an environment in which we can all succeed. In fact, one of the most important things we can do is to keep working to develop this environment, the setting in which we can best succeed.

"Individually, the students are all beautiful, each in their own way. It's when we put them in groups, with the all-powerful peer pressure, when we put them in situations that make them feel uptight or stupid—that's when battles begin. Disruptions aren't solved by rules and more rules, but by a more appropriate environment. Our role is to look at every student *as an individual* and to help him or her grow. That means not only educating them in the three R's, but we've also got to teach them how to think for themselves, make decisions, solve problems, and be ready for the world."

As Littky talked, a couple of teachers sitting near the back muttered cynically under their breath.

Littky ignored them. "The amazing thing came when I was talking to students about cutting out the study halls, adding a new tenth-grade math requirement, and making enrollment mandatory in five courses—I didn't get any flack, none! Most of these kids know why they're here, and as long as they're our students, we'll work them *hard*.

"There's an irony that keeps coming to my mind. Kids look at coaches as people who help them get better, people who work to help make the team win. But what happens when we teach? Kids think we're *against* them, that we're trying to trip them up. This has got to change. Our kids should regard teachers as coaches who'll help them learn to think critically. It'll happen because we'll *make* it happen. I hope you'll join me in this quest."

Val Cole and Barb Eibell looked hopefully at each other. A couple of teachers rolled their eyes like the teenagers they so disliked.

"I'm here because of my commitment to the town," Littky said. "I didn't plan any of this. Becoming principal was far from my mind. But now it is the only thing I think about. This is *our* school. I can't do it alone. I need every single one of you to make it work. There'll be times when I get all the credit for the great projects you do, but I'll also get the blame for the stuff that doesn't work. But if the school works as a whole, everyone will benefit.

"I'm ready. I feel strong. You must be open to me. If you don't like things I am doing—let me know! I won't strike back. The answers are somewhere between us. I'm going to have you evaluate me at the end of the year, so I can get a clear picture of how you feel about me and the things I'm doing. If I push too hard, you can tell me to slow down. I know you've got enough to do, but it may seem sometimes like I've forgotten that. Ask poor Barb Eibell—every time I see her, I ask her to do something else."

Barb smiled and nodded her head deliberately up and down.

Littky smiled back at her.

"What is exciting is that I have a dream, and the plan will develop with us. My philosophy is to get the best people and let each of you grow. There are no sacred programs—everything will develop out of you and the students.

"I'm excited about the possibilities. I know there'll be hard times. But Thayer High will become a model for what education should be—a place where we all want to be.

"Dr. Robby Fried of the New Hampshire state department wrote a letter to the U.S. Department of Education that said, 'A year from now, you're going to hear a lot about Thayer High, in Winchester, New Hampshire.' Let's prove him right. I look forward to getting to know all of you—and you to know me. Let's put our faith back into education. Amen."

Barb wanted to leap to her feet and cheer. She settled instead for enthusiastic clapping. The applause was scattered at first. Slowly it grew, until everybody joined in.

Barb came to school early on the second day of the workshop. She brought a box of plants and hung them in front of the windows. She tacked posters on the walls, stacked books and records, and put pictures of her family on her desk.

The first day of the workshop had turned out better than even she expected. She knew there would be a gush of positive energy from Dennis, and she'd expected to be charged up by it—he had that effect on her. What she hadn't expected was the positive reaction from the other teachers. There were skeptics, cynics who would scoff at *any* change, especially if it made them dig up and dust off the tattered shreds of hope they once had for the teaching profession. Many were critical of Littky, particularly his appearance.

She didn't delude herself into thinking the skeptics had been converted by Littky's inspiring words the day before, but she couldn't miss the growing excitement. She'd overheard one of Littky's critics say, "After thirty years, I didn't think I could get excited about school—but I am!"

It was more hope in one day than Barb could remember having had in years. She knew she was in for a lot of work. But she was ready.

A reporter from the *Keene Sentinel* spent a day at the workshop. He'd been tipped off that Thayer High School, the joke of the region, was undergoing a renaissance under its new principal. The story was to run the day after the workshop ended. Excited, Dennis drove to the diner downtown to buy a paper.

The story was on the front page, right below a photo of Dennis talking to Nick Collins, who sat atop a ladder working on his second mural. The article's lead stopped him dead.

"DENNIS LITTKY . . . PLANS TO SINGLE-HANDEDLY REVERSE THE WAY WINCHESTER RESIDENTS AND THAYER STUDENTS PERCEIVE THEIR TOWN AND SCHOOL," the story said.

"Oh, God!" Littky cried. "I can't believe this. That's exactly the opposite of what I'm trying to convey. I just spent three days telling those teachers that I can't do it alone, and now here I am on the front page of the paper grabbing all the glory. Where did that damn reporter get *this* idea?" He slapped the paper with the back of his hand.

That night he wrote a letter to the *Sentinel* news editor complaining about the lead, criticizing the reporter for leaping to a conclusion that couldn't be farther from the truth.

Understandably, the story hit several teachers wrong. Some of their comments worked their way back to Littky, but he knew that most of the talk would be said behind his back. He planned to mention the article at the next meeting, but that wouldn't be until the day school started. It wasn't the kind of thing he wanted to dwell on. Besides, his backtracking wouldn't gain him any points with those teachers who'd already decided that he really *did* want all the glory.

On the first day of school, the sun rose orange and full as a harvest pumpkin.

Cars roared into the parking lot on tires the size of steamrollers. Students streamed out of long yellow buses. Some ran and laughed, others were dark and brooding. Littky stood at the end of the sidewalk, shouting hellos, tossing his arm over students' shoulders, talking incessantly.

Karen Thompson clambered off the bus with a couple of her chums.

"Oh, Gawd," she said. "I hate the first day of school. Everybody's so, so . . . you know."

Her friends knew and agreed. They cut across the lawn, but they couldn't get by the new principal before he wrapped his arm over one girl's shoulders. He addressed Karen by name.

"Jeez," she said when they were clear of him. "How'd he remember my name? I've only met him once."

Inside the school, the first thing to hit her was the smell of fresh paint. The sulphur-colored walls, graffiti, and peeling paint were gone, replaced with a bright white. The brown-stained, broken ceiling tiles were gone, replaced with new ones. The floors were refinished. The whole place looked new.

Littky stayed outside, hurrying kids along.

"You've got five minutes to get to your homeroom," he bellowed. "C'mon, let's get going!"

He went up the front granite steps two at a time and crossed the hall to his office. At 8:50 A.M. he rang the second bell.

School had begun.

The eight seniors in Littky's advisory were scattered around his office. Littky had decided to take an advisory of his own as a way to cultivate friends who'd help him keep up with what was going on in school. As the oldest students, seniors held the most sway in any school. That's why Doc wanted to work closely with them.

One girl took a mandarin orange jelly bean from the community bowl on Doc's desk and popped it in her mouth. A boy reached into the bookcase and grabbed a magnet from among the gadgets and gizmos on the shelf. "It's like an amusement park in here," the boy said to another boy, who was fiddling with an Etch-A-Sketch.

Littky's office was a hodgepodge of the bizarre. It was impossible to absorb all the details at once. There was a museum of hats lining one wall. Littky would pick one and plunk it on his head on his way out the door. He'd come back the next day with a different one on his head. There was a tattered top hat, a safari hat, a Civil War cap, a Chinese construction hat made of straw, an African tribal headdress, a coonskin cap, a yellow hard hat with a head-light and siren, and the ubiquitous navy blue baseball cap of the Detroit Tigers. The hats represented a sort of road map of his travels and home ports.

Under the hat collection were shelves loaded with an assortment of brain teasers, games, and other objects of bemusement. A Nerf ball and basketball net were stashed in the corner. There was a giant Rubik's Cube and a lava lamp. On the desk was a clock that drew power from a fresh apple. Littky loved to explain how the acid in the apple charged the electrodes wired to the clock. Without realizing it, students would get a lesson in the basics of battery power.

A bulletin board was cluttered with pictures—kids paint-ing the lockers, Marcia flipping eggs, Nick and his Pegasus. A bent black-and-white photo at the bottom of the board showed a young, clean-cut boy sitting in a front-row desk flanked by other youngsters—boys with brush cuts, girls with ribboned ponytails. The boy sat straight and tall, attention fixed on a copy of *Our New Friends*, like every child in the room. A prim and lovely teacher presided gracefully over the tight, straight rows, smiling. The picture had appeared on the cover of a September 1951 issue of the

Detroit Free Press. The boy in the photo was Dennis as a second grader, the boy his classmates would vote the one most likely to succeed.

There was a Superman poster on the closet door; a photo of Albert Einstein was tacked to the wall. There were hundreds of books—on education, yoga, history; there were volumes of poetry and some favorite novels—*The Pigman, The Snowwalker, The Catcher in the Rye.*

His desk was an organized clutter, but only Littky could see that. A basketball-sized Rolodex held the telephone numbers of every person and place he knew. There were hundreds of cards. Next to the desk was an easy chair from his childhood home and a rug from his travels to the Caribbean. Littky's office was a museum of his past and his enthusiasms.

One of the students in his advisory, star of the basketball team, all six feet and four inches of him, pushed two gaudily painted wooden trains back and forth over the conference table. One of the trains was in the shape of a hot dog on a bun.

Littky grinned and pointed at the train.

"Some kids at my old school on Long Island made those in art class and gave them to me," Doc said. "My dog keeps trying to eat the hot dog train, so I thought I'd rescue it and bring it here."

The basketball star picked up the wooden hot dog and opened his mouth, as though he was about to take a bite out of it.

Littky laughed. "At least I *think* I rescued it by bringing it here."

The seniors laughed.

"Welcome to your homeroom—hereafter called 'advisory,'" he said. "Today's gathering will be a lot longer than usual because we've got a lot of stuff to do before you go to your first class—such as tell you where your first class is going to be. I'll also spend some time describing what advisory is all about and how it can work for you." He passed out each student's schedule.

"I think you'll notice a lot of changes in how things operate here. Your input is very important. I chose to be a *senior* adviser in part because I'll only have one year to get to know you and this will be a good way to do it. I also chose you because the rest of the school looks up to seniors in general, and many of you in particular. You're people I want to be in touch with.

"I picked each of you for a reason. If this school is going to succeed, it'll have to have your support. You're the ones who will make it work."

They were listening, Littky could see that clearly, but he couldn't tell if they were buying what he was saying. His gut feeling was that they weren't.

Littky made a point of being out in the hall between classes that first day. He cut short a phone call with an official from the state education department to make sure he did his "hall time." His presence set a standard he wanted to continue throughout the year.

Phone calls, letter writing, paperwork were all activities Littky took care of on weekends, at night, before school. Paper work especially, was something he saved for the solitude of his cabin. During the school day, he wanted to be *in* school.

"It's the only way I can keep my fingers on the pulse of things here," he told Phil Hamm. "If something's going to break out, I want to be there to stop it. I want to know what's going on. It's also an ideal way to get to know the students. I want to learn everybody's name and something about them—dialogue is everything. If I can get them to feel comfortable talking to me about little things, then maybe when something big is bothering them, they'll feel comfortable coming to me."

Marcia Ammann was waiting anxiously in the hallway when the bell rang and students started flooding in. She hadn't been in the school with students since her substitute teaching fiasco. That was then, this was now—she wanted to start *this* school year as much a part of the Thayer High scene as possible.

Marcia backed up until her shoulders touched the wall. The kids all looked so huge and imposing. She saw the broad-shouldered boy who'd intimidated her so much when she was a substitute. He sauntered nonchalantly down the hall talking to a tall, attractive girl and didn't notice Marcia at all. She stared after him. He had changed. His shoulders were broader.

She spent her first period in the library with Judy Knox and her group of apprentices. Next to Dennis, Judy was the one person at Thayer with whom she truly felt comfortable. During the workshop, Marcia and Judy couldn't help feeling alienated. Neither were part of "the fold." Both felt the other staff members were suspicious of them and the roles they were to play in school. Some people called them "Littky pawns."

Fifty students were jammed into the small book-walled room. Judy was responsible for placing every one of them in an apprenticeship job within the week. One hundred eyes stared at her expectantly as she laid out their roles and responsibilities as apprentices. With her roiling energy, she talked about the experience as though she was preparing them for a rafting trip down a Colorado rapids.

"Your work place will be your classroom," she said. "Instead of reading and studying about the world from afar, you're going to be in it up to your belly buttons. You'll be working with professionals, experts in their fields. You'll watch them, work with them, and try to make some sense out of what you see.

"This program is new. That means its success depends on you and me. As with any job, you're expected to be on time, dress appropriately, and work to the best of your ability. If you don't, just like with any job, you stand a risk of being fired.

"You'll be out in the community every day. What you do and how you act will reflect not only on you, but the whole school."

Judy had their attention.

The first day back in school was a ritual that never ceased to excite veteran teacher Val Cole. The kids seemed to start the year intent and interested. Val wanted to grab hold of that energy and keep it alive as long as possible.

The breakfast meeting that morning was a nice touch, she thought. She liked starting out eating breakfast with her colleagues and taking care of last-minute details before being inundated by students. It was much better than the usual "just showing up" for the first day back.

She also liked spending the first half hour of the day with the students in her advisory. They were all seniors, and several of them had been in her classes in the past. She felt comfortable with them. On the face of things, the advisory concept suited her. She just wasn't exactly sure what her role was supposed to be. Littky said he would form committees to work on various aspects of the school—one group would study and develop the advisory program. Maybe that was something she should consider joining. The building and grounds committee also interested her. So much had been done to the appearance of the school over the summer—she wanted to make sure it continued.

Val ran her classes that day much the way she did any year, except the classes ended differently—there were no bells. Littky sounded bells at the start and end of the day, but that was it. He said teachers and students were fully capable of keeping track of time, and the bell system was an insult to everyone. Littky had increased the passing time in the halls from two minutes to five, and she heartily approved of that, too. She liked not having that rude bell end her classes, and the halls were less congested when students didn't have to race to their next class the instant the bell sounded. Littky also refused to use the public address system. It disrupted classwork. And besides, he said, it was incredibly impersonal.

For Barb, the first day back was anxiety-producing. Even with her fresh optimism and excitement about the new principal, it was still possible that the students might not share any of the new energy. The kids were creatures of habit. Why wouldn't they simply pick up where they left off last year—taking pleasure in making her life miserable?

But her first day was fine. And, it turned out, her eighth-grade language classes were her favorites. All of the faces were new—it was like looking at a fresh slate.

At the end of the day, Littky called an assembly. He wanted to begin building a common bond with students and staff as soon as possible. Whenever he could, he wanted to remind everybody that they were in this together.

"Yes, I was nervous last night," he told the crowd. "So were many of your teachers. Why? Because they want to be good, they want the school to be good, they want to be liked—just like you do. My idea of a school is one where students and teachers are working together. The goal of the school is to teach you how to learn and get ready for those fifty or so years after school. Last year there were 270 failure notices sent out; students dropped out left and right. The staff didn't feel good about last year. This year, I'd like to see things change."

He ran through the list of changes already made, then he focused on the rules.

"The most important rules to remember are respect for people and respect for property—everything else stems from that. For the time being, we're keeping the same rules as in the past. But as we get farther into the year, I'd like all of you to help me and staff come up with a new set of rules."

A murmur of voices filled the auditorium.

"I firmly believe you know when you're doing right and wrong. The success of this school depends on all of us. Let's stop problems before they start. Everyone's been talking about Winchester. I think we'll put it on the map as the best school around. It'll provide the best education for each of you, whether that means learning to read, building a farm, constructing a dome, or learning advanced computer technology.

"Already people all over New England are responding to us. An award-winning artist called and offered us ten pieces of her art work. You can see them—they're hanging in the main office and several classrooms. Marlboro College gave us a dome, which we're in the process of rebuilding. A husband and wife who have traveled the world have named Thayer High School in their will, donating their house and all its contents to us when they die. That's only a small part of the list of donations to the school.

"During the coming weeks, I'll be taking pictures for a slide show to show your parents at open house later this month. Anyone who wants to dig in—let me know!

"All I ask is for you all to give the school a chance—get to know me and the teachers as people who are here to work *with* you. I am proud to be here. I hope you are, too. I'm excited to get to know all of you. Stop me anytime during the day. That's why I'm here."

The gymnasium erupted with applause.

14

"Making It Together"

KAREN THOMPSON AND THE OTHER members of the Group were juniors now. In the natural hierarchy of high schools, that made them even more formidable than they had been the year before. They were tough—even some of the upperclass boys were afraid of them.

It didn't take long for Erica Miner, the new home economics teacher, to understand the Group's notorious reputation. The members represented a majority of her second period class. That had been their plan. They'd heard it was Erica's first teaching job and had looked forward to giving her a hard time. But Erica was determined to keep order in her classroom. She thought that if she could keep them in line from the start, maybe they wouldn't get out of control. She was wrong.

The more rules and structure she imposed on them, the more flagrant their resistance became. They walked into class talking; no amount of yelling, prodding, coaxing, or ignoring could get them to stop and pay attention. If it were only one or two students misbehaving, she could simply eliminate the distraction by sending them to the office. But this was the whole Group—eight girls. If she sent them all to the office, she'd be sending most of her class. She appealed to Littky.

"I don't know what to do," she confessed. "They only listen when they want to. They walk in and out of the classroom like they own it. I'm pretty sure they go to the girls' bathroom in the basement to smoke. It's like they own that room too. And then there are some days when they're just fine, they listen and really get involved."

Littky rubbed his beard. "On the days when they listened, what were you teaching?"

"Let me think," Erica said. "They were real attentive during a cooking demonstration the other day. I got one to assist making crepes and then the whole class did it."

"Any other times like that?"

"Yeah. That was during a cooking class, too."

"So think about what you did differently during those classes as compared to the ones when they acted up."

Erica spent the rest of the day, then the entire weekend thinking about what to do. She labored over lesson plans, trying to find ways to engage her students. By Monday she was prepared.

After lunch, when the students spilled into her class, Erica was eager to get started. She began laying out what was to happen that day. Two girls in back of the room kept right on talking.

"Girls," Erica said, "would you please be quiet?"

The talking continued. At first Erica tried to ignore them hoping they'd be drawn into her lesson. The voices got louder.

"Girls, I'm not going to ask you again. Would you *please* be quiet?"

One of the girls spun around.

"Get the hell off our backs, you bitch!"

Erica gasped. No student had ever sworn at her before. She felt her throat tighten as hot tears welled in her eyes. She strode over to the girl, slapped her hand on the desk and spoke through gritted teeth.

"Get out of my room!"

The girl shrugged her shoulders, got up, and walked out.

A few days later, Doc saw Karen in the hall. He drew her aside and talked softly to her. "Karen," he said, "I hear things got a little rough in Mrs. Miner's class the other day. What's the deal?"

"I dunno. We just have things to talk about, so we talk."

"You know, you're really upsetting Mrs. Miner. Do you know why you do it?"

"I dunno. There are times when I really like her class. But sometimes I don't."

"When do you like her class the most?"

"I guess when we're cooking. Everybody seems to listen pretty well when she does that."

"Does the fact that everybody's listening help the class any?"

Karen shrugged. "Yeah, I guess it does."

"She likes you best when you guys are listening. You seem to like her best when you're listening. It's a two-way street. Do you think you could get your buddies to take care of their conversations outside the classroom?"

Karen thought for a moment.

"I could try, I guess."

"Good. That's all I can ask."

For a while things calmed down some in Erica's classroom. But just when she would start feeling comfortable, there would be another outburst.

Littky met with Phil Hamm and Erica to try to come up with ways to deal with the Group, short of taking them out of home economics and putting them in other classes. They decided the girls needed a set time every week to get together and talk about what was on their minds.

Littky asked Barb Eibell and Margaret, a graduate counseling intern from Antioch and also Littky's girlfriend, to conduct the class for an hour every week.

Meanwhile, Erica came up with an idea of her own—she

gave the Group the task of planning and preparing a complete Thanksgiving dinner—for the entire Thayer faculty. When she proposed the idea, they were excited.

The weekly sessions began to work. Where before the girls held court when and where they liked, they suddenly found themselves holding their anger and grievances until their weekly session. There, in the controlled environment set up by Barb and the counseling intern, they could work through their problems.

One time, Karen and several others were fuming mad at Heidi, one of the girls in the Group, for "messing around" with their boyfriends. Heidi knew her recent activities had kicked up a lot of dust. It hadn't been her intention—it had just, as she told Mrs. Eibell, "sorta happened."

"Didn't you realize they'd get mad at you if you fooled around with their boyfriends?" Mrs. Eibell asked.

"Yeah. I think I did."

"Do you know why you did it?"

Heidi spoke quietly. "I think because I was embarrassed."

"About what?"

Heidi pulled at a section of hair, her attention fixed firmly on the floor. "Because I was . . . a virgin. Mostly I tried to pretend I was, you know, experienced."

"So you thought you'd try the real thing with your friends' boyfriends?"

"I didn't really think about it," Heidi said. "I just did it."

"Using your body is no way to gain friendship or acceptance," Barb said.

"I know that now. If anything, it's a good way to *lose* friends."

"Do you think you can tell the Group that today?"

"They're all so mad at me."

"If you don't talk it out with them, they're only going to get madder, you know."

Heidi nodded her head.

"It's going to be a tough session. You up to it?"

Heidi gave her a weak smile. "What choice have I got?"

When Karen walked into Mrs. Eibell's classroom that day, she sneered at Heidi, and muttered under her breath, "You slut."

The girls moved the desks into a big circle, readying themselves to chew out Heidi. But Barb and Margaret came up with a plan to help deflect some of the anger. Going around the circle, they had each girl say one bad thing about Heidi and one good thing. The exercise helped drain the girls' anger and, at the same time, redirect their thinking about Heidi into a positive vein.

At the end of class, Karen knew she would always hate what Heidi had done. Nothing could change that. But her rage was gone. In its place, she felt kind of sorry for Heidi.

Littky called them TGIF memos. They were a carryover from his years at Shoreham–Wading River Middle School. The memos went out every Friday to all the staff. The pages were filled with his reactions to the events of the past week and comments on things to come. He described his educational philosophy and his vision for Thayer. He also included tidbits of general interest.

The first memo came out on September 4, 1981:

Dear Staff—

This is the first of 40. Each week I will try to write my feelings, thoughts, and ideas for you to read and react to. I will also list the meetings and activities of the coming week.

I would like each to be interesting to read so I need help. What are questions that need asking? Problems to think of? Ideas that worked? Good quotes, excerpts from student writings or things they said. Let's make this a community sharing memo. I put them together each Thursday evening, so drop me a note by each Thursday or mention something

to me. Most of my meetings will be set up the week before—
so if you want to sit down and talk let me know before each
Thursday.

My reactions after the 1st week—

I have been truly excited at the cooperation of everybody—students and staff. Everyone seems open and willing
to work together. . . .

The school open house on September 16 would be the
first public event under Littky. The plan was to present a
ten-minute slide show about Thayer High School before and
after the recent changes. Following that, Littky would talk
to the parents for another ten minutes, then send them to
meet with their child's adviser and pick up his or her
schedule. Parents would be encouraged to visit the school's
classrooms and offices.

The Wednesday before the open house, Littky used the
regular staff meeting to preview the show. Dark, brooding
music set off the slides depicting the sorry shape of the
building when Littky took over. Frame after frame showed
the broken windows, stained ceiling tiles, broken lockers,
corners piled with accumulated trash, and scarred lunchroom tabletops.

Then the music changed; the speakers blared out "Eye of
the Tiger." The slides were brighter—Thayer students
brushing glossy paint on the lockers; Jim, the custodian,
sitting on a ladder, fitting clean ceiling tiles into place; the
CETA crew replacing the battered old tabletops with new;
Nick Collins in the many phases of his painting of the
Pegasus. The students were intent on their work, smiling,
laughing, hamming it up in front of the camera.

The show made its point succinctly—the school was
changing.

Val Cole was as pleased as anybody to see these changes,
but she couldn't throw off the resentment she felt toward
Littky. In the teacher's lounge the day after the slide show,

Val decided to say what she sensed others were thinking.

"If you ask me, Dennis Littky has done a magnificent job of making us teachers look bad. He makes it look like we were sitting on our duffs all last year, complacently watching the school fall apart."

Her comment worked its way back to Littky, who responded with a quick jab to Phil Hamm.

"What was I supposed to do? Make a replay of last year so as not to hurt her feelings?" He took a deep breath and calmed himself. "That's the very thing I wanted to avoid," he told Hamm. "I wasn't criticizing them for conditions here. The fact is, the school didn't have a strong leader, so things fell apart. That's not the teachers' fault. I think when they see me criticizing my own programs or making changes in my changes, they'll begin to trust me more."

His apology to Val and the others who shared her view appeared in the next TGIF memo.

> I am very happy where the school is right now. . . . I have faith in what each of you is doing in the classroom. Any statements I make about last year are nothing but repeating things you have told me. I realize that many of you performed very heroically just to keep the school going each day. Teachers went way beyond the call of duty. I do not discredit this. In fact I admire it—lesser people would have laid down and called it quits. You are here because you care—what I hope to do is to help lead the group to use that energy and creativity in a positive way, in a building way—not just being reactive.

One thing Littky couldn't get used to at Thayer was the way everybody fled from the school at the end of the day. It was as if they were running from a burning building. The students were gone in a flash, and most teachers stayed only as long as they were absolutely required to.

It hadn't been like that on Long Island. There it was

usual for teachers to arrive at school before sunup and leave after sundown. Many spent weekends working on projects or took groups of students on after-school outings.

But Shoreham–Wading River Middle School was brand new and wealthy. Littky had handpicked every member of the staff, looking for high-energy teachers willing to immerse themselves in an experimental school where they could use their ample energy. Most of those teachers had been young and childless. It was a situation that lent itself to complete commitment.

Things were different at Thayer. He'd inherited most of the staff, so almost none of them were there because of Littky and his plans for the school. Many teachers were exhausted after the stress and tumult of the previous several years. Many were bitter, suspicious of reforms, and antagonistic toward Littky and what he was trying to do.

That's why, on the day of the open house, he was so delighted to have three girls ask him if they could stay after school and paint some banners for the event. "Of course," Littky said. As soon as the final bell rang, they dashed to the art room for paint, brushes, and rolls of paper.

WE'RE ALL MAKING IT TOGETHER, they painted in big bold letters. DR. LITTKY IS GREAT!

The girls carried their work to the front lobby and taped it neatly on the wall, then raced to Littky's office.

"Come see what we've done!" they sang out happily.

Doc followed, curious and excited. The "making it together" sign caught his eye first. "That's great!" He gave them each an affectionate squeeze around the shoulders.

"Look behind you!"

Littky turned to the other wall. As he stared silently at the other poster, his smiled washed away.

"Thanks, girls, but it's a little embarrassing." Their enthusiasm turned to frowns."What's wrong with it?"

"I appreciate the compliment," he said. "But in a way, it's

a real insult to the teachers—it leaves them out, and that's just the opposite of doing it together." Their sad looks touched him. "I'm sorry, but I'll give you a choice—you can take that down or make one for every teacher in the school."

Two hours later the girls finished the last teacher poster. When Doc saw the signs festooning the walls, he beamed.

Following the slide show at the open house that night, Littky talked to the parents. He told them about all the work Jim Burns and his crew did that summer, about Nick Collins and the Pegasus.

"I talked to students this summer. Some of them said that flying horse wouldn't last a day. Well, it's only two weeks into the semester, but so far nothing's been damaged. The kids seem to *care*. One said to me the other day, 'The school would have been wrecked by this time last year.' The kids care because we care and they know it.

"We worked all summer to take the good that was here and get rid of the things that were problems—and then we added more good. Yesterday a boy said to me, 'Do you think the parents will believe this is Thayer High?' There's a different attitude here—the students have changed from not trying, to feeling that teachers are on their side—and that's a big change from last year.

"We're not perfect—students still sneak out of school and still get in arguments with teachers—we'll never be perfect—but we'll try to be the best we can be. I'm proud to be here. I'm proud to live in Winchester. Three years ago I came here to vacation for a year or two, but now this is my *home*.

"As the girls wrote on the poster, 'We're all making it together'—and that means you, too. In the past parents bad-mouthed school at home, which just made it harder for us. We need you to support the school. If you have questions, call the school and ask for Marcia Ammann, call your neighborhood person, or ask for me to come over and talk about the school's discipline policy or whatever interests you.

"As I've said, we're not rich in money, but we're rich in resources. We need wood, we need paper, we need tutors, we need drivers. We're going to try to give the students the best education we can—and that doesn't mean the most expensive. If we share, we can do it without our taxes skyrocketing."

Littky had barely ended his talk when about a dozen parents swarmed around him. One woman, the wife of a teacher, shook his hand. "I just wanted to thank you," she said. "My husband is a new man since you arrived."

A couple introduced themselves and thanked Dennis for saying hello to their boy every day and remembering his name.

All the while, a large woman in a worn housedress stood apart from the crowd. When the circle around Doc thinned, she approached him tentatively. "Hello, Mr. Littky," she said carefully. She was the mother of one of the girls who painted the posters.

"I just wanted you to know," she said, "that this is the first time my daughter's ever liked coming to school."

The art teacher had no matte board to frame students' art work, so Littky turned to the person he usually relied upon to fill such requests. He breezed past Marcia Ammann's office and shouted, "Marcia! Find some matte board, get some matte board!"

Marcia shouted back, "I'll get right on it!"

When Littky went on his way, Marcia reached for the dictionary. "I don't even know what matte board is."

A few days later a truck pulled up with 2,000 pounds of matte board, donated by a local paper company.

The outpouring of attention from the community

amazed Littky. Hardly a day passed that someone didn't contribute something to the school. It was as though people were just waiting for an invitation to help.

At the end of September, Littky was notified that Thayer had been picked as one of twenty-five schools in the country to receive a $26,500 federal grant to help fund the apprenticeship program. The New Hampshire Charitable Foundation awarded Thayer a $4,000 grant to help start businesses in the school. Littky wanted to set up a computer business to help support the in-school computer program.

In October, he learned that his school on Long Island had been given the Presidential award by the National Institute of Education. The school was also featured as one of four "outstanding schools" in the country in meeting the needs of its adolescent students in a book titled *Successful Schools for Young Adolescents,* by Joan Lipsitz. The author concluded that although each of the four schools had its own characteristics, the one thing that stood out in common was "there was joy in each school." Littky's Shoreham-Wading River Middle School, in particular, was seen as "an example of what creative policy-setters, administrators, and staff can do with a lot of money, energy, and community participation. On the continuum of excellence from optimizing what is best about American schooling to redefining it, Shoreham-Wading River has gone furthest toward redefinition."

In November, Littky was invited to speak to fifteen superintendents in southwestern New Hampshire Topic: "The process of developing a school responsive to the students and the community." He was chosen as the keynote speaker for the annual meeting of the Monadnock Health and Welfare Council in Keene. Ironically, he would conclude the year as keynote speaker at the annual New Hampshire Principals Conference at Bretton Woods, the same conference he was almost excluded from for lack of a suit and tie.

Littky wrote in a TGIF memo: "I'm proud of these invitations and hope to instill in others the hope for what schools can do. People are watching our school—an example of what can be done in education. We should all be proud."

If the energy and attention Thayer High was receiving continued, Littky was confident that everything else would follow—the school would make a rapid recovery. Turning Thayer High into a model of good education appeared inevitable.

Littky had high hopes for the agricultural program. Other than the apprenticeship program, it was the only major structural innovation in place that moved the whole school in the direction he wanted it to go. Reconstructing the dome was only one part of the daily class. The students were also working on plans to set up a farm.

On a Wednesday afternoon at the end of September, the agriculture class held an organizational meeting. The get-together was attended by the county agricultural agent and several local farmers, including State Representative Elmer Johnson. Energy was high. By the end of the meeting, a dairy farmer offered the use of ten acres next to the school for raising feed corn for the farm animals, which he also planned to donate. The county agent volunteered his expertise to the class two to three times a week. Earl Beaman, who owned a prosperous lumber company in Winchester, told the class that a Keene construction company owned a barn close to school that might be available.

After the meeting, Littky, John Belcher-Timme, and the class tromped outside to survey the area that was to become their working farm. Littky suggested they construct a boardwalk over the marshy land between the school and the barn. The students buzzed with excitement, discussing how they'd clean up this and construct that, how they'd turn the ramshackle barn into an operating dairy farm and maybe even supply the school with milk, how they'd call themselves the Future Farmers of Winchester.

Before the day was done, Littky got permission from the Keene company to refurbish and use the barn. A few days later, a truck arrived to deliver a load of railroad ties for the boardwalk—the lumber was donated by Earl Beaman.

In the first month of school there was practically no vandalism—only two minor incidents:

A girl was caught in the girls' locker room writing on the walls with magic marker. She was given a bucket of paint and a brush and told to repaint the wall.

A toilet paper dispenser was kicked in on the wall of the boys' washroom. Jim Burns fixed it immediately.

Meanwhile, Pegasus still reigned unsullied and supreme in the cafeteria. The new table tops were scrubbed smooth and shiny every night.

Littky walked the halls, his eyes peeled for places that needed attention.

On one round of the building, he decided to relocate the pay telephone. It was in the gym lobby, a fairly untraveled area, making it a good place for kids to gather to use the phone and do whatever they wanted—smoke cigarettes, skip class, make out—pretty sure they would not be observed.

The cafeteria, on the other hand, was the hub of activity and, as such, was regularly supervised. Whenever possible, prevent a problem before it becomes one, Littky insisted. He moved the pay phone into the cafeteria.

Dennis focused his attention on "building environments." Everything he was doing was designed to be both preventative and nurturing.

I strongly believe in building environments, whether that's a classroom, a schedule, a meeting—whatever has the best chance of gaining the best results. The Advisory is a preventative environment—the school building looking good is a preventative environment—me being around the halls is a preventative environment—exciting classes are preventative—individual and group meetings are preventative.

Phil Hamm had prepared Littky well for the school's most volatile students. Littky wanted to do everything he could to keep them under control. Hamm said that a ninth grader named Glenn was particularly troublesome.

Littky made a point of talking with Glenn regularly. He wanted the boy to get to know him on friendly terms, so that if and when he got out of control, Littky could be more effective in dealing with him. Glenn's biggest problem was his explosive temper—anything could set him off, even having someone look at him "the wrong way."

During the second week of school Glenn lost it: he got mad at a teacher, stormed out of the classroom, and left school. After a few hours his anger evaporated and he came back. Dennis caught him in the hall. "Your teacher just told me you stomped out of her classroom because you got mad about something. She's not even sure what. Glenn, you can't just leave school whenever you feel like it."

"She asked me a question. I didn't know the answer," he said. "She made me feel stupid."

"You've got a lot going for you," Doc said. "If you could just learn to control your temper, I think you could go a long way. There's something I've been thinking about that might help you. I'd like you to meet with Mr. Hamm and me, say, once a week, to help teach you how to control your temper."

Glenn looked skeptical. "How can you teach someone that?"

"Well, do you know what a simulation is?"

"I'm not sure."

"It's when you try to re-create a real-life situation in a controlled environment. Mr. Hamm and I would try to make you mad, you would respond however you respond, and then we would step back and try to learn from it."

"You want to do that . . . with *me*?"

"Yes, if you're willing. I think it could help you a lot."

Glenn thought for a minute, studying Doc. "I'll give it a try. When do you want to do this thing?"

"What's wrong with today?"

They met in Littky's office.

"Okay, Glenn," Doc said. "Do you understand the ground rules?"

Glenn looked from Littky to Hamm and back again. "You guys are going to do whatever you can to make me mad, and then I'm going to respond."

"That's it," Littky said. "Then we're going to talk about your response. You ready?"

"Yeah."

Phil took the first shot. "Glenn, you're such a pain. Why can't you learn? If you weren't so lazy maybe you wouldn't be so worthless."

Doc chimed in. "Glenn, you idiot. I'm sick and tired of you talking all the time. I don't want idiots in my classroom wasting everybody else's time."

At first Glenn snickered. But as the barbs dug deeper, he got more and more agitated until suddenly his temper ignited. Fists clenched, he lurched to a stand.

"Goddamnit!" he roared. "Get the hell off my case!"

Littky leaned forward. "You're not acting," he said softly. "Are you, Glenn?" He put a comforting hand on the boy's shoulder.

Glenn was livid. "Damn right, I'm not! *Nobody* talks to *me* like that! Nobody gets away with calling me an idiot."

Littky's voice was soothing. "Calm down, Glenn, calm down," he said. "Just take a step back for a second and think—think about what's going on here."

Glenn was breathing hard, trying to control his anger.

Doc put a hand on his shoulder. "Tell me—what's going on here?"

Glenn took a deep breath. He looked a bit dazed. Slowly, the tension began to drain. He gave Doc a half-smile. "I think I see what happened. I let you guys get to me."

Hamm nodded. "What would have been a better way to respond?"

Glenn thought for a moment. "I think . . . I think I should've told you politely to go fuck yourselves."

Littky and Hamm looked at each other, then burst out laughing. "Well," Littky said, "at least you're on the right track. It's not a real good idea telling anybody, let alone teachers, to go fuck themselves. But staying calm and politely telling someone you don't like the way you're being treated is the smart way to respond. Do you think you could come up with a different line?"

Glenn nodded. "How about this? 'If you don't like what I'm doing, just say it. I don't think you have to insult me in the process.'"

Doc picked up on Glenn's words and continued the simulation.

"Glenn, I'm sorry for losing my temper," he said. "I'm just tired of you always talking and disrupting class. Would you please be quiet and pay attention?"

"I'm sorry," Glenn said earnestly. "I'll try a little harder."

"That's great!" Littky said. "Do you think you could do that for real?"

Suddenly Glenn hesitated. "I don't know," he said. "Can we do this again?"

Littky and Hamm set up weekly simulations with Glenn. In the meantime, until he gained better control over his temper, Glenn agreed to carry an orange flashcard with him to all his classes. If he felt himself losing his temper, all he had to do was flash his orange card at the teacher, get up, and leave the room. Once he calmed down, he could return to the classroom. If he did this successfully, there would be no reprimands.

Doc was convinced that most behavioral problems couldn't be blamed on the students alone. If a kid misbehaved, everything had to be considered—the teacher, the class, the subject matter being taught, the teaching methods, the student's home life, and so on. When there was an outburst that required his intervention, Littky called in everyone involved and tried to sort out what had happened and deal with the real problem.

Most of all, he didn't want the student to walk away feeling that there was something wrong with him or her as a person. The only thing he wanted to focus on was the behavior and the reasons behind it.

Despite some successes, Littky often felt frustrated. He had a vision he wanted the school to realize. But over and over again, he found that vision being swallowed up by the day-to-day management of the school: he felt as though all he was doing was putting out fires. He stalked the halls, ears tuned for an outburst, a fight, a teacher shouting for him. No sooner would he stop one fight than someone elsewhere in the building needed him to handle another.

One day a fight broke out in a classroom where the teacher had given the class twenty minutes of free time. "Twenty minutes of free time is *way* too long for these kids," Littky told the teacher. "You weren't watching the whole class. A lot of the kids just had nothing to do, so they came up with something. An outburst of some kind was almost inevitable."

A few older students were having trouble; it was clear they would not make it to graduation. "A seventeen-year-old who hasn't passed ninth grade sees no light at the end of the tunnel," Littky said. "They're a strain on the staff, and they certainly aren't doing themselves any good by sitting through long days in the classroom."

Littky worked to convince the school board to approve hiring an aide. The aide would work two or three hours a day tutoring those students, preparing them for the high school equivalency exam.

"We're not here just to keep students in high school for four years," Littky told the board. "They aren't earning a diploma based on the *time* they put in. As far as I'm concerned, if I can make it easier for them to get in the army or get a job and keep it, that's the important thing. The truth is, some kids just aren't going to make it no matter what we do. But maybe if they remember they were treated well here, then we've accomplished something."

The board approved the program.

Doc studied faces. If a kid looked extremely tense or stressed out, Littky made a point to talk to the student and try to root out the problem. He became more attuned to teachers who had problems controlling their classes. Each day he stopped by every teacher's class and observed, even if for only a few minutes. Then, one by one, he held individual conferences with staff members, beginning the long process of making them more self-aware as instructors and disciplinarians. It was hard to break teachers of habits that had been formed over many years.

"If a kid doesn't understand what you're doing in class, he's likely to act up, rather than be embarrassed because he can't answer a question," Littky counseled his teachers. "If he's kicked out two days in a row, he misses two days of information and falls even farther behind. Then there's no way to keep his attention in class. Acting up becomes a way of life, a reputation that kid is *expected* to keep up."

One of Barb Eibell's eighth graders was getting out of hand so much that he was making learning impossible for the rest of the class. She didn't want to do it, but she sent him out of class. The second day it happened, she, Littky, and the troublemaker met to discuss the problem.

"Is there some reason you'd rather spend your days in my office than in Mrs. Eibell's classroom?" Doc asked.

The boy shrugged his shoulders. "I got trouble with English, how am I s'posed to learn another language?"

It was a revealing comment. He was over his head in Barb's Spanish class. Littky looked at Barb—the message was clear: she had to change her class so that this boy and others like him could learn.

As a mandatory eighth-grade course, the language classes drew all students—accelerated, average, and remedial. That was new for Barb, since language courses were typically the domain of college-bound students. Though she was used to dealing with problem students, she wasn't used to kids who had learning disabilities.

"The boy's right," Doc said. "You've got to decide what this child can get out of your class. Maybe you could involve him in map-making, watching slides, or learning about customs. Come up with projects that will make Spanish relevant to him without lowering your standards.

"*All* kids should be actively involved—no matter how slow or how smart they are. Right now, you're doing all the work. You stand in front of the room, talking at the students. They sit there passively—some are listening, some aren't."

Barb nodded. "I guess I have to learn to shut up more."

Doc spent several weeks intensively observing Barb teach. They had a daily dialogue about what worked, what didn't. Barb began to look forward to Doc's visits.

But others weren't so eager to change. Littky's regular observations of teachers in class made him realize how far many of them had to go. Many teachers stood lock-kneed at the front of the room, talking. Occasionally they'd toss out a question. Sometimes a student would answer, but more often than not the teachers answered their own questions.

To Littky's way of thinking, that kind of teaching reinforced the notion that learning is a dull and passive process—exactly the opposite of what he had in mind. His dream was to open up the structure of the day completely, eliminating the cast-in-stone, subject-by-subject, fifty-minute class period. Real life didn't come packaged neatly. Why should school? He wanted to integrate the learning experience, mixing science with English with math with social studies. He wanted teachers to work in teams, blending and balancing—playing off each other's specialties. Students would be compelled to make essential connections—plugging in mathematical knowledge to answer a social science problem, using composition skills to learn about biology. He wanted students to think of the *world* as their classroom, not four walls and a chalkboard.

Mostly he wanted Thayer students to experience what they learned. Books, lectures, desks in neat rows—all these things had their proper place, but they rarely triggered the kind of engaged, active learning he saw as the hallmark of good education. Thayer High had a long, long way to go before it reached that goal.

Doc was ready to start cracking down.

My emphasis up to now has been to get to know students and let them know and understand me and what I stand for. My emphasis has been to help set direction for staff, respecting the past and moving on. The time has now come for me to be more direct with students who are not responding or who are abusing us and the system. I will continue to try to set up programs that bring the best out of students, but we only have so much manpower to start new programs. I will also begin to have students coming to school ½ days if they can't handle the entire day or to put students out of school for a day or more if they continue not to respond. I'm beginning to set controls with students about their behavior.

The time has also come to begin giving teachers more feedback about their classroom so we can get better and better together, supporting each other, and finding ways to use each of us in the best manner. In the next three weeks I will meet with every staff member and try to tell each the areas that I think are strengths and areas that I feel need working on. I expect each staff member to do the same for me, so I too can grow and stay in touch with how I am doing. It is something I would even like teachers to think of doing with their students.

During the first weeks of school, Littky had met with the staff nearly every day. Morning conferences between advisers and students were delayed until Dennis felt confident that every staff member was ready. He wasn't fond of meetings, but there was no better way to deal with the new responsibilities teachers were taking on.

He outlined his thoughts in a letter to the school board. "I expect staff to wear many hats—that of teacher, adviser, school community member, subject area specialist, a constant learner and more."

The way he saw it, teachers weren't doing their jobs if they limited their involvement in the school to the classroom. Several teachers disagreed with that. Littky had long been aware of a group of teachers who resisted nearly everything he tried to accomplish. He called them the Skeptics. They held a lot of sway with the other teachers.

What made the Skeptics so formidable was that they had the power to pull the plug on the energy Littky had managed to build with other teachers. Hours of discussion and demonstration could be short-circuited by a well-placed comment from one of their number. At meeting after meeting, they sat in the back, whispering among themselves and tossing out caustic remarks. They were unrestrained when it came to the advisory program.

"It's not our job to play that kind of role," one Skeptic

declared. "I was hired as a teacher, not a psychologist."

"We don't have time to meet with every kid individually. We have too many meetings already!" said another.

"This isn't in our contract!"

Littky welcomed questions and criticism as a healthy way for a group to learn and grow. But there were limits.

He carefully explained that as advisers they were counselors, but they were academic counselors, not psychotherapists. If a student had an emotional problem, it would be referred to Phil Hamm. Advisory was intended to make the school friendlier, more accessible, to kids.

In a TGIF memo, Dennis wrote:

> Each student should have something special in school, be it band, sports, the chess club, a class he/she loves, a teacher he/she is close to, etc. The advisory was set up to begin to key into this. The individual conferences give us and a student a chance to talk and work together, be it to help a student find a college or a job or to put the family in touch with a counselor. Although our classes will mostly be with groups, our guiding and supporting will be with individuals.

He spent hours talking about the program. But just when most of the teachers seemed to be catching on to the concept, the Skeptics repeated their same tired arguments.

Littky sought out Marcia Ammann. "This resistance is really getting to me," he told her. "The Skeptics all sit in the back in a bunch. One or two seem to set the tone for everyone else. Just when I think everybody is with me, they repeat their complaints and we're back at square one."

"I could have predicted who they'd be," Marcia said sympathetically.

"The simple fact is Thayer High *will* have an advisory system. We will do it, but how we do it will be determined by the staff. I've decided to form a committee of teachers to help determine the specific role advisers will play at Thayer. I'll make sure I've got people who support the advisory system, then pepper it with the strongest critics. They'll be less likely to sabotage a program they helped design.

"The teachers have got to see results—good, positive results. And they've got to feel the community is behind what they're doing. If the community stops blaming them for everything that's wrong at school and starts complimenting them for what's going right, then maybe they'll buy into my vision."

Resistance to the academic advisory system persisted. He talked, cajoled, and argued advisory's merits. He put Robbie Fried of the state education department on the committee. Fried was an articulate, persuasive educator who firmly supported the advisory concept. That didn't work, either. Teachers poured more passion into arguing against the program than in trying to make it work.

Littky wanted staff members to meet with each student in their advisories for half an hour four times each semester. Few advisers were even close to complying with that. Their attempts to meet with students were halfhearted at best. The standard response was, I don't have the time to be a teacher *and* an adviser.

Then in January the advisory committee issued a survey to the staff members asking their opinions and suggestions regarding the advisory concept. The survey helped set up a constructive dialogue among teachers about advisory, as well as other issues of concern. Criticisms were no longer directed against Littky for "imposing" the advisory role on staff; instead, teachers looked for the good in the program, tried to weed out what wasn't working, and then set out to improve it.

In June the committee summed up the philosophy: "The Academic Advisory system is formed to establish and maintain a close link between the school, parent, student and teacher in order for each student to have a successful school experience and to plan realistically for his/her future."

The committee and staff worked out the responsibilities: each adviser would be expected to work with ten to fifteen students, conduct morning attendance, and meet with each student for thirty minutes eight times a year about his or her academic progress. In addition, advisers would be expected to spot students' academic strengths and weaknesses and to coordinate the grades on their report cards.

One of the biggest concerns teachers had about their role as advisers was in dealing with students' personal problems. The committee stated very clearly that while it was important for the adviser to recognize that a problem existed, the teacher would be responsible only for referring students to the proper person for help.

Finally some of advisory's toughest critics were drawn in. The difference, it seemed, was that the points had come from staff, rather than from on high. Though the concept had come from Littky, the content was theirs.

Littky was delighted.

At the October 14 staff meeting, Dennis did something he'd never done before—he let someone else run it. The subject was the discipline code, something he'd chosen not to tackle until school was well under way.

Littky believed rewriting the rules of discipline was key to making the school run more smoothly. The old rules had lost their meaning because they weren't enforced. If the school—the *whole* school—took part in reviewing and rewriting the rules, they stood a chance of being followed and enforced.

This meeting with the teachers was the first step in the process. Certain problems concerned Littky more than others—fighting, disrespect toward teachers, vandalism, drug abuse, tardiness, and skipping school. Littky simply would not tolerate students drinking during school. If he caught a student in such a state, his first move would be to get the offending student out of view as soon as possible. Then it meant automatic suspension from school and extra-curricular activities.

Students could wear hats and chew gum, he said. But if a teacher didn't want either in the classroom, that was up to the teacher, and students would have to abide by the class-room rules. "My point is not that I love hats and gum," he told the school board, "but I feel there are more important things to fight about."

Littky, though opposed to students smoking, decided not to become militant about the problem. While smoking needed to be moved out of the restrooms, it wasn't an issue on which he wanted to expend endless energy. If the kids grew to respect the school and the people in it, such prob-lems would eventually correct themselves.

After working out a consensus with teachers about the rules, Doc met with the class officers. Questionnaires were passed out to every student through advisory. Karen Thompson, who'd been elected junior class vice president, and the other class officers spent weeks gathering and reading through the responses and suggestions. With a handful of students, Karen collated the information into a tidy package for Doc to review.

When it came to setting the rules, the kids tended to be tougher than the adults. By the time the discipline code was finished, the rules were clear and well known to everyone. Five things would not be tolerated under any circumstance: fighting, drugs or alcohol, swearing at teachers, theft, and vandalism. Violation would result in one to five days of automatic suspension, depending on the infraction.

Public display of affection (PDA) was an issue that drew a lot of attention from students and staff. After weeks of work, Doc pulled together a set of guidelines reflecting the majority opinion. Holding hands was fine, kissing and "mauling" were not. He didn't hesitate to pull students apart when he felt they were overstepping the bounds. "I'm not opposed to kissing," he said. "But school just isn't the place for it."

When the rules were completed, Doc wrote a letter to the students:

> . . . There are some cases where the student is absolutely wrong, i.e., swearing at a teacher, fighting with another student, disrupting a class. There are some cases where the teacher is wrong, i.e. accusing a student of something that he/she didn't do, or cases where both the student and teacher are part of the problem—both being disrespectful to each other. If the problem occurs in the classroom, it is up to the teacher to deal with it, which may be a detention, a zero, a call home. If the problem continues, then I should be brought into it. I will listen to both sides and decide not only what to do at the moment—suspension, call home, etc., but also what to do in the future to prevent the problem from happening again.

On October 15, as usual, all advisers were given the day's announcements to be read during their morning advisory. This day the announcements included an item that Littky wasn't ready for. Neither, it turned out, was the rest of the school.

At the bottom of the page was a letter addressed to "Dear Tabby." The column was a takeoff on Dear Abby, created by Phil Hamm and three students as a forum where kids could air their problems and concerns. Though Littky had approved the idea in general, he had not seen the letter until it appeared at the bottom of the announcements:

"Dear Tabby—My boyfriend and I have just started having sex. What should we do for safety?" The letter was signed "Wondering."

"Dear Wondering: There are many kinds of safety precautions you could use. The pill's the most common, but there's also the diaphragm, foam, gel, etc. First thing you should do is talk it over with your boyfriend and talk it over with your doctor. If you're under age, you'll need your mother with you."

Within minutes, Littky's office was filled with outraged teachers.

"I had no idea this was going to be in the announcements. I'd already started reading it to my advisory before I realized what it said. Then it was too late!"

"I can't believe this. Am I supposed to start teaching sex education now?"

Dennis agreed with them. Their complaints were legitimate. He tracked down Phil in the guidance office. "Don't do *anything* like this without telling me you're doing it!" Littky barked.

Phil Hamm was defensive. "I thought you approved of what we're trying to do."

"In general terms, I do. But you don't just dump something like this in teachers' laps without any warning."

"I'm sorry," Phil said. "It wasn't my intent to start a controversy, but to help kids handle some of their problems. I figured if teachers didn't feel comfortable reading the letters to their advisory, then they wouldn't. I had no idea it would cause this kind of stir."

By the end of the day, the news had leaked out. Marian Polaski phoned Littky to say that angry parents had called her about the incident. Littky called a meeting of the Key Communicators to explain the situation to parents. But the damage had been done. Those who already disliked Littky and his methods would not forget.

15
Thayer Spirit

TRADITIONALLY, ON THE FOURTH WEEK of school, teachers sent out notices to let parents know if their son or daughter was failing in a class. Littky rejected the practice out of hand.

"In most cases I don't believe negative stuff gets things done," he told the staff at a Wednesday meeting. "Why pick on the negative? If we say something negative, I feel we have a responsibility to say something positive. I feel that four or five weeks is too quick a time to send out warnings. We will be meeting with parents November 6. If a student is doing very poorly, please drop a note to the student's adviser. The adviser can decide if a call home is necessary or not.

"Most families dread the note or call home from teachers or the principal's voice on the other end of the line. No wonder parents feel threatened by school! The majority of calls or notes are negative. I hope we can change this. I don't want our first communication home about a child to be negative. That is not why we're here, and in most cases warnings don't do much but get kids angry."

Littky asked teachers to give him names of students who were doing well in class or had done something special. Those names would be announced at the staff's weekly breakfast meeting on Mondays, then followed up by Littky or Marcia Ammann, who would call or write a letter home.

"They're not going to come," several teachers insisted.

"The whole day will be a waste of time."

Parent Conference Day was a sore topic.

The idea was for teachers to meet individually with their advisees' parents. Report cards would be handed out in person to parents, then discussed. Littky saw the approach as plainly personal, direct, and constructive. It forced parents to focus on their children's development and future, and it gave them a direct link to school. Advisers were to collect the grades for each of their advisees, then confer with teachers about each student's performance. That information would then be passed to the parents.

The assistant principal and the teacher's union representative were adamant.

"Technically," said the union representative, "our contract says the day is designated for teacher workshops. It's union rules."

Littky tried to appeal to her sense of reason. "What's the big deal?" he said. "The parent conferences will help our relations with the community and will be a big help to students. I thought that's what our job was all about. Do you want it or not?"

The union rep couldn't dispute Littky's claim—she liked the idea of meeting with parents. Her problem was, as union representative, she had a contract to uphold.

At staff meetings, the battle raged.

"If we allow this breach of the contract, then it's just going to set a precedent," one teacher griped.

"It's a violation of our contract, plain and simple. We're not going to allow it," said another.

Finally Val Cole spoke up. "Hey, guys. You're fighting about semantics. I think everyone's agreed that parent conferences would be a good thing. Why don't we just sign something that says there's no violation of the contract going on here and get on with it?"

Littky arranged a compromise. He invited a communications specialist into the school for the day as a resource person to help the staff. That fulfilled the workshop stipulation in the contract. The staff then presented a signed letter to the school board that said that Parent Conference Day was not violating the contract. The board accepted the letter. Parent Conference Day could go on.

"Thank God for Val Cole," Littky sighed. "She is the strongest positive force. She's respected; she doesn't say anything wild. She doesn't speak a lot, so when she speaks it counts."

However, some skepticism lingered. Marcia got a note from the assistant principal that said, in effect, "It ain't going to work. It'll be a waste of time."

Marcia didn't know who was right, but she knew she didn't like the negativism.

Since Marcia was in charge of community relations, organizing Parent Conference Day fell on her shoulders. Her main concerns were to get the word out to parents and to get them to show up. It was a real problem: how could she possibly ensure good attendance when most parents worked at jobs where they punched a clock? How could they just skip out of work to come to school?

Her first plan was to contact parents by mail, giving them the date of the conference and what it was intended to do. The clincher was that the only way students could get their report cards was for their parents to come to the conference.

Next she and her apprentices wrote reminders to parents in the new monthly Thayer High newsletter. She put announcements in the *Winchester Star* and the *Keene Sentinel*. She wrote letters to all the employers in the area asking for their cooperation in letting parents off to attend their conferences. Within the week, she heard back from fifty-five businesses. They were happy to accommodate. Marcia was ecstatic; maybe there'd be a good turnout after all.

But the teachers themselves were a stumbling block. Advisers were responsible for setting up appointments with their advisees' parents. She was distressed to learn that some teachers were making no effort whatsoever to accommodate parents' schedules.

When Littky heard about it, he fumed. He let out some of his anger in his journal:

> I'm tired of people saying they're spending too much time working—tough shit! If this is going to be a special place, they're going to *have* to work. What do they think? This is going to just *happen?* I'm getting *unbelievable* resistance over this parent conference business. 'You're making us do too much,' they keep whining. It just makes me so damn mad! Sometimes I think they're fighting me because they *want* me to fail.

He made his point to teachers in the October 16 TGIF memo:

> We have a long struggle ahead of us. I feel the most resistance from staff. The parents seem to be very supportive, the Board of Ed is supportive, and I believe the students are trying. I get most frustrated when we know what we need to do, but people are resistant. This school is going to take more of your time than a regular school. It will be a great school, not a regular school.
>
> Let's get excited about meeting with parents and discussing their children. Let's take it as a challenge to see how many we can get to come in. All I ask is that people have a positive attitude about solving any problem that arises. If we don't have this attitude, then we should not be educating our youth.

Marcia was up at dawn on Parent Conference Day. She set up a table at the front door, loaded with coffee and doughnuts. She wanted parents and teachers to feel welcome the moment they stepped into the school. She met the first teachers at the door.

"Good morning!" she sang out. "Have a doughnut for some positive energy!" She got hopeful smiles in return.

As parents started to arrive, Marcia greeted them energetically, offering them coffee, doughnuts, good humor, and directions.

"You know, this is the first time I've been in this school since I graduated," one man said to her.

The response startled even her. Parents were coming! In droves they were coming! Teachers got caught up in the energy.

By the end of the day, roughly 90 percent of the parents had shown up. As Marcia smoked a cigarette in the teachers' lounge, talking and laughing with some teachers, she realized it was the first time that year that she really felt accepted by her colleagues.

The next day Marcia got on the phone to the handful of families who hadn't come in and made special appointments for each of them. Some grumbled, but eventually all but a handful of parents came in.

For days following the parent conferences, Littky could see a change in the school's mood. Many teachers thought parents would take students' bad grades out on them, but that hadn't happened. Many were afraid that the parents simply didn't care. They'd begun to believe the kids who'd told them over and over again, "My parents don't give a damn. They could care less what I do." That wasn't the case. Most parents appealed to their child's adviser, asking what they could do to help.

Two days after the conferences, Littky, Marcia Ammann, and school board president Marian Polaski attended a coffee at the home of a parent. They were heaped with happy responses from everyone present. The parents said they'd been impressed with *everything*—the teachers, the way the school looked, the way the whole staff seemed to pull together for the event.

To Littky, it was a turning point.

But two weeks after the parent conferences, Littky was at Flat Street, a Brattleboro night spot, when suddenly, a tough-looking young man with a brush cut accosted him.

"You're Littky," the young man said. He pushed Littky's shoulder with the flat of his hand. "I just got home from the marines and I'm going to use every skill I've learned and I'm going to kill you!"

Dumbfounded by the assault, Littky studied the young man. He had never seen him before. The marine was either drunk or crazy. He hurled himself at Littky. His words shot out with flicks of spit. "You made my mom lose time at work because of your fuckin' parent conferences!"

A friend of Littky's stepped between Dennis and the young man. He looked him straight in the eye and spoke calmly, slowly. He called the young man by name. "You don't want to beat this guy up," he said softly. "What good would it do you? C'mon, let's get out of this room. Loosen up."

Littky kept quiet.

His friend led the young man away. He stayed with him for a few minutes, then worked his way back across the dance floor toward Littky's table.

"Let's get out of here," Littky said.

The young man pointed at Littky and shouted across the dance floor, "I'm gonna *get* you, fucker! I'm gonna *get* you!"

Littky and his friends hurried out the door toward their car. But before they got there, the marine and another young man came up behind them.

"We're going to kill you!"

Just then, a cop pulled up and flashed his lights.

"What's going on here?" the cop said.

"It's okay, officer," Littky said. "Everything's fine. We're just leaving." The cop watched them get into their car and drive out of the parking lot. At the first traffic light, Littky looked down at his hands. They shook.

"Look at that," he said with genuine wonder. "I can't stop them. I think I'm afraid to go to my cabin. I'm afraid to go home."

It was the first time Winchester didn't feel like home.

Christmas vacation was over and second semester had begun. Doc wanted to take advantage of the momentum the school had built following parent conferences and direct it into something entirely positive. The state basketball tournament gave him the idea—Thayer's boys' varsity team was on its way to state competition in early March. Littky wanted the celebration to be bigger than a pep rally. He wanted to recognize more than just the basketball team—he wanted to celebrate *everybody*.

When the topic came up at a Monday morning breakfast meeting, Val Cole shook her head. "No way am I going to get involved in that," she muttered.

Overloaded with energy, Littky bobbed around the meeting room tossing out ideas and asking for volunteers.

"It'll be a chance to stand up and be proud," he said, "a chance to honor ourselves and our accomplishments and to honor the students who've put out in a positive way. Let's really get into it! Let's make an entire evening of it—we'll honor seniors, honor roll students—"

"How about the VFW's Voice of Democracy winner?" a teacher shouted out.

"Good!" Dennis said.

"The band members!"

"Yes!"

"The other sports teams!"

"Yes!"

"Everyone in the senior play!"

"Great!" Littky scribbled down the ideas. "We'll need a committee."

Against her will, Val Cole was drawn in. She joined the committee, became its spokesperson, and found herself seized with enthusiasm. "We want to make it an all-day festival," she said. "An up-with-Thayer day! We'll have competitions, exhibits, games. The evening portion will be open to the entire community—demonstrations, pep rally, honors assembly, slide show."

Though pleased with Val's energy, Doc was worried Spirit Day was getting *too* big. An all-day fun day for 350 kids could be difficult to manage.

"Not if it's well-organized," Val countered. "We've worked up a list of activities. Listen to this one—we're calling it 'As Classes Match Wits.' We'll pit classes against classes to see which one can answer the most Thayer High School trivia questions."

Littky couldn't bring himself to squash the committee's enthusiasm. Better to cheerlead, he thought, than be the voice of doubt. But others were less hopeful.

"Kids'll just take off whenever they feel like it," some teachers said. "They'll end up wandering around downtown—and then it'll be our necks. I thought this was a school, not a carnival."

Val pressed teachers into action. Farm program teacher John Belcher-Timme offered to have his students give wood carving demonstrations. Shop teacher Dale Courtney arranged for a drafting demonstration. Erica Miner's students were prepared to give sewing and cooking demonstrations.

Staff members came up with hundreds of questions for the quiz bowl. Littky took his camera everywhere to collect pictures for a slide show. Two boys volunteered to give a weight-lifting demonstration. A softball-in-the-snow game

was organized. The excitement grew exponentially every
time someone new got involved.

February 26 glistened white, a fresh-snow day. The instant anyone, student or faculty or staff, stepped through the
door, he or she felt the difference in mood. This was a
different sort of day. They were the same kids who were
there yesterday—Littky knew every one of them—but they
were different today. They were engaged, and that made
them look a little older somehow. He smiled as they gave in
to the music and boogied about their business.

Streamers and balloons by the hundreds festooned the
gymnasium. Jimmy Karlan's science classes set up a blood
pressure booth, complete with diagrams of the human
circulatory system. Erica Miner's students tacked up sewing
projects and recipes and set out pastries, cookies, finger
sandwiches, and other goodies.

The competitions began: softball-in-the-snow and tug-
of-war outside; spelling bee and quiz bowl inside. During
the quiz bowl, the questions came fast and furious.

"Which faculty member has the longest beard?"

"That's easy—Doc!"

"Wrong. Sophomores, what's your answer?"

The sophomores huddled quickly. "Mr. Wessels," one of
them shouted out.

"That's correct!"

The tug-of-war attracted the brawniest from the junior
and senior classes. They lined up and flexed, basking in the
sun and attention, knee-deep in snow.

The flag dropped. Each side dug in and pulled for all
they were worth. The onlookers cheered.

Just before lunch, a loud sputtering sound beat down on
the school. On schedule, a plane crisscrossed the blue sky
above Winchester.

The whole school—everybody—spilled into the crisp,

cold afternoon. In fifteen minutes, 350 students and teachers arranged themselves on the snow and spelled out "THAYER SPIRIT." As the plane passed over, the students and teachers raised their arms, letting out a cheer that could be heard by the photographer as he tripped the shutter on his camera.

That night, cars and trucks jammed the parking lot. People flooded the school, milling around the gymnasium and the lobby. They took their time looking at the exhibits and watching students draft, carve wood, sew, paint with water colors, weave, and work a potter's wheel. A booth sold fresh carnation corsages by the hundreds. Parents pinned the flowers to their lapels, jackets, and dresses. Girls fastened them in their hair.

Littky wanted attendance to be high, so he built an incentive into the night. Students were awarded points for every person they brought with them. The class with the most points would win free pizzas from Deano's Diner. It didn't take long for the stands to fill up. Then people crowded the floor of the auditorium to watch the parade of cheerleaders, athletes, honor students, clubs, and class leaders. By the time the recognitions were done, nearly every student had been called to center stage at least once.

A man in denim overalls studied the proceedings intently from the bleachers. At one point he squeezed the hand of the woman next to him, then leaned forward and tapped the shoulder of the man in front of him.

"That's the third time our boy's been called up there," he whispered and smiled. "Not only that—his class won the quiz bowl!"

A group of high school girls had worked for weeks preparing a dance routine. For most of them, their Spirit Night performance would be the first time they ever appeared in front of an audience. The crowd cheered as the girls ran out. Several blushed, one tripped and almost fell. Stoop-shouldered, heads down, they moved through their routine.

When it was over, the crowd roared its approval, stamping feet against the bleachers. As one girl ran back toward the sidelines, she brushed the hair away from her cheek and looked up at the crowd for the first time—her face beamed.

The crowd "Oooohhh'd" and "Aaaaahhh'd" as two boys demonstrated their strength and the discipline of weight lifting. The two-screen slide and music show followed.

The events came one right after the other, fast, upbeat, ebullient. The crowd loved it.

Then Littky grabbed the microphone. "Gimme a T!"

"T!"

"Gimme an I!"

"I!"

Until they spelled out "TIGERS!"

The roar was deafening. On the wall opposite the bleachers, Nick Collins's latest mural—a roaring tiger—exploded with color, meaner and bigger than life.

A few days after the event, Littky received a letter. It was from the superintendent of the district, who was not his immediate boss and had communicated with him only once before. The superintendent was perturbed; how could Littky have frittered away an entire day to hype a basketball tournament—especially so close to budget time? Littky read the letter to the staff at the Wednesday meeting. Then, in front of everyone, he ripped it into tiny pieces and threw them over his shoulder.

16
The Gang

PREVENTATIVE ENVIRONMENTS BECAME THE BUZZ phrase of Doc's second year as principal. Prevent a problem before it becomes a problem. . . .

The problem: eight tough boys.

Littky had been forewarned about this pack of boys entering junior high from the elementary school. Some said they were unteachable. They had learning problems, emotional problems, family problems. Other kids avoided them. For years, they had been shifted from one special education teacher to another, but nothing had worked to get these kids on track. At a time when most of their peers were in high school, these boys were just leaving grade school.

"We already know they aren't going to fit into the mainstream," Dennis told Phil Hamm. "We need something different for them. We've got to give them their own space, a place they can be proud of. If we don't do something extreme from the beginning, I can guarantee they'll get out of hand. They'll get bigger and stronger and more disruptive. And then where will we be? They'll take more and more of our time and resources. In the end, they'll probably just drop out."

"I was thinking about how well Findlay's alternative class worked," Hamm said.

The year before, science teacher Bob Findlay had taken charge of a group of seven disruptive junior high school boys, organizing them into a sort of school-without-walls in the community center. The boys did everything as a group, voting democratically and learning discipline through cooperation. The program had been extremely successful for them.

Littky combed the town for space outside the school. He finally found it in the historic United Church of Winchester for a monthly rent of $150. Next, Littky had to find a teacher to work with the boys full-time.

Don Weisburger had been Thayer's soccer coach the previous year while finishing a master's degree in education from Antioch University. Littky liked Weisburger's enthusiasm and energy. He knew that working successfully with the boys would take a lot of both.

During the summer, Don visited the homes of the boys who would make up his class. Littky wanted the families to know what was happening; their support was crucial.

"Ultimately, it's the parents' decision if they want their child in this classroom," Dennis told Don. "That's why it's important they meet you and that you give them a clear understanding of what the program is all about."

Don, who'd grown up in Scarsdale, a wealthy suburb of New York City, was apprehensive about his ability to convince the boys' parents. Winchester was a world apart from his cloistered and cultured upbringing. His father was a successful insurance executive who owned his own company. Don had been expected to carry on the tradition, but chose teaching instead. He'd never taught at the high school level or worked with special education students. Now here he was, a nice twenty-three-year-old upper-middle-class Jew trying to convince working-class parents in rural New Hampshire that *he* was the one who could straighten out their troubled kids.

In eight kitchens, Don, a non–coffee drinker, drank coffee; a nonsmoker, he breathed the smoke-filled air with relish, smiled a lot, and talked about his plans for the alternative class. Only one family said no to the class.

One on one, Don thought he could handle them. But seven tough, rebellious boys in one room worried him. "I don't know," he confessed to Littky, "it scares me." "It should," Dennis said. "I'm not going to snow you into thinking this is going to be easy. It ain't. I hired you because I think you've got the energy and stamina. I've seen how well you work with the boys on your soccer team. They worked hard for you because you respected them and they respected you. They knew you were working to make them into the best team possible. That's your role as coach. It's no different in the classroom. Failure is what these boys know best. You've got to change that. You've got to make them feel good about themselves. Make them into a gang, a good positive gang. That's your challenge."

They spent the first week making their space theirs. "You can outfit it any way you want," Don told the boys.

Already it included a stage, a kitchen, a piano, and ample floor space. Weisburger took the boys to Thayer's basement storage room, where they rummaged around for discarded furniture and other odds and ends. By the end of the week, the gang had pulled together an impressive booty—eight lockers, a wrestling mat, two soccer balls, several cans of bright paint, a book shelf, a table, nine desks in various stages of disrepair, some chairs, a chalkboard. They hauled it all to their space.

Armed with mops, sponges, paint scrapers, screwdrivers, and hammers, the boys scrubbed and cleaned the room, repaired the desks and chairs, hung the chalkboard, and painted the sulfur-yellow lockers light blue, bright orange, and green.

Each boy staked out a spot for his desk. David, a chubby boy, staked out a spot near the kitchen. Buddy, small and quiet, picked a lonely corner of the room between the wall and the book case. Shawn, the leader, put his desk on the stage, sat down, and folded his arms across his chest. A couple of boys looked up at him enviously, hesitated, then carried their desks to the stage too, carefully situating themselves behind Shawn.

"This place is really special. Nobody else has what we have," Don told the boys over and over.

To Don's relief, the first couple of weeks went well. The novelty of the church basement and the work outfitting it kept outbursts to a minimum. But when Don tried to settle them into a routine, incorporating reading, writing, and math into the daily plan, he met immediate resistance. Their levels of learning were all over the spectrum, making group lessons virtually unmanageable. Some were reading at a first-grade level. Some at fourth-grade. Some not at all.

"Doc, they're driving me crazy," Don confided one day. "They don't want to read. They don't want to do math. All they want to do is horse around, wrestle, play soccer, and goof off."

"Why don't you use soccer and wrestling as a reward for doing work?"

"I've tried that. I can't even get them to *open* some of those books, let alone read them."

"Maybe you've got the wrong reading material. Give them something to read that they want to know more about."

The next day, Don brought in a comic book. Immediately, several boys surrounded him. "Which one is it?"

"Lemme see."

In the afternoon, during the last period of the day, the Gang crammed itself into Don's car and toured the town in search of cans, which they could sell to the dump for twenty cents a pound. On Fridays they turned their earnings into comic books or model cars and airplanes. Then they hunched over their new acquisitions, devouring the comics, mulling over the instructions for the model airplanes.

Don read them *The Outsiders*, a book about a gang of inner-city kids. Then they went to Keene to see the movie based on the book.

"We're just like them," Buddy said. "Different from everybody else."

"We're outsiders, too," David said.

The boys regarded the comic books, the models, and the outings as fun. Don saw it all as valuable learning. They were reading. They helped plan the road trips. They were working as a group. Soccer and wrestling were the high points of most days. Don used those activities as incentives. If everybody got their work done, then they could play soccer or wrestle. If a boy lagged in his work, the others helped him or got on his case. Weisburger wanted them to work as a team in everything.

Still, the boys were unreliable. If Don spent time working with one boy, the others would get into a fight. Shawn remained his biggest enigma. Tall and lanky, he was the leader of the Gang. He didn't say much, but when he did, the others listened. Don made constructive use of Shawn's natural leadership skills and appointed him head of cleanup. The other boys followed his direction unquestioningly. But there was another side to Shawn—an explosive, unpredictable temper. His frustration level was frighteningly low. Anything could set him off.

"Dennis, I need help," Don pleaded. "There's just no way I can keep all those boys active simultaneously. At least once a day there's an outburst that stems from boredom or because I wasn't paying enough attention to one of them. I just can't be everywhere every second."

Doc tracked down apprenticeship director Judy Knox. "It's going to take a strong person to deal with them. Got anyone in mind?"

Judy thought for a moment. "Yeah, I think I do. I think I have just the person."

When Judy described the job to Karen Thompson, Karen

hesitated. She didn't know Mr. Weisburger, but she knew the boys. Her apprenticeship with the second graders the previous year had been pleasant; but the prospect of working with emotionally and mentally handicapped teenage boys was daunting. Even as sixth graders, they were well known as little hellions who spooked younger and older kids alike. Yeah, they were tough—but she was tough too.

"Sure," she told Judy. "Sure I can handle it."

Karen worked on her résumé, turning over in her mind the things she would say to convince Mr. Weisburger she was right for the job. Karen had completed nearly all her requirements for graduation, so she had a fairly open schedule. If she got the job, she would spend two hours every morning assisting the boys in reading, writing, and math.

On the day she was to meet Weisburger, she put on her favorite high-waisted pants and a freshly pressed blouse. At lunch, Judy took her to the cafeteria and introduced her.

"Hi," Don said. He shook hands quickly and turned his attention back to the lunchroom. Though put off by Weisburger's abrupt manner, Karen wanted to make a good impression.

"I'm really excited about working with your boys," she said. "I think I'll do a good job."

Don turned toward her. "Look," he said. "This is a pretty serious job. I need to know you can handle it. Come over tomorrow morning after advisory. I'd like to see how you interact with the boys and also see how well you and I can get along."

"Okay," Karen said. "I'll be there."

But Karen wasn't at all sure she could get along with Mr. Weisburger. He seemed so cold, so disinterested. Had she made a good impression?

The next day, Karen showed up as promised. The boys obviously had been prepared for her arrival; they swarmed

around her, calling her by name. "Okay guys," Don said.
"Give Karen some breathing space. I've got to interview her,
then you'll have your chance. Until then, I want you to
work on your reading."

The boys, charged by Karen's presence, did stunts on the
wrestling mat, poked each other, and laughed shrilly before
settling down to read. Karen looked at Weisburger. He
smiled. She let out her breath and smiled back.

"Is this enough to scare you off?" he asked.

"Heck, no. I thought they were going to be a lot worse
than this."

"Let me assure you. They can be," he said. "By the way,
sorry I was so distracted yesterday. It's hard to eat during
lunch duty, let alone conduct an interview."

"That's okay. That's what I figured."

"I understand you worked with second graders last year as
an apprentice," Weisburger said. "My background's in elementary education, too. In fact, there's a lot I did with those
kids that I've been able to apply here."

"One thing I see in common is they have the same kind of
wild energy," Karen said.

"Yep. But it can take on a different form when you're
dealing with thirteen- and fourteen-year-olds. In many
ways, it's the toughest age group to deal with. They're
heading toward adulthood, but they're still really kids.
They still like to roughhouse, play games, go wild, but it's
different at their age. They're bigger and stronger, they
know more stuff, but they haven't got the responsibility to
know how it should be used. Let me just throw out some
possible scenarios. You tell me how you would respond."

"Okay," Karen said.

"What would you do if two boys were fighting on this
stage right here and four others were cheering them on?"

"I'd try to split them up."

"What if that didn't work?"

Karen thought for a moment. "I'd get the kids on the sidelines to help me."

"You mean give them some responsibility."

"I'd tell them I need their help to stop the fight."

"Okay, Karen. The fact is, you're a senior in high school. You're attractive. What if one of these boys tries making moves on you, or if the Gang makes comments about you?"

"I'll just tell them it's not appropriate. It's not, that's all there is to it."

Don was impressed with Karen. He liked her sure, strong answers. She had a nice way about her—tough and gentle all rolled into one. "I'd like to work with you," Don said. "If you want the job, it's yours."

"When do I start?"

"Tomorrow, same time."

"C'mon over here," David said, poking at Karen's arm. "I put this together myself." He pointed at a spaceship that hung from the ceiling. The boys moved around her like puppies, each one grabbing for her attention.

"Hey, look at this!"

"Karen, will you help me?"

"Watch me, Karen. Watch!"

Buddy was the exception. Karen glanced at him several times, wanting to go over and talk to him. He stayed at his desk, head down, bent over the pages of a book. The other boys kept monopolizing her attention.

"How does it feel being a novelty?" Don asked her as two boys tugged her arms in opposite directions.

"Novelties wear off after a while, don't they?" Karen laughed.

"Maybe. . . . Maybe not."

Karen let out an exaggerated sigh. "I better, or there's going to be nothing left of me."

Karen spent mornings with Don's gang, then returned to

the high school for English, math, and science classes. After a couple of days, the boys calmed down. She and Don were able to focus on doing some work with them.

"The first part of every day, I just let them talk and do whatever they want," Don said. "It's something I learned as a substitute teaching third grade. Kids would come in after recess all worked up over something that happened on the playground. There's no way a kid is going to pay attention in class if he's still mad as hell at the kid sitting next to him. So if I sensed something was up, I'd deal with the problem right then and there in front of everyone.

"With this gang, it's the same theory. They come in here in the morning with a hundred things on their minds—cars, racing, basketball games, whatever. I can pretty much guarantee it ain't going to be reading, math, or science."

"How much time do you give them?"

"As long as it takes—within reason. Sometimes they only need five minutes, sometimes fifteen, sometimes an hour. Sometimes they want to talk about something as a group to me. So I let them. But as soon as they're done, they know it's time to do school work, and they're ready."

The next morning, Karen saw this. The boys spilled into the room buzzing with excitement. David had to tell his friend about his tour of the fire station. Shawn was upset about a game the Celtics lost the night before.

Karen watched Weisburger watch the boys.

"Okay, guys, time to get to work."

A couple of boys pulled books out of their desks. Weisburger handed some reading material to the others. Karen watched Buddy as he ran his hand over the backs of the books lined up on the shelf next to his desk. She walked over to him.

"I like these the best," Buddy said, without looking up. Karen studied the titles. *Mister Happy, Mister Big.*

"They're called the Mister Men Series," Buddy said.

"Would you read one of them to me?" Karen asked.

Buddy pulled *Mister Big* off the shelf and sat down on an oversized pillow against the wall. Karen sat next to him. He opened the book, bit his bottom lip, then started reading. "Will you read this page?" Buddy asked.

"Sure." As Karen started reading, Buddy moved closer. He was small enough that he fit under her arm. He reminded her of a little boy.

"You read the next page," she said when she was done.

After that, hardly a day passed that Karen and Buddy didn't sit together and read. Sometimes Buddy read to her. Sometimes he just leaned up against her and listened.

"It's like he's starved for attention," Karen told Weisburger. "He cuddles up next to me like I'm his sister or his mother."

"In many ways you probably are," Don said.

"Hey, Karen!" Don said one morning. "I've got to swing by the school and meet with Doc this morning. Can you hold down the fort?"

"Yeah, sure," Karen said without thinking. Then she hesitated. She'd be alone with the Gang. If anything went wrong, it would be on her shoulders. But Don was already out the door.

Her eyes darted from one boy to the other. Suddenly one of the boys shot across the stage shouting like a banshee. David screamed at him from across the room, "Shut up!"

Karen leapt up on the stage and grabbed the boy's arm. "Now cut it out," she pleaded.

He pulled away and ran back across the stage the way he had come. Shawn was waiting for him.

"Si'down," he said. The boy stopped in his tracks. "I said, si'down." The boy walked to his desk and sat down.

Karen stopped her trembling. She walked over to Shawn. "Thanks," she said.

Shawn nodded.

The Outsiders had given Don the idea first. He saw how

awed his boys were by the streetwise gang portrayed in the book and film. Why not take them there, to the Outsiders' turf, to his hometown, New York City?

The idea took.

"When do we go?"

"Will we see the Outsiders?"

"We're going in the spring," Don said. "Provided we work hard this winter and earn some money to get there."

The Gang shoveled snow and collected newspapers. The man who ran the dump gave them permission to set out a box to collect the papers. Out of scrap lumber and metal sheeting scavenged from the dump, the boys built a box with a sign, "PUT NEWSPAPERS HERE." Every morning, the boys weighed the refuse on a scale Don had brought in, then figured out how much money they would get at twenty cents a pound for aluminum cans and $40 for nine hundred pounds of newspapers.

After a couple of weeks, the Gang had earned an impressive stash of change and crumpled dollar bills. Don dumped the treasury on the stage in a great clatter of silver and copper. The boys sat down to count. It took time, but the boys organized the change into tidy one-dollar piles, smoothed out the dollar bills and counted them.

"Thirty-four dollars," David said.

"And sixty-five cents," Buddy added.

"Okay, everybody outside. We're going to the bank," Don said. Don and Karen had extended the lesson to include bank accounts and interest earnings.

"We want to open an account here," one of the boys told the teller.

"Under the name Thayer Junior High School Gang," another boy caroled.

They deposited $34.65 in the account, then ran all the way back to the church.

"Why don't we go lookin' for cans at Nigger Camp?" one of the boys proposed one day.

"What was that?" Don said.

"Nigger Camp's always got trash in it," another boy responded.

"Do you know what you're saying?" Don asked.

" 'Course. It's true. There's usually a lot of trash and crap there."

"How'd it get that name?" Don asked.

"What name?"

"Nigger Camp."

"Oh, that . . . I dunno."

"Do you even know what you're saying?"

It was clear they didn't.

"Look, you guys," Don said. "You go to Harlem and call someone 'nigger,' and I can guarantee you won't make it out whole."

"What's the big deal?"

"That's about the worst thing you could call a black person."

"What's so bad about it?"

"It'd be like somebody calling you Polack or spick or redneck hick."

"I'd punch anybody who called me a redneck hick!"

"Why?" Don asked.

"Because . . . because it bites," the boy said.

"Same exact thing calling someone a nigger."

One afternoon during a regular round of the dump, the Gang saw their box—busted. Someone had run over it.

"Who did this?" David shouted.

"Some friggin' asshole!" Shawn stormed toward the remains of the box. "I'm going to find who did this and break their balls."

Don tried to calm the boys. "Chances are we're never going to find out who did this. So how's it feel being on the receiving end of vandalism?"

RIGHT: Dennis Littky. BELOW: Winchester, a town of contrasts, displays evidence of prosperity as well as the brunt of economic hard times in its historic Main Street buildings. A town of 3,700 people. Winchester was hit hard by the country's economic downturns, with several major plant closings, high unemployment, and a relatively large welfare population. *(Michael Moore photo)*

ABOVE: Stacks of firewood almost obscured Littky's mountaintop cabin the first winter he lived there, in 1979. A wood-burning stove was his sole source of heat; light came from oil lamps. He had no running water or indoor plumbing. BELOW: The Amarosas, owners of the local hardware store, befriended Littky when he first came to town and remained unwavering supporters throughout his political ordeal. *(Michael Moore photo)*

ABOVE: Thayer High School, built in 1922, had to make do with one of the smallest school budgets in New Hampshire. RIGHT: This scarred tabletop was a symptom of the conditions Littky found at Thayer High during his first summer as principal. Littky, student workers, and a new custodian cut new tabletops and scrubbed, painted, cleaned, and redecorated the school—all on a shoestring budget. BELOW: Student Nick Collins transformed a wall of graffiti in the cafeteria into an artistic mural of a flying Pegasus. A dropout the previous year, Nick reentered school that summer. By the time he graduated, he had completed two more murals in the school and was bound for college.

TOP: English teacher Valerie Cole, at first skeptical of Littky, became one of his most ardent supporters. Cole is one of four teachers involved in the new Spectrum program, an interdisciplinary approach to teaching and learning. *(Michael Moore photo)* LEFT: Language teacher Barbara Eibell takes a "student as worker" approach to teaching, rather than the traditional lecture/listen format she used before working under Littky. *(Michael Moore photo)* BELOW: Doc meets with his advisory in his office, part of the ritual that begins every school day for all Thayer students and teachers. OPPOSITE, TOP: Dovetail teachers and students construct a post-and-beam barn behind the school as a learning project and to add classroom space. The program did away with the fifty-minute subject-by-subject teaching structure and opened up the school day. Math, science, English, and social studies teachers worked together integrating subjects and challenging students to view the world as their classroom.

BELOW: Don Weisburger relaxes with members of his seventh-grade self-contained classroom after an outing. (Karen Thompson photo) RIGHT: Karen Thompson Marsh, a recalcitrant student when Doc arrived at Thayer, became a teacher's assistant as a senior in a self-contained classroom of troubled seventh graders. (Michael Moore photo)

TOP: Doc greets a student in his office with a warm handshake. LEFT: Theodore Sizer, head of Brown University's School of Education, selected Thayer High School under Dennis Littky as the first high school to join his prestigious Coalition of Essential Schools, a secondary school reform movement aimed at empowering teachers and students. *(Michael Moore photo)* BELOW: As part of Thayer Spirit Day, organized during Littky's first year as a celebration of the students and teachers, 350 Thayer High School students and staff join hands to form the words *Thayer Spirit* on the school lawn.

ABOVE: Susan Winter, Bobby Secord, and Allen Barton (left to right), the three school board members who fired Littky, listen to testimony at his superior court hearing. *(Michael Moore photo)* RIGHT: Francis Gutoski (foreground), an implacable and outspoken Littky critic, worked tenaciously to remove Littky from his job as principal. *(Michael Moore photo)* BELOW: Winchester school moderator Elmer Johnson reads off ballots under the eye of board member Marcia Ammann. Simultaneously heralded by educators across the nation and lambasted by his own school board, Littky faced an uncertain future at Thayer. *(Michael Moore photo)*

RIGHT: Terri Racine, who nearly dropped out of high school as a pregnant tenth grader, not only received her diploma with her classmates, but became an honor student and senior class president. "I don't think I would have stayed in school if it wasn't for Doc," she said. *(Michael Moore photo)* BELOW: Doc surrounded by teachers and friends within seconds of learning that his supporters had won election to the Winchester School Board. *(Michael Moore photo)*

"It sucks."

"Right," Don said. "It sucks real bad."

October 27 was Shawn's birthday. Don came in with a card and model airplane. Karen brought a homemade cake. They got the boys secretly to sign the card. At the appointed time, they assembled around the piano. One of the boys pounded out a crude version of "Happy Birthday" and everyone sang. Shawn stood stone silent, fighting back tears. Then the Gang tackled him to the floor, spanking him— fifteen times.

Of the four entries Don made in his journal that year, he took a page and a half to describe this event—it's the longest entry in the book.

> Today was Shawn's birthday. . . . This afternoon the kids tackled Shawn to the floor & all got to spank him (me too!!!) 15 times. I didn't know quite how Shawn would take it. To say he loved it would be an understatement. . . . Every once in a while you can have free 'dibs' on Shawn. When he is in the mood, he is absolutely amazing! The greatest kid in the world, when he is on. When off—bye, bye!!!
>
> One of the best days yet.

One day in January, Don and Karen were working with the boys on their math workbooks. They spent about a half hour every day on math. On this day, they had been at it about twenty-five minutes. Don went over to Shawn's desk to see how he was doing. Shawn was bent over his workbook, gnawing hard on a pencil.

"What's going on here?" Weisburger asked.

"Nothin'," Shawn said.

"C'mon, Shawn. I want to see some work out of you."

"I don't get it!" he said, pounding the table with his fist, breaking the pencil in the process.

"Shawn, we've been over and over this—"

Suddenly Shawn jerked to his feet. "I don't get this god-damn stuff!" He pushed his desk over. It crashed loudly to the floor. All eyes were on Shawn.

Don reached toward him, trying to calm him down. But Shawn pulled back, his anger incendiary.

"You fuckin' asshole, I ain't doin' this crap!" Shawn grabbed a chair and heaved it over his head. He took two steps toward Don. Don backed off and motioned to Karen.

"Get everybody out of here. Right now!"

Karen moved quickly. "C'mon, you guys. Let's go." The boys responded, backing out of the room.

Shawn's face was red. He was sweating, his neck muscles tense.

"Shawn!" Don shouted, looking him straight in the eyes. "You throw that chair at me and I swear you'll be out of this place so fast it'll make your head spin." Shawn hesitated. Don lowered his voice and spoke as calmly as he could.

"You can throw it, but if you do, understand that everything we've worked for together is over."

Suddenly, Shawn's whole body started to shake. He looked wild-eyed at Don. Don braced himself. Sweat dripped into Shawn's eyes. He blinked. He put the chair down, then bolted out of the room.

The Key Communicators made it clear to Littky that they wanted more information on the seventh-grade alternative program. Rumors were rampant: the boys were getting credit for smoking cigarettes, reading comic books, collecting trash, and playing soccer.

Littky scheduled a meeting with the Key Communicators at the church so they could see for themselves how Don's class operated. Don, Karen, and the Gang cleaned the room top to bottom and put their work on display.

The ceiling looked like a space-age garage—shuttles, rockets, jets, and airplanes hung off fishing line as though in suspended animation. The boys had written research papers, which they tacked neatly to one wall. On long tables were clay models of New York City landmarks. David was making the Empire State Building; Buddy, the Statue of Liberty; Shawn, Grand Central Station.

Don and Karen were on hand to field questions.

"What's this I hear about one of your students getting credit for smoking?" one of the Key Communicators asked.

"Here, let me show you," Weisburger said. He walked over to the wall on which hung the eight papers. He took one down.

"I had all the boys pick a topic they wanted to research, something they were personally very interested in. I didn't want to assign topics to them, since that's the fastest way in the world to turn somebody off to writing. The boy who wrote this paper loves to smoke cigarettes. I've also made it very clear to the group that I don't approve of smoking and won't allow anyone to smoke in class. But everybody has a right to their passions, and cigarette smoking happens to be this boy's. He was actually excited about doing the project.

"I took him to Small-Eaze Grocery so he could study the brands of cigarettes and their various levels of tar and nicotine. Then he investigated what tar and nicotine was and what it could do to the human body. The result of all this was a five-page paper written by a boy who was reading at a third-grade level last year. He's jumped two reading levels since the beginning of the year. We even turned the investigation into a math assignment. I had him figure out how many cigarettes in a pack, how many in a carton. Then I had him calculate how many packs he smoked a week and what that cost. I'm trying to promote learning. I'm trying to endorse coming to school. I don't care what gets them here, as long as they want to learn."

A Key Communicator raised her hand. "I hear they're reading comics and getting credit for that."

"They're getting credit for reading," Don said. "As far as I'm concerned, reading comics is better than not reading at all. All it is is a device to catch their interest. If they're excited about reading a comic book, then maybe they'll be a little more receptive to reading a science book or a book about New York City or whatever. In a mainstream classroom, these kids would be reading Dickens or Shakespeare. It's not that I have anything against good literature. But I can tell you right now, these boys couldn't care less about it. If the kid loves the Celtics, I'll give him every book ever written about the Celtics. The goal is to get him to read. If he does that, then Dickens becomes a possibility."

Karen gave the Key Communicators examples of ways they had made math relevant to the boys, such as the assignment in which the boys had marked out a basketball court. "They learned how to read a tape measure. They had to add and subtract. They had to figure out how to draw the arch for the shooting zone and everything. We didn't tell them it was a math assignment, but it certainly was. I think they learned more math in those three days than we've been able to teach them all semester out of workbooks."

When the meeting ended, several Key Communicators complimented them on the program.

"Jeez, what a switch," Karen said to Don when the group had left. "We came in braced for the worst, and they end up thanking us for running such a good program."

One day, Shawn was standing in the lunch line. A girl came up behind him.

"Hey, fuckin' Jew," she said.

Shawn whipped around. "What'd you say?"

"I said, 'Hey, fuckin' Jew.'"

Shawn's face shot red the moment before he hauled back and pummeled the girl in the face. Several teachers ran

toward Shawn and tried to restrain him, but he pulled away,
flailing his arms. A student ran to get Littky.

"There's a bad fight going on in the lunch room!"

"Who is it?" Littky asked.

"Shawn."

"Run and get Mr. Weisburger."

Littky knew enough about Shawn's explosive temper to
know that a fight involving him could be serious. He also
knew that if Shawn would respond to anybody it would be
Weisburger.

Littky got to the cafeteria just as Shawn broke loose from
the grip two teachers had on him. He bulldozed past Littky,
then out the front door of the school.

"He went out the door," Littky told Weisburger.

Don was pretty sure he knew where to find Shawn. He
headed out the entrance toward Marian Polaski's yard.

Shawn was pacing Marian's lawn, hands shaking, smoking a cigarette. Don slowed his own pace, so that Shawn
would have plenty of time to see him approach. Then Don
stretched out his arms and gave Shawn a warm hug.

"Thank you," Don said.

"She called me a fuckin' Jew—"

"I know. And I know you struck her because you know
I'm Jewish."

"It's just not right. It's like callin' someone a nigger."

For a moment they said nothing. Don kept an arm over
Shawn's shoulders; he felt him relax.

"I know it was your way of showing you care about me.
But you also know that fighting is against the rules."

"Yeah, I know I'm gettin' suspended. I just couldn't let her
get away with sayin' that."

"I know you couldn't, but was there another way to let her
know other than hitting her?"

"I guess."

"What else could you have done?"

"I dunno, I s'pose I could have told her she was full of it or somethin'."

"That would have worked. It also would have kept you from getting into trouble because of her."

"It's just hard."

"I know it is."

"I coulda done that. Yeah . . . I guess that's what I shoulda done."

Don looked Shawn in the eye. "How about I buy you an ice cream cone?" he said.

The Gang spent the last period every day that winter earning money for their trip to New York. They shoveled driveways, collected cans and newspapers, did any odd jobs. They laid out an itinerary, voting on the places they would go. They each wrote a paper about New York City and finished making their landmarks.

"It says here the Empire State Building is nearly a mile tall," David said.

"Anybody know how tall that is?" Weisburger asked.

Within an instant, the class was involved in a math assignment, trying to mark out how far a mile was.

"Jeez, that's tall!"

"How could they build something like that?"

"I can hardly wait to see it!"

On the day they were to depart for the Big Apple, five boys showed up at the high school parking lot. Shawn was not among them. At the last minute, he'd decided against going. Buddy's dad drove up and walked straight to Don, leaving Buddy standing alone next to the car.

"I don't think Buddy should go," he said.

"Why not?" Don asked, surprised.

"He doesn't have the $25."

Weisburger had asked each boy to bring $25 in spending money. Don pulled out his wallet.

"It would be my pleasure," he said, "to give Buddy the money." He handed the crisp bills to Buddy's dad.

Buddy hadn't moved from his position next to the car, but his eyes never left his dad and Mr. Weisburger. When his father motioned to him, Buddy hesitated.

"Get your suitcase," his father shouted.

A smile broke out on Buddy's face. He threw open the door, grabbed his suitcase, and ran to the other boys.

They rode the train into New York City and got off at Grand Central Station. The boys stuck close—very close— to Don and Karen. They cut across the main lobby, winding their way in and out of the press of people to the main door. Then they walked out into New York City.

"Where's the sky?" Buddy whispered to Karen.

Karen craned her head back as far as it would go and pointed. "I think that's it up there."

"I never seen anything like this. People, buildings everywhere. It makes me feel so . . . *small*."

During the two days the Gang was in the city, they attended pro basketball and hockey games, took a tram from Manhattan to Roosevelt Island, rode the subway, went to the top of the Empire State Building and the World Trade Center, toured the United Nations and Museum of Natural History, walked through Central Park, watched a bum propose marriage to Karen, bought hot dogs from a street vendor, sampled New York bagels, ate Chinese food with chopsticks, saw Weisburger's high school, played soccer in the backyard of Don's parents' home, and huddled in their sleeping bags talking quietly late into the night.

On the last day, as the Gang walked through Central Park, the boys pulled away from their teachers. Karen and Don watched the boys huddle, dig into their pockets, and fish out the change and crumpled bills that remained after two days in the city. Buddy, clutching the wad of money, broke away from the other boys and ran to a vendor. He came back wearing a smile as big as the city and carrying two fistfuls of yellow tulips. "These are for you," he said, handing the flowers to Karen.

Buddy was wild about the Philadelphia 76ers. He followed the games, memorized point averages. Most of all, he loved Moses Malone. Even Karen, lukewarm on sports in general, had fun chattering with him about "the amaaaazing shot Moz made last night!"

Thumbing through a book called *Famous People Stories*, Karen stumbled on a piece about Moses Malone. Excited, she showed it to Buddy.

"Look what I found, Buddy!"

Buddy's eyes lit up. "Moses," he said. "Let's read it!"

Buddy and Karen hunkered down at their usual spot. Buddy started reading, diving into the copy like he was eating a peanut butter sandwich, his all-time favorite food.

"Few players in the National Basketball Association have moved around as much as Moses Malone," Buddy read almost without halting. He looked at Karen. "That's true, you know. I knew that, too."

He kept reading, stumbling only a couple of times. "Moses was a shy, quiet boy when he was growing up with his mother in a tum . . ."

"Tumbledown," Karen prompted.

". . . in a tumbledown old house with holes in the walls and no plumbing. Now, he's still a shy, quiet man, but he has a new sort of self-con . . ."

"Self-confidence," Karen said, carefully sounding out the syllables.

"What's that?" Buddy asked.

"Self-confidence is when someone feels good about themselves, when someone feels like they can do whatever they set their mind to."

He kept reading: ". . . self-confidence which comes from knowing he is extremely good at what he does. He has accomplished a good deal so far, including one of the things he wanted to do most—buy his mother a new house."

Buddy looked up at Karen. "He's shy just like me. And look at what he became."

"Not bad."

"Not bad at all."

Karen looked down at her young friend. "Hey Buddy, did you know that you're reading at a sixth-grade level?"

"I am?"

"Yep."

Buddy pushed himself closer to Karen and smiled. "Not bad," he said.

Karen smiled back. "Not bad at all."

Graduation was nearing. Karen was torn. She had debated long and hard about whether to go to college or not. She'd been accepted at the University of New Hampshire and planned to study special education. But she wasn't sure. She *was* sure that she was in love with her high school sweetheart Jack Marsh. If she went away to school, her relationship with him would be put on hold. Besides, she had options. She'd been offered a position with the Keene School District's regional TNT program, a self-contained classroom for emotionally disturbed children. She could get some more practical experience in special education and then maybe go to college after that.

As the days grew closer to graduation, Karen savored every day she spent with the Gang. "I love every last one of them," Karen told her mother. "They've done so much for me."

"I think it's you who have done so much for them," her mother said, recalling the Christmas fruit baskets Karen had taught them to put together for their families and the dinner she and Karen had held in the Thompson kitchen.

"No," Karen said. "They've shown me good things about myself that I never knew existed."

It was going to be hard to leave them. Karen wanted to be able to say good-bye to each of them individually, in some way that would be more meaningful than just a good-bye on the last day of school. She decided to give each boy an hour to spend with her any way he wanted. A couple of the boys wanted to have breakfast with her at the diner. One of them wanted to have lunch at her house. Buddy asked if she would go on a bicycle ride with him.

"That's a good idea," Karen said.

The day they rode off together was cool and sunny. Spring was just getting a foothold. They crossed the Ashuelot River by way of the covered bridge, then tooled along the country back roads. Then they headed toward town. Karen was in front of Buddy, pumping hard to get up a long, gradual hill at the top of which they would go their separate ways. She looked over her shoulder. Buddy came up behind her, red-faced.

"It's okay to cry, Buddy," Karen said.

"I don't want to say good-bye," he said.

"I know. I don't either."

Buddy got back up on his bicycle and rode slowly away from Karen. Then he looked over his shoulder and shouted to her. "I'll be at your graduation. I'll be there!"

Karen cried all the way home.

17
Dovetail

DENNIS WAS ON THE EDGE of his seat, not wanting to miss a word.

It was near the end of school of his second year at Thayer. Littky was at an education conference in Massachusetts for teachers and administrators.

Ted Sizer, the keynote speaker, finished his talk. Dennis threw himself from his seat and ran up to him. "I just want to tell you, I just want you to know—I'm *doing* what you're talking about! I agree with everything you're saying."

Sizer extended a hand. Dennis seized it, pumping it hard and fast, as though trying to draw water from a dry well.

"I can't talk right now. I've got to go," Dennis said. "But I'd like to talk to you again."

With that, Dennis headed back to his hotel room.

Truth of the matter was, he was just plain too excited to talk to Sizer. When he got to his room, he was roiling with energy. He tossed on his jogging clothes and ran out the door at full tilt. He didn't stop until he'd thoroughly spent himself. Then he threw up.

When he got back to Winchester the next day, he wrote a long letter to Sizer, describing the ideas, programs, and methods he had used at Shoreham–Wading River Middle School and was working on now at Thayer. They were exactly the kinds of reforms Sizer had proposed at the conference.

Theodore R. Sizer, formerly dean of the Graduate School of Education at Harvard University and headmaster of Phillips Academy, Andover, was completing a massive study of high schools. The study was cosponsored by the National Association of Secondary School Principals and the Commission on Educational Issues of the National Association of Independent Schools. He was in the process of cataloging his findings and suggestions for reform in a book, to be released the following year. Then he planned to organize a coalition of high schools that would work to implement the principles laid out in the book.

At the conference, Sizer condemned what he called the "Model T" structure of high schools today as "profoundly flawed, fundamentally inefficient, and not based on common sense or on what we know about how people learn." He said the heart of a good school is good coaching. Educators must change their attitudes toward adolescents— schools need to empower students, he said.

Littky had listened to Sizer's words as though hearing himself talk.

"Less is more," Sizer kept saying. "A lot of content doesn't mean anything. What is important is *how* students use their minds. We should be teaching youngsters how to learn," he said. "Incentives are the key."

"Learning must be built around mastery, not attendance. Teaching must be individualized. It must be made clear that it is in the students' interest to learn what you want them to learn. We must develop a variety of ways to test. Class ratios must change by using staff in new ways. There must be time for staff to talk to each other about kids. Change must be decentralized—the individual school must make the change."

When Sizer received Littky's letter, he wrote back that he had been on the seventh draft of a book about the dilemma of the American high school and was struggling to finish; Littky's letter helped motivate him.

Dennis phoned him to describe some of the programs and reforms at work at Thayer, and Sizer understood instantly what they were about, often finishing Littky's sentences for him. Dennis felt as if he'd known Sizer for years— a "soul brother," as he put it, albeit in a suit and tie.

When Sizer described his plan to organize a coalition of schools to pursue the goals he'd espoused at the conference, Littky said, "Why not look at us?"

Before the conversation ended, Sizer had agreed to attend the conference Thayer was hosting that October. "Doing More with Less" would be the conference title.

"Learning doesn't necessarily have to take place in a traditional classroom," Sizer told Dennis.

"I know," said Dennis. "It's like when a student builds a house. The idea isn't to teach house building per se, but to teach math and other skills that students must know to do the job well."

"Exactly. That way, the knowledge is more real, more flexible. Under that kind of system, there's an even more intense belief in the importance of traditional subjects."

The conversation recharged Dennis. He wanted to make things *happen* at Thayer. Sizer's encouragement was the push he needed.

Richard Lawson, Thayer's outdoor science teacher, was begging Dennis for a new class schedule that would give him more time with his students. They would scarcely get to the field site to begin work on a science or building project before the hour was over and the students would have to rush back to the high school. Lawson was stymied by the schedule.

"What I'd really like to do is to teach outdoor science all day for ten weeks," Lawson said.

"Why not do it the whole year?" Dennis asked.

"You're serious?" Lawson said.

"Yeah. Why not completely free up the day, but still

combine all the disciplines? If you want to spend a week on a science project, spend a week. If you want to go into the woods, go into the woods."

Sizer's words still rang in Littky's ears: "Don't play around. *Do* it!"

Before the end of the 1982–83 school year, Littky had arranged for four teachers—Richard Lawson (outdoor science), Bob Findlay (math), Ben Nicholson (English), Marcia Ammann (remedial education)—to create and run the new program in the fall. The program would be called Dovetail.

The Dovetail teachers interviewed tenth, eleventh, and twelfth graders interested in the program, examining the prospective students' motivational levels. A letter was sent to parents explaining the program and asking for support.

The school board was irritated.

"Dennis," Marian Polaski said, exasperated, "it's not that we object to the program. We object to the way you put it into place. You have to clear things like this with us first!"

In a letter to the school board dated June 16, 1983, Littky apologized: "I'm sorry if you felt that I moved too fast. I am confident that you will be proud of the productivity of these students. I will keep you posted."

This wasn't the first time Littky had set the wheels in motion on a project before letting the board in on it. And it wouldn't be the last. When Littky wanted to move on a project, he moved.

By the end of the year, fifty students had been accepted into the Dovetail program. Their skill and ability levels varied widely, so each student was given his or her own schedule. In addition to the Dovetail curriculum, some had regular classes, such as chemistry, trigonometry, and language; others scheduled all their classes within the Dovetail program.

Lee Gamache, a 15-year-old boy from Northfield, Massachusetts, would attend the program. He'd had a rocky time in a string of public and private schools in Massachusetts, and he was failing school across the board. Tests revealed, however, that he was a gifted student. His parents hoped the Dovetail program might be the answer to Lee's problems. The tuition they would have to pay was a small price, they figured, if the program worked.

Littky and the Dovetail teachers had the summer to set up the program. Unfortunately, three of the four teachers had full-time summer jobs. Coordinating work sessions was difficult. Though there was a lot of talking and dreaming, it wasn't until the night before school started that the Dovetail teachers figured out the nuts and bolts of running the school within the school—namely, the daily schedule.

In the first year, Dovetail would have two major undertakings—the construction of a post-and-beam barn that would be used as the school's environmental study center and an elaborate historical survey of the neighboring town of Richmond.

Under the program, all fifty students would be required to participate in the construction of the barn. Lawson, who directed the construction class, coordinated math work with Findlay. Nicholson and Ammann organized *Shavings*, a student-produced community newsletter that detailed elements of the Dovetail program. The students wrote the articles, took the photographs, and did the typing, layout, and design. The first issue came out in October, answering one of the most-often-asked questions: "What is Dovetail?"

This program, designed for sophomores, juniors, and seniors, allows each student to move through his/her studies at an individual rate of speed, studying for and passing competency exams in each area.

Because part of the Dovetail philosophy is to relate appropriate learning to real life, several other areas are added to each Dovetail week.

First, the Richmond Research Project (located just off Whipple Hill) includes the Barrus Cemetery, dating from 1774, a soapstone quarry, and several cellar holes. The now-deserted settlement provides a wealth of local history to research. Eventually students will be able to depict accurately the lives and livelihoods of the people who once lived there.

Construction: We began with a need for classroom space. All students have been actively involved in the building of a post-and-beam structure behind the elementary school, which will eventually become part of an entire Dovetail village. Students who are interested in learning construction as a potential life skill will continue to work in crews on various building projects in town.

Apprenticeships: About 18 students applied for apprenticeships as part of their Dovetail experience. Their schedules allow for larger blocks of time at the apprenticeship site, to resemble an actual work day, rather than apprenticing an hour at a time throughout the week.

Business: Owning and operating businesses will be another part of the Dovetail experience for some students. Supervised by Dovetail teachers, students will learn research, production, marketing, and sales skills that can also be used in later life.

The goals of Dovetail are twofold: to prepare students more appropriately for life, and to involve students actively in designing, carrying out, and taking responsibility for their own learning.

The year before, Lawson and his rural science classes had studied post-and-beam construction and had fashioned several hand-hewn beams for a barn. This work was an extension of the agricultural class Littky had started for the dozen juniors his first year as principal. The plan had been to construct a barn on school property to house farm animals. In addition to preparing the beams, the rural science students had laid the foundation for the barn. But the work stopped when nearby landowners objected to the placement of the barn within sight of their own property. With the help of the Winchester planning board, the school found a place behind the elementary school to construct the barn.

The work from the previous school year gave the "Doves" a solid head start when school started, and time was of the essence. The program needed its own classroom space. When the weather turned cold, the large tent they had erected on the school grounds would no longer serve, and the dome, which was being used for Dovetail English classes, wasn't big enough for the entire group.

The students learned to use tools as well as follow architectural plans. After building a fieldstone foundation, they erected a post-and-beam frame with mortise-and-tenon joints fastened with wooden pegs.

Terms like *girts*, *plates*, *rafters*, *R-32 insulation factor*, and *stress skin panels* became a comfortable part of their vocabulary as the barn took shape. Lawson was intent on finishing before the first snowfall. But the more time the students spent on construction, the less they could spend on other areas.

"I need all of the kids working full-time," Lawson insisted. "Winter's coming, and we're not going to have a place to work."

Lawson had his sights set on completing the barn by the November 7 open house. The program needed something concrete, something impressive to show the community what Dovetail was all about.

Some teachers objected to the curtailment of regular studies, and Littky found himself regularly fielding comments from passersby and parents, who wondered: "What are all those kids doing loafing around under the trees?"

"I see a lot more sleeping going on than learning."

"What about math? What about English? What about reading? I don't think those kids are getting the basics."

The lack of preparation and coordination among the Dovetail teachers was beginning to show. But as the date of the open house neared, Dovetail students and teachers buckled down trying to make the deadline.

"The kids are really pulling together," Marcia Ammann told Dennis one day. "It's as though they know that the survival of the program depends on them getting this barn done and getting it done well.

"What's really interesting," Marcia said, "are students like Lee Gamache. I really had my doubts when I first met him. I took one look at him and said, 'Uh-oh. This kid's going to be a real troublemaker.' In a regular classroom, I'm certain I would have been right. But out here he's become a leader. You should see him work."

On November 7, the barn was finished.

All day the Doves and teachers worked to prepare for the open house. The students set up booths to give demonstrations of the tools and methods used to raise the barn. Details of the historical survey of the neighboring town of Richmond were also on display—architectural history, maps, demographics, math lessons that tied in with the survey work. Several students rehearsed speeches for their demonstrations. The pathway to the barn was lined on both sides with candles in sand-weighted paper bags. The barn was made to look like an eighteenth-century home.

That evening, more than a hundred visitors were guided to the new barn along the lighted path. Once inside, students carrying kerosene lanterns led the visitors to the demonstration areas. The faces and the room glowed in the soft light.

Marcia Ammann stood next to the mother of a teenage boy who was bent over a shaving horse, demonstrating its use. The woman whispered to Marcia. "I didn't know he knew how to do that. He doesn't talk much, you know. Not to me or anybody."

Marcia nodded.

Then the boy looked up, quickly scanning the crowd that had formed to watch him work. He began a detailed explanation of how the shaving horse worked. Marcia looked at the boy's mother. She was staring at her son, mouth partially open, shaking her head.

"Well, I never!" she said.

Eliot Wigginton was the founder of the famous Foxfire program in Georgia. He and his high school students had put together the Foxfire series of books that had sold millions of copies worldwide. The books were a compilation of student articles and photographs on the area and its Appalachian mountain people. Littky decided to call him.

"Hello, Eliot. You don't know me, but give me five minutes," Littky said into the phone.

"Okay," Wigginton said.

In five minutes, Littky told him who he was, about the community conference the town was hosting in October, about Ted Sizer, about "doing more with less," about using community resources to turn a poor rural high school into an innovative, vital, changing place. Thayer students would help run the conference, the townspeople would provide accommodations. "Will you come?" Littky ended, out of breath.

Wigginton was regularly besieged with invitations to speak at institutions and organizations across the country. He got hundreds of them a year. Out of necessity, he'd become careful about which invitations he accepted.

"We can't pay you much—" Littky started to say.

"That's okay," Wigginton interrupted. "I'll speak for free, and I'll bring a student with me."

By the time the Winchester School Board was informed, conference arrangements were well under way. Once again, the board was miffed. Though the members knew Thayer was to host a conference—that had been part of Thayer's proposal in receiving the $30,000 federal grant for the apprenticeship program—the details of the conference were presented to them *after* they were in place. Once again, Marian Polaski admonished Littky. Once again, Littky assured her that the conference would have resounding importance, that leading educators from all over the country were participating.

"Dennis, it's not that we object to the conference in general. We object to you bypassing us once again. You just can't assume that we'll support everything you do."

In addition to Ted Sizer and Eliot Wigginton, Littky got the National Educator of the Year, Lee Hay, to come, as well as a lineup of other high-powered educators—among them, Jonathan Sher, author of *Education in Rural America;* Faith Dunne, Dartmouth College professor; Don Davies, president of the Institute for Responsive Education; and Mary Kohler, founder of the National Commission on Resources for Youth.

More than a hundred people from the eastern United States signed up to participate. The conference was held in the school gymnasium and surrounding classrooms. Food was prepared by the cheerleaders, the ninth grade, and high-school history classes. The money they raised would be used to pay for field trips. The signs and decorations were made by art students. Out-of-town participants stayed at private homes in Winchester. Most of the homeowners returned the $50 housing fee to the school scholarship fund. None of the speakers asked for a fee.

The conference was aimed at action. Participants divided into groups after hearing a speaker. The speeches were designed to motivate the participants to plan for needed change at their home schools.

Wigginton talked about his experiences setting up the student-run Foxfire program:

> There is real wisdom in utilizing the community and the real world inside our schools.
>
> John Dewey made the very careful distinction about education, especially as it impinged on basic skills, back in the twenties. . . . "You don't learn about basics as a student by studying the basics, by sitting there and doing endless exercises in those workbooks that so many people are making so much money from. You learn the basics rather by doing projects where the basics have to be utilized." . . .
>
> Using the outside community gives us the golden opportunity to answer the question that is implicit behind the eyeballs of 100 percent of our young people as they look at us every day in our classrooms. "Why are you making us sit here and do this? If you can't show me that this is going to be of real utility in my life when I walk out the doors of this school, you can't expect me to get excited about what you're standing up there in the front of the room talking to me about. What's it for?"

The weekend of the conference was the height of New England's autumn color season. Outside, the hills burned with color. Inside Thayer High School's cafeteria, some thirty people sat at lunch tables, talking about "spreading the message": "Wealthy schools aren't the only ones that can afford to individualize education. Money doesn't make the difference. People do!"

Betty Hall was as much a fixture at Thayer as the blackboards and desks. Her hair was chalk white, pulled back in a braid that she coiled into a bun. Pursed lips, glasses, tailored suits, wide-heeled shoes, she had long held the reputation of being a strict teacher, a fussbudget, a stickler for details. Sooner or later, all those who would graduate from Thayer would sit in her class. She taught U.S. history, a required course. Facts were facts, commas were commas, words had particular spellings. That was the law in Mrs. Hall's class.

Everyone was amazed when Betty Hall agreed to get involved in Dovetail's Richmond project.

The Dovetail students had mapped out the study area—a two-hundred-year-old village. During their investigation, they had stumbled on a cellar hole of what appeared to be a home and mill. They sorted through records, deeds, and old maps to determine exactly what had stood there. Then they sifted through the dirt in search of clues. That's when the Dovetail teachers decided to enlist Hall's help.

Betty Hall's passion was archeology. She took college courses on the subject and spent vacations engaged in digs. She was thrilled to get involved in the Richmond research project and agreed to work one day a week with students at the site and on their independent studies of U.S. history. Soon she was often seen on her hands and knees sifting through the dirt, wearing blue jeans, her white hair loose on the breeze.

The Dovetail students meticulously cataloged the location of the artifacts they found—glass bottles, bits of leather, horseshoes, broken pottery, nails. The cemetery, which dated back to the 1700s, also became a source of information. Students took rubbings of the stones, and each selected a person buried in the cemetery to investigate. After exhausting the local libraries, they journeyed to the Cheshire County court house in Keene to look through historical records. By tracing land sales, family holdings, descriptions of property, and circumstances of transfer, the students were able to piece together a picture of each person and the community he or she lived in.

"It's absolutely amazing," Marcia said to Dennis one day after returning from the courthouse. "Those kids didn't want to leave. Before this Richmond project, if I'd suggested spending the day at the Registrar of Deeds office and reading through those long tedious documents, they would all have said 'yuk.' *I* might even have said 'yuk.' Now they're begging me to take them back."

Lawson's students now took on another building project—constructing a private timber-frame home, the revenues from which would go toward buying needed equipment and other supplies to keep the program going.

The undertaking proved exhausting. The winter was hard; students found themselves chopping timbers out of the ice so they could be cut into beams. Tools were powered by a generator. The time available to work on the house during school hours simply wasn't enough. Students began working after school, vacations and weekends for nominal wages. The meager profits from the venture helped finance the establishment of Dovetail Housewrights, Thayer High School's own timber-frame business.

In no time, Dovetail Housewrights lined up projects that filled the docket for the remainder of the year as well as the following year. Soon the students had cut and raised an addition to a house, cut the beams for a two-story cider mill, and submitted the winning bid for constructing a house.

The idea was to run Dovetail Housewrights like a regular business, with a board of directors made up of students and local businesspeople. Books would be balanced by accounting students. As students gained experience and expertise, they would take on the duties of supervisors, and so on.

For those like Lee Gamache, these projects made a real difference in their lives. For the first time, he was involved in school, eagerly learning and leading. In a mock graduation speech, he wrote:

I was the first and only student to ever pay tuition to come to your school. I came here to attend the Dovetail Program. I learned more in one year of Dovetail, than I can remember ever learning in all my other years of school. Dovetail was fun, we did do some fooling around, but the work we did we had pride in, and by doing it with our own hands, I can still remember it very well. . . . You'll always learn more by doing than you will by seeing.

But for the Dovetail program as a whole, things didn't work out as well.

The planning had been inadequate, and the sought-after integration of disciplines was uneven, an unevenness exacerbated by personality conflicts within the Dovetail staff. Students, unless highly self-motivated, fell into patterns of storm and rest. Many did more resting than storming.

In the end, the math teacher, Bob Findlay, bowed out of the program. In a letter, he summarized his feelings about Dovetail:

> What started out as a noble experiment has ended as just another program. The ideas, enthusiasm and time needed to put such a program together did not manifest itself in the Dovetail staff. The concept of integrating curriculum throughout an entire operation means first that the curriculum lends itself to integration and that the staff meld together into a cohesive unit. This did not happen!
>
> From the outset Dovetail tried to be all things to all people. Our planning meetings in the summer of '83 were filled with idealistic dreams instead of concrete planning. . . .
>
> The staff was ill-conceived. Instead of dissolving into a homogeneous solution, we remained a loose mixture. Though the four academic areas were covered on paper, there was no "dovetailing." Curriculum planning took more than wild dreaming. . . .
>
> Still not all of the Dovetail project was a bust. . . . The concept of competency based curricula at Thayer High has its roots in the Dovetail courses of math and history.
>
> I'm sorry that I'm not going to be a part of the program

next year. Yet, I don't think that it will ever achieve its
potential until a group of energetic, innovative, far-sighted
teachers are allowed to take the program over again. Next
year's Dovetail is going to suffer from myopia.

Nicholson and Lawson continued Dovetail the next year
with Marcia Ammann working half-time in the program
and the other half as a junior-high crisis counselor and
tutor. The number of students in the program was reduced
by half and the Dovetail schedule scaled down from all day
to three hours a day. The year after that, the program was
cut completely.

Doc took Dovetail's disbanding in stride. The concept
was good, but the mix of personalities had been bad. Next
time, he thought, the key will be to find a team of teachers
who work well together and, perhaps, to shift the emphasis
away from vocational skills and more toward academics.
Still, Dovetail was an important step in heading the school
in the direction of teaming and integrating subjects.

18
Learning Comes Alive

"SUMMARIZE THE ESSENCE OF YOUR class in one sentence," Littky said.

Barb Eibell sat on Littky's deck along with a few other Thayer High School teachers. Her mind reeled. It was just the kind of thing Littky loved to spring on the staff.

Twelve of Thayer's teachers—nearly half the staff—participated in the three-session workshop in July 1984 at Littky's cabin. *Horace's Compromise*, Ted Sizer's book on the dilemma of American high schools, had just been published by Houghton Mifflin Company.

"Let's look at this book in terms of its relevance to Thayer," Littky said. "It does a good job of stating clearly some of the directions we'll be taking."

The workshop marked an important step for the staff. Littky, who was beginning his third year as principal, saw it as a test. Would the teachers support the changes he wanted to make? Would they have the energy, enthusiasm, and stamina it would take? Without their support, nothing could go forward.

He decided the best way to answer the question was to pose one. "What is real learning?" he asked the teachers.

The question was loaded. He wanted to know if they shared a common ground. Each teacher was asked to relate a good learning experience he or she had had with a student.

Jimmy Karlan, formerly a Thayer junior-high science

teacher, had returned to Thayer after a one-year absence to head the apprenticeship program started by Judy Knox. His example of real learning charged Littky. He described a Thayer eleventh-grade girl who had taken an apprenticeship at the *Star*. The young woman was a poor student and had low self-esteem. She'd been doing layout at the *Star* because she lacked the confidence to write articles.

With Karlan's encouragement, she telephoned a sports reporter at the *Boston Globe* to ask if she could watch him cover a story. The reporter agreed and offered her a press pass so she could follow him while he covered a Boston Celtics game—her favorite team. Afterward, she wrote a forty-five-page paper about the experience and also wrote articles for the *Star* and the school newspaper. Both articles made the front page.

Karlan's example was perfect. Exactly the kind of "common ground" Littky was after.

In a memo summarizing the workshop, Littky wrote:

> I realized how hard my work with the community will be if they are concerned about discipline and the toughness of courses. If the community has been happy with the development over three years . . . why change? I must (along with students and teachers) help them to see what real learning can be, not to accept the status quo.
>
> The hope is that the kids will know when they are having an important learning experience and pass this on to their folks. The poor have been asking for equality with the rich. It has been their model. We are asking them to throw out what they give the kids in good suburban schools (their idea of good) and to try something different. This will be hard. It will also be hard to change the image of what a teacher does with the day. Meeting with other teachers and one on one work will not be looked at as teaching. Lecturing is seen as teaching. We need national help/publicity to begin to educate people to have higher standards about learning.
>
> It also became clear to me that I cannot ask my teachers to

do what we are expecting on their own time. We must do it within our school time.

... The summer course served as a wonderful gathering of teachers in a relaxed atmosphere to discuss educational change. We left with a common understanding of a direction. We left feeling an empathy for each other's anxieties. We left committed to trying to change.

Ted Sizer, now head of the education department at Brown University, was in the process of organizing the Coalition of Essential Schools. The coalition, based at Brown, was intended to draw together high schools from all over the country that were actively pursuing educational reform. The coalition would serve as a support group and offer member schools financial and human aid whenever possible. Thayer High School under Dennis Littky was one of two schools that topped the list. All of a sudden, it seemed, Thayer was taking center stage.

On April 18, 1984, the Carnegie Foundation and the National Association of Secondary School Principals announced that Thayer would receive a $3,000 grant to pay teachers for planning in the summer that would focus on team teaching and integrating subjects. Out of 1,675 applicants, Thayer was one of two hundred schools—the only one in New Hampshire—awarded a grant. On May 4, New Hampshire Governor John Sununu sent a letter congratulating Thayer. Shortly after, the school received a $7,000 grant from the New Hampshire Charitable Foundation to be used for staff and curriculum development.

"We are moving on our own," Littky told the staff. "The grants just give us a few bucks and a pat on the back, telling us that two important educational organizations not only feel we are moving in the right direction but also that we have the capacity to make change. I feel we can move in whatever direction we wish."

The school and its maverick principal became the focus of media attention. Reporters from the *Christian Science*

Monitor, the *New York Times, Yankee Magazine*, the *Boston Globe*, and New Hampshire public television stalked the school. Thayer was on the precipice of change. That was exciting. But it was also daunting.

With or without the Coalition, with or without the grant monies, Littky was prepared to launch a massive restructuring of the school. Nationally, education had become the hot topic. The National Commission on Excellence in Education had just released its controversial report *A Nation at Risk: The Imperative for Educational Reform*. The report was an indictment of education in America. "For the first time in the history of our country, the educational skills of one generation will not surpass, will not equal, will not even approach, those of its parents," the report began.

Ernest L. Boyer, former United States Commissioner of Education and president of the Carnegie Foundation for the Advancement of Teaching, concurred with the commission's grim assessments in his book *High School: A Report on Secondary Education in America*.

Sizer, Boyer, the commission, and others all stressed the importance of strong leadership from high school principals. All decried the impotence of teachers to decide the substance of their own teaching. All discussed the need to professionalize teaching, increase salaries and benefits, and empower individuals. All reached the same conclusion: in order for schools to pull themselves out of their slump, reform was imperative.

In a May 4, 1984, memo to his staff, Littky listed Sizer's five imperatives for better schools:

1. Give room to teachers and students to work and learn in their own appropriate ways.
2. Insist that students clearly exhibit mastery of their work.
3. Get the incentives right, for students and for teachers.
4. Focus the students' work on the use of their minds.
5. Keep the structure simple and thus flexible.

Littky kept in mind Sizer's dictum: "The particular needs of each student should be the only measure of how a school gets on with its business."

Bobby Secord was a newly elected board member that spring, replacing Marian Polaski, who, after seven years on the board, had decided not to run. Secord, a local boy, was a soft doughnut of a man. He'd graduated from Thayer and had been chosen prom king in 1967. He later married a woman whose ancestors had founded Winchester. He was an enterprising businessman and owned a convenience store, a restaurant, and a soft-serve ice cream stand and was constructing a strip mall off Route 10 at the edge of town.

His roly-poly homeboy image, however, was offset somewhat by his penchant for blue serge suits, red ties, and briefcases. His thick black beard was close-cropped and meticulously trimmed. He went about his business in a black Cadillac and lived in a cavernous green clapboard house high on a hill above Michigan Street.

Bobby Secord's presence on the school board was cause for some concern. His twin sons weren't enrolled in the Winchester school system. They attended a Christian school in nearby Swanzey. Rumor had it, he was on the board to get Dennis Littky out.

That summer, Dennis wrote a lengthy letter to the school board outlining his goals for Thayer and speaking of the "new directions" he hoped the school would take.

Marcia Ammann was worried that Secord would find fault with that letter. She had resumed her old position as community coordinator, in addition to continuing as a remedial reading instructor, and felt it was crucial that the board support Dennis and his plans. Otherwise, it would be nearly impossible to sell the plans to the community.

Dennis arranged for an informal meeting of the board on August 27 to discuss the letter. On the day of the meeting,

Marcia found Dennis sitting on the front steps of the high school. "Bud Baker called to tell me he couldn't make the meeting," Dennis said. "He told me he read the letter several times and that he supported me."

Baker was a veteran of the Winchester School Board. He was a trusted politician, but not power-hungry. A small, nervous man who had spent his life in Winchester, he was a plain-talking, blue-collar townie through and through.

Board member Cindy Nelson—ninety-eight pounds of energy—wheeled into the parking lot, grinning broadly. Secord drove up, clad in suit and tie and carrying a briefcase. Cyndy Ryder came in her Bronco truck, only her gray bun showing over the top of the steering wheel. William Strenkert, the other new board member, walked over from his white colonial across the street.

As the meeting began, Secord and Strenkert bluntly stated that appearances were bad. Kids were regularly seen smoking on school grounds, leaving trash and cigarette butts on the sidewalk outside. "Maybe the rest of the building is immaculate," Secord said. "But some people only come here for basketball games, and that's what they see."

Dennis repeated what he'd said in the letter. He planned on invoking a stronger no-smoking rule that year. "I think we're at a point where we can effectively enforce a no-smoking rule," he said. "Before this, I don't think it would have worked."

That got Dennis going. He talked about "getting tougher" that year. "If a kid wants to be here, I'll do anything to help. But if he doesn't and he gets in the way of other kids trying to learn, he's gone."

"What about posting a list of rules on the bulletin board by the front stairs?" Cindy Nelson suggested.

"That's not the best place for rules and regulations," Dennis said. "It's designated as a place to honor kids. It should be a completely positive place." At the start of school, and each month thereafter, a student-of-the-month would be named and his or her picture posted on the bulletin board with a brief explanation why the student was chosen. It was a conspicuous display reflecting new student attitudes: it's cool to be good.

Then Dennis moved on to a topic of serious concern. "Should we be handing out diplomas to students who haven't mastered basic skills, like reading, writing and arithmetic?" he asked. "Diplomas are devalued every time a student graduates from this school without having mastered those basic skills. I know there have been kids who slipped through when they shouldn't have. I think we should start looking at competencies."

"What about using the New York Regents exams," suggested board member Bill Strenkert, a former New York City advertising executive.

"I like the idea generally," Cindy Nelson said, "but what would happen when a student reached the basic competency level long before graduation? Where would teachers find the time in their busy day to teach the few who had arrived at that point?"

"That's the scary part," said Dennis. "That's where restructuring time comes in. It's also going to be tough developing good measures of competence."

The negative flavor of Secord's and Strenkert's comments were all but washed away by the constructive conversation that followed. Before long, it was past 9 P.M. and time to break up. Secord left first because of another commitment. Marcia wasn't so sure he'd been won over, but Dennis shrugged his shoulders. "I'm not going to spend a lot of time worrying about how he feels and what he thinks."

The new school year began that September with a special community assembly. Ted Sizer came in person to announce to the large gathering of Winchester students and parents that Thayer was the first school named to his national organization, the Coalition of Essential Schools. The crowd stood and applauded.

Littky knew that membership in the Coalition would go a long way toward helping Thayer along the road of reform. Staff members at Brown University would offer workshops and help with curriculum development. Affiliation would give Thayer national recognition. Belonging to a network of schools similarly engaged in reform would help them to exchange ideas and learn from each other. Membership might also help secure money from outside agencies to pay teachers to work on curriculum and to buy materials.

Littky also liked membership in the Coalition because it wouldn't cost the town anything, and it didn't oblige the school to take orders from the Coalition.

Littky was utterly committed to exploring new curriculum, new ways to integrate teaching, better ways to evaluate students. He got permission from the state and local board to clear one Wednesday afternoon a month for staff development meetings. Beyond that, there were after-school workshops, weekend meetings, conferences. From the grant monies, Littky was able to pay teachers for their extra time. Some teachers, however, were frustrated by the additional demands and feared burnout.

"My hope is that when you talk about burnout you don't just mean working hard," Littky responded. "If you are working hard and have great satisfaction, you don't have burnout. We do celebrate, too. My job is to keep people up. I know people are exhausted at times, but that's part of the excitement of growing. And I know I push too hard sometimes and have to pull back."

For the moment, though, there was no pulling back.

The four teachers Littky named to the problem-solving committee demonstrated the first signs of a new creativity and energy. "The problem-solving group," wrote Littky in

the September 28 memo, "tried to solve the problem of how
they would become experts in problem solving and then
help the rest of us. They divided up the ten books and
materials I had gathered and then contracted with me (the
grant) for $500 to study on their own and have a plan of
attack at the end of October."

The energy and enthusiasm were there.

As a starting point for his discussions with staff, Littky
used the nine principles developed by the Coalition of
Essential Schools.

COALITION COMMON PRINCIPLES:

1. The school should focus on helping adolescents to learn
   to use their minds well. The school should make no
   claim to be "comprehensive"; that is, it is not to be a
   center offering a wide variety of social and vocational
   services to adolescents, at least at the expense of its central intellectual purpose.
2. The school's goals should be simple: that each student
   master a limited number of centrally important skills
   and areas of knowledge. While these inevitably will
   reflect the traditional academic disciplines, the program's design should be shaped by the intellectual and
   imaginative powers and competencies that students need,
   rather than necessarily by "subjects" as conventionally
   defined. That is, the school should not bind itself to the
   existing complex and often dysfunctional system of isolated departments, "credit hours" delivered in packages
   called English, social studies, science and the rest. The
   aphorism "less is more" and the virtue of thoroughness,
   rather than mere coverage of content, should guide the
   program.
3. The goals of the school should be universal, the same for
   everyone, while the means to these goals will vary as the
   students themselves vary. School practice should be tailor-made to meet the needs of every group or class of
   adolescents.

4. Teaching and learning should be personalized to the maximum feasible extent. Efforts should be made toward a goal that no teacher have direct responsibility for more than eighty students. To allow for personalization, decisions about the details of the course of study, the use of students' and teachers' time, and the choice of teaching materials and specific pedagogues must be unreservedly placed in the hands of the principal and staff.

5. The governing practical metaphor of the school should be student-as-worker, rather than the more familiar teacher-as-deliverer-of-instructional-services. Accordingly, a prominent pedagogy will be coaching, to provoke students to learn how to learn, and thus to teach themselves.

6. Students entering secondary school studies at this school are those who are committed to the school's purposes and who can show competence in language, elementary mathematics and basic civics. Students graduate, receiving a diploma, when they formally exhibit their mastery of the school's program. There is, therefore, no strict age grading and no system of "credits earned" by "time spent" in class; the emphasis is, rather, on the students' demonstrating that they can do important things. Students of traditional high school age but not yet at appropriate levels of competence to enter secondary school studies will be provided intensive remedial work to assist them quickly to meet these standards. A final demonstration of mastery for graduation—an "exhibition"—should be the joint responsibility of the faculty and of higher authorities, and represents the latter's primary and proper influence over the school's program.

7. The tone of the school should explicitly and self-consciously stress values of unanxious expectation. ("I won't threaten you but I expect much of you"), of trust (until abused) and of decency (the values of fairness, generosity and tolerance). Incentives appropriate to the school's particular students and teachers should be emphasized, and parents treated as essential collaborators.

8. The principal and teachers should perceive themselves as generalists first and specialists second; staff should expect multiple obligations (teacher-counselor-manager) and a sense of commitment to the entire school.

9. Ultimate administrative and budget targets should include, in addition to total student loads per teacher of eighty or fewer pupils, substantial time for collective planning by teachers, competitive salaries for staff and an ultimate per pupil cost not to exceed that at traditional schools by more than ten percent. To accomplish this, administrative plans will inevitably have to show the phased reduction or elimination of some services now provided students in traditional "comprehensive" secondary schools.

At each workshop, Littky focused on one or two of the principles. In October, he scheduled a workshop to focus specifically on integration of subjects, team teaching, and competencies. Littky waltzed into the teacher's lounge brandishing doughnuts and orange juice. A dozen teachers were seated comfortably on the couches and chairs. A couple sat cross-legged on the Oriental carpet. Littky had bought the furniture and rug as Christmas presents to the staff the year before, replacing furniture that one teacher described as "dilapidated enough that I would be embarrassed to put it out at the street for garbage collection."

The room was comfortable, resembling a basement rumpus room: handmade blue curtains, old round-cornered refrigerator, two rows of coffee mugs on a rack on the wall, painted ceiling pipes, and a sticker on the door that said, "Teachers are our best hope for a better world."

Once he established "the challenge" of the workshop, Doc used a careful blend of cajolery and prods to get minds working on the problem. "What basic skills do students need to succeed in school?" and "What constitutes mastery of a subject and what ways might a student demonstrate that mastery?"

When the discussion reached a new level of understanding, Doc divided everybody into small groups. Each group was then responsible for coming up with a practical, concrete solution to the problem. Gradually, he was preparing the staff for the big step: implementation.

Littky wanted to try integrating curriculum on a schoolwide basis. He wanted teachers from diverse disciplines to work together, teaching by theme rather than subject. Teachers worked on ideas. Doc began to gather the ideas into a grand plan that would get teaching out of the classroom and into the world.

Gradually, Doc introduced the plan to the staff. He knew from experience that dumping a revolutionary idea at a staff meeting invited negative posturing. The knee-jerk reaction would be to find fault, to complain about why it wouldn't work, the extra time it would take, etc. Before the workshop, Littky had made a point to talk individually with teachers about the plan. Their enthusiasm kindled his. By the time the workshop rolled around, teachers, far from being resistant, contributed new ideas of their own. On the other hand, if the enthusiasm hadn't been there, Littky wouldn't have pursued the project at that time. The one-on-one, behind-the-scenes work was what made the difference.

"If we suspend classes for two weeks," Val Cole suggested, "we can *do* those things we've been talking about. We can get at the basic skills from the list! What we need are topics. We need to come up with projects that will integrate all the disciplines and incorporate those basic skills we've been working on."

In *Share*, the school's newsletter, the staff printed a list of skills it had settled on as important for students to acquire: communication skills, problem-solving skills, organizational skills, management skills, and cooperation skills.

Finally, the staff pulled together an eight-page summary of Thayer's philosophy and goals, asking, "What do we want for our students?"

We want to prepare them to achieve, to produce, to reason, to be happy, to be responsible, to communicate. We want to develop the desire for continuous learning in all of our students. If they seek a job, we want them to be as well or better qualified than other applicants. We want to challenge the academically gifted. We want to educate your children in the most appropriate way so that they can become the best they can be. We want all of our students to *choose* a place in life, not be *forced* into one because they lack skills.

It detailed the range of critical skills students must acquire to earn their diploma, including reading, oral and written expression, problem solving, computations, computer literacy, personal economics, the arts, field and laboratory methodology, world issues, and survival skills such as child-rearing, stress management, knowledge of local government, primary first aid, the employment process.

TGIF October 26, 1984:
As I sit exhausted Thursday night, I think of your jobs, the work each night and the consistency of your teaching. Someday I believe people will respect our work and pay for it accordingly.

We are doing so very much. I hope everyone realizes it. Running the school well this year and at the same time working on the next year is an awesome task. That is why most schools don't change. That is why I am so proud to be working here. That is why educators from afar think we are so special.

TGIF November 9, 1984:
There is no one else trying to undertake what we are doing. This is frustrating because we will create the answers for ourselves.

Littky continued his behind-the-scenes work to get the Two-Week Project going. Each time he talked to someone about it, the plan became clearer in his own mind. On Wednesday afternoon, November 29, students would be released from school to free up the staff for a workshop. At the meeting, Littky divided everyone into groups of three, based arbitrarily on the color shirts they were wearing. Each group developed ideas that would incorporate everything the staff had been working on to date: integrating disciplines, team teaching, competencies and mastery, basic skills, exhibitions, out-of-school experiences.

Then he passed out a ballot: "I would like us to do this two-week course this year"—yes or no.

The tally: twenty-two yes, two no.

Littky then sought approval from the school board. The vote was four to one. Bobby Secord's was the lone no vote.

During the next several months, the Two-Week Project took greater form. Teachers formed teaching teams, determined specific course objectives, skills, and assignments, then created a curriculum that would integrate subjects and provide a range of methods for students to exhibit what they had learned—through journals, speeches, and other demonstrations. Each teacher team would have six hours each day to work with its small group of students. Teachers nailed down field trips, ordered films, purchased supplies and equipment. Advisers introduced the concept of the Two-Week Project to their students during morning advisory meetings. Littky wanted to be sure the program was presented in a very positive way.

TGIF March 8, 1985:

The difference between the two weeks and our regular program hopefully is more than just time. The time should give us the flexibility to help the students get very involved and to use their minds and hearts in learning. I hope the learning is deeper and longer lasting than most. When we say less is more, this is what we mean, a chance to go deeper into a topic and to know something very thoroughly.

Jimmy Karlan, chairman of the Two-Week Project, drafted a letter to students and parents:

All courses share similar qualities and goals and will be taught by a team of teachers. Each team has worked cooperatively to design an integrated two-week curriculum that will help develop and strengthen what we are now calling "Exit Level Skills" and "Basic Skills."

Basic skills consist of a very specific list of skills (not courses), that we, as educators, consider necessary for a student to master in order to succeed in high school. (For example, a student must be able to add, subtract, multiply, and divide whole numbers, fractions, and decimals.)

Exit level skills also consist of a very specific list of skills (not courses) that we, as educators, consider necessary for a student to master in order to earn his/her diploma. (For example, a student must be able to demonstrate a basic knowledge of computers or be able to measure and calculate the area and volume of common geometric shapes.)

By early spring, eleven two-week courses had been designed by the teacher teams. One course, called A Week in the Life of New Hampshire, was designed as a journey through time from 1623 to 2100, making use of historical, sociological, and psychological studies of New Hampshire. Students would practice creative writing and acting and would do dramatic reenactments of significant events in New Hampshire life. The course would include a trip to the state capital to meet with the governor and observe the legislature in session.

Another course had as its theme mountains and mountaineering. Workshops would be set up to teach rappelling, first aid, and survival skills. Students would organize an overnight mountain climb in the White Mountains. The course would also include class lectures, readings, and discussions about mountain geology, geography, topography, and biology. Students would study Nepal and the Nepalese to understand the sociology of a mountain culture.

A third, called "On the Road Again," was a study of art, literature, and the poetry of Melville, Wharton, Frost, and Dickinson. Students would test their own creative powers through sketching, photography, poetry, writing, and calligraphy. They would also visit the Clark Art Institute; the homes of Wharton, Melville, and Dickinson; and a planetarium.

The Two-Week Project lifted the fifty-minute, subject-by-subject structure and allowed students and teachers to think about teaching and learning in new ways. Teachers brought together math, science, English, history, and art and challenged students to make their own connections.

Marcia Ammann worked with the home economics teacher, history teacher, and science teacher on trying to make New England history come alive. Students conducted an archeological dig and "adopted" a tombstone. They did research at the county probate court, learned stenciling, quilt-making, and hand-hewing lumber. They visited several historic New England villages.

In her journal, Marcia recalled the first day: "I'm not sure who was more nervous that April morning—36 white faced, sleepy high schoolers, or the four of us (teachers). We had planned and dreamed for this day, but it all seemed far removed and strangely separated from this reality."

Marcia had never seen students and teachers work so well together. The students didn't stand back waiting for instruction, they dug in. Each day, they wrote in their journals about their learning experiences and insights. One student wrote: "In regular class they tell us and tell us, but here *we* discovered it."

An eighth grader, whose theme was Young Inventors, came back from the Boston Museum of Science ready to embark on the major goal of that group—to invent or elaborate upon an invention viewed at the museum. The student wrote:

> I believe I was truly inspired to do this project on the Van de Graaff generator because of what I saw in the museum. I was thrilled watching the air being heated up by electrons zooming through gaps in a circuit, heating the air so easily. It was just like lightning only smaller (one hundred times smaller.) I never dreamed lightning could be so powerful, so devastating! It was incredible. Right there I knew what I was going to try. The very thought of making my own lightning—that very thing—is what inspired me to do the Van de Graaff.

At the end of the second week, Thayer was alive with students exhibiting and demonstrating what they had learned—they gave speeches, aired self-produced videos, read poems, short stories, and plays, displayed four-by-four-foot oil paintings and wax sculptures. The young inventors exhibited a wave tank model, a modified rocket, a door-light that glowed when the knob was turned, a bubble machine, a probability machine, and a cattle catcher.

One of the teachers in that group wrote:

> To observe these students so engrossed in working on their projects was truly a wonderful thing. . . . There was group participation, independent learning, creativity and problem solving all happening at once. Real learning was taking place. . . . It was also a learning experience for the teachers because we had to stand back and let ourselves be used as a reference.

Littky saw the Two-Week Project as the first successful school-wide demonstration of integrating subjects, team teaching, and altering the five-period day. He saw in teachers and students "a new excitement, a new braveness."

He saw it as a major step toward permanent restructuring.

A key to Littky's success as a manager was that he provided his teachers an environment to take ideas and run with them. His role was to clear the way for teachers and students to exercise their creative and productive energy for the good of the school. The more power teachers exercised, the more creative and productive they became. But Littky is a practical man. Time simply doesn't permit all teachers to participate in all decisions. For example, rather than ask teachers, "What do you want the final schedule to be?" Littky would say, "This is going to be the final schedule; if there are any problems or suggestions, we'll address them on Friday." On the other hand, for most projects, Littky played the role of the generalist—talking theory, playing devil's advocate, making suggestions; the projects themselves belonged to the teachers.

A gray area existed between where Littky's leadership ended and teachers' empowerment began. Teachers' success depended on the support and freedom their principal gave them. Littky's success depended on the energy and ability of his teachers to get things done.

In addition to the Two-Week Project, teachers were consciously trying to make learning come alive for students during the regular school day. For example, Erica, the home economics teacher, secured $23,000 in grants in two years to help pay for two computers for her classes and to construct a greenhouse. Students used the computers to produce a cookbook that they sold in town. Three students worked side by side with an expert to design and build a greenhouse on the back of the school. The greenhouse became a working experimental classroom teaching students the basics of heating, cooling, and insulation, as well as growing and canning vegetables and fruits.

In an effort to help ninth graders better adjust to high school, Val Cole asked her tenth-grade students to write letters to them about the transition into high school. The ninth graders then wrote back.

Betty Hall incorporated some of the learning methods she used in Dovetail to make United States history real for students in her regular classroom. She had the students set up their own self-government and ran the class through a democratic system.

One student described his history project this way:

"It started out as a lecture and book course. It didn't work out for lots of people in class, so she [Mrs. Hall] decided to individualize. She gives us chapters and a project for each unit. We work independently, she checks our projects, asks questions and suggests. It's better. I'm interested in Ireland, so I'm doing my project now on the Easter Rebellion."

Five students from Don Weisburger's advisory gave a presentation about the advisory system to a school district in Vermont. Students set up a Christmas card business. A junior high class developed a game to see who could teach topography the best to elementary students. A contingent of students traveled to Fall River, Massachusetts, to talk at a conference of two hundred principals and counselors about the apprenticeship program and Dovetail. After the conference, one student wrote of the experience:

That was a *real* speech before 200 principals and teachers. What we've done here [at Thayer] prepared me for that. We were telling them how we felt about Dovetail. I explained that I have a lot more self-motivation this year. Last year, people working in Dovetail would *ask* to do things; this year *we* are doing it. We are learning on our own and we love doing it. The principals really like hearing about it, you could tell from their reaction.

The school was more than on its way, in Littky's eyes. At a staff meeting, he told his teachers that Thayer had passed "the breakthrough point" in progress a year earlier than he had predicted. The news brought cheers from the staff.

Thayer continued to bask in the limelight. Visitors came from all over the region—Brown University, Antioch, the state education department—to observe life at Thayer. More articles appeared in national newspapers and magazines detailing the educational successes at Thayer under its eccentric principal. Three national education magazines—*Education Times, Education Weekly, Executive Educator*—featured Thayer. The Coalition of Essential Schools commissioned an educator to write an assessment of Thayer to be used to help monitor change at the school. The thirty-page report was overwhelmingly favorable:

> Most striking—and most respectful of students—is the Thayer School faculty's determination to enable and motivate Winchester young people to learn basic skills that will give them choices in life. They also seem determined to open students' eyes to the world beyond Thayer.

Helen Martin Eccles, the report's author, talked to teacher Val Cole, who told her: "I teach 16 and 17 year olds; 90% of them don't finish college, and I don't know of more than five or six who have been English majors. So my goal is to teach enough about the fine things (literature, writing, speaking) so that when the kids are out there in the world they aren't happy just seeing 'The Avengers' on TV, and they want books with more to them than just a plot. My business is to interest children in being able to write and speak clearly, communicate effectively, and enjoy life and to have the ability to locate the answers to their questions."

Statistics confirmed the glowing assessment: In 1981, the year before Littky took over, the absentee rate was 17 percent. In the first year under his administration, the figure dropped to 12 percent, then 8 percent the following year. By the beginning of the 1984–85 year, it was down to 4 percent.

College-bound students went from a low of four out of the

1981 graduating class of thirty-six students to one-third of the 1985 graduating class of thirty-eight.

California Achievement Test scores in 1985 showed that students in every grade at Thayer improved over the year before by at least one grade level, and in some cases by three. All grades at Thayer were at grade level or above, especially in the area of communication skills.

When Thayer High School began the new year in 1985, it was riding the crest of success.

Dennis drove into the Thayer parking lot early for a board meeting one night. He spotted Bobby Secord's black Cadillac, with Secord in it, parked near the elementary school. Littky swallowed hard, got out of his jeep and approached the Cadillac. He tapped on the driver's side window. Secord, with what struck Littky as tortured reluctance, opened it.

"Bobby," Dennis said softly. "I understand you don't like me.

Secord, visibly taken aback by the question, took a few seconds to respond. "I don't have anything against you," he said. "It's just your ideas."

"What's wrong with my ideas?"

"Too liberal."

"Which of my ideas are too liberal?"

Secord gave him no answer.

19
The Opposition

CINDY NELSON AND CYNDY RYDER wanted to be reelected to the school board. Two other names also appeared on the ballot—Allen Barton and Susan Winter.

Susan Winter was, by some estimates, a handsome woman, well put together; others saw her as hard, overly concerned with appearances, a social climber. She was a loan officer at First Northern Bank in Keene and a Winchesterite by virtue of her marriage to Richard Winter, whose family was deeply sewn in Winchester's fabric. Her father-in-law was a member of the town's police force. She and her family attended church regularly. Her two daughters, one in elementary school and one at Thayer, were growing up pretty, feminine, and especially well-dressed—they were girls who worried about keeping their dresses spotless and their hair tidy. The Winters lived in a customized, luxury trailer off State Route 10. During the next two years, they would build a garage, pave their driveway, install an above-ground swimming pool and a satellite dish, build a deck, and purchase a power boat and three new automobiles, including a Grand Am for their eldest daughter.

In the last town election, Susan had run for clerk and lost. Now she was taking a stab at school board.

Allen Barton was relatively unknown. He was new to town. He lived on the outskirts of Winchester, just over the Massachusetts border. He was elderly, a farmer, and taught engineering part-time at Springfield Technical College in Massachusetts.

Barton was running with Winter. Their object was to unseat Nelson and Ryder, whom they saw as liberal-minded overspenders. The Winter-Barton platform was one of fiscal conservatism and a return to educational basics. Their politics caught the attention of two townies—Ernie Royce and Marilyn Nolan.

Royce, a rough-speaking veteran of the Vietnam War, owned a gem shop and convenience store, which he would later call Cha's, for his Korean wife. The family lived in the rooms behind the store. From first to twelfth grade, Royce attended school in Winchester. He dropped out in 1954, one semester before graduation, because he got into an argument with a teacher. After working for five years, he joined the army, where he worked his way up through the ranks. He fought on the front line in Vietnam, eventually becoming a mustang officer. On the GI bill, he attended night school, graduated from high school, and earned two years of college credit. He retired from the army as a captain.

Royce was not a man caught up with appearances—his hair, though short, was rumpled, as were his clothes; several of his bottom teeth were missing. He was also not one to mince words. When he had something to say, he said it. If he didn't like something, he didn't stand back and hope it would change—he did something about it. Royce didn't like the treatment his son was getting in the local elementary school. So he did something about it. The educators there, he said, had labeled the boy a problem learner. As Royce saw it, if anyone had learning problems, it was those educators, not his son. So he had his son tested in Massachusetts, where it was revealed that the boy had an IQ of 140. Royce removed him from the system and enrolled him in the New York Military Academy, where he excelled. Royce's disdain for local education didn't stop at the grade school. By his estimation, the entire system was out of whack, and Dennis Littky was a major part of the problem.

"He's an ultraliberal," Royce said. "He's not teaching children, he's *guiding* them. He tries to educate by offering students rewards. I feel that he has failed miserably."

Marilyn Nolan had never met Susan Winter or Allen Barton in person, but she wanted to. She rented a farmhouse from Elmer Johnson, where she lived with her daughters, several grandchildren, and a husband who worked on the line at the paper mill and cleaned part-time at the local post office. Nolan had not left her house for several years because of poor health—a combination of respiratory problems and obesity. But education, for her, was a sort of obsession. She had kept meticulous records of goings-on at Thayer since 1983. Kerry, the youngest of her six daughters and the only one still in school, acted as her eyes and ears at Thayer. Her files were thick and getting thicker, lining nearly an entire wall of her dining room, on which hung a pair of praying hands made of copper and a painting of Jesus Christ on black velvet.

Something had happened to her since the early days at the *Star* when Littky had recruited her. Back then Nolan had sent a letter to the paper saying, "If you're going to write about things and people you ought to at least print the truth." Littky sent her a handwritten note saying he liked her style and asked her if she'd work for the paper. Though years had passed, still she recalled vividly her first meeting with Littky.

"I opened the door and there's this bearded wonder. I almost didn't go in." Marilyn Nolan hated hippies. As far as she was concerned, if you looked like a hippie, you were a hippie. She'd had a hard time with her own daughters during the seventies. They had fought with her, skipped school, dropped out; one ran away from home.

Nonetheless, she had tried to overlook Littky's hippie style because she wanted to write for a publication. She wrote several stories for the paper and typed up the local calendar of events each month.

Though Littky hadn't seen her in years, he remembered her as a meticulous and reliable worker. He often acted as her cheerleader, encouraging her, trying to convince her of her abilities as a writer. He certainly didn't consider her a threat.

But Nolan was more than a little suspicious of all that cheerleading. "People like that are phonies," she said. "They've always got to be flattering people and touching them and pumping them up. And the women loved that. They shined, they glowed. When he walked into the office, it was like God was walking in. They listened to his every word. 'I'm Dennis Littky. This is what I'm doing. You're going to help me.' "

Nolan became possessed with her desire to unmask the "real" Dr. Littky. She traced his career, made phone calls, sent for any information written by or about Littky. She would even track down a copy of Littky's doctoral dissertation.

At one time or another, Marilyn Nolan would invite various townspeople, newspaper reporters, and school officials to her home to review her material. Using an easel, she would display elaborate charts and diagrams she had drawn, produce stacks of papers, assignments, dates, and content of telephone calls, and other evidence to prove her case against Dennis Littky.

"He had a plan," she said. "His thesis is his master plan, to get his ways of teaching into a community. He says right there in his thesis, you find the power and how to influence it. He's doing this to be the great education reformer, because he's interested in manipulating the children. It's so very obvious. But it's more than Littky here. Littky has a lot of help.

"The whole picture is shocking and it's frightening. It has nothing to do with better education. Charismatics command almost an instant following, especially from females. Hitler was a charismatic and he started in the schools. Humanists start in the schools. That's where they teach, in the schools. That's where education changes society. Society does not change education. Jim Jones was a charismatic. Power corrupts. Too much power corrupts really bad."

Littky was permitting "obseenities," as she called them, at Thayer, obscenities that were corrupting the children. "I'm tired of schools allowing kids to do things parents wouldn't permit," she said. "He's teaching them to have new values. He's destroying our children."

Parked like a fixture in her home, Marilyn Nolan was building a case against Dennis Littky and the school he had created. If Susan Winter and Allen Barton were Littky critics, Nolan was their supporter. She invited the two candidates to her Warwick Road home, along with some friends and others she wanted to convince to vote for the pair.

Just before the election, there was a rally at the local VFW hall. The hall was wall-to-wall people, all apparently there for the same reason—to hear about the rampant overspending of the current school board and the two incumbents who were leeching the already overburdened taxpayers to support Dennis Littky's experimental educational programs.

Winter, Barton, and their patrons, including Elmer Johnson and Francis Gutoski, insisted that all these experimental programs were costing the town and its people big bucks, even though the fact was the reforms had brought in far more money than they had cost the district. Since Littky's first year as principal, the school had received hundreds of thousands of dollars in grants and donations. But they knew the quickest way to a voter's heart is through the pocketbook. Winter, Barton, and their people made money *the* issue.

Meanwhile, Cyndy and Cindy were confident that they faced little threat from Winter and her unknown sidekick. After all, Winchester Schools had experienced dramatic changes for the better over the previous four years: a desperate school had been transformed into a showpiece of successful reform. There was the Carnegie grant and award for excellence in education. Thayer had been the first school in the country to be asked to join Ted Sizer's prestigious reform movement. And, of course, there were the kids themselves— for the first time in recent history, they actually wanted to be in school and were doing well.

On the night of the rally at the VFW, Marcia Ammann and Cindy Nelson sat at the Ammanns' kitchen table. Marcia, plying her craft as a prognosticator, was reading Cindy's cards. Nearly every card she turned up smacked of politics. None of them looked good. She foresaw a long string of terrible events.

"I'm real nervous, Cindy. I think maybe we should have gotten out there and done some serious campaigning."

"It's too close to the election now," Cindy said.

The next day, they pulled together a list of people to call, hoping to drum up support. But their list wasn't long. Their efforts, Marcia knew, were token at best.

The school board was seeking a 16 percent hike over the previous year's budget. The board maintained that much of that would be needed to cover expected increases in negotiated teacher contracts, as well as to keep pace with inflation and growing numbers of school-age children living in the district. Winter, Barton, and their supporters said that was hogwash. The schools had gotten along fine on the current budget, they said, so they ought to do just fine with the same budget for the next fiscal year.

At the annual Winchester school district meeting on March 21, voters decided the 1985–86 budget and the winners of the two school board seats. Susan Winter and Allen Barton swept the election by a four hundred-vote margin. Then, on Winter's motion, residents voted to raise $1,962,559, some $200,000 less than the amount requested. The new board cut the budget increase back to 4 percent, leaving it with almost no increase after a deficit payback. The cut also made no allowances for expected pay increases in teachers' contracts. The March district meeting stood in glaring contrast to the standing ovation in the same gymnasium six months earlier when Ted Sizer declared, "You are now members of the Coalition!"

What had gone so wrong? Everything had been going along so swimmingly, it had never really occurred to anyone to mount a defensive campaign. Everyone assumed parents would turn out in droves to support the programs and people who were doing so much for the town's children. But the Winter-Barton camp had done a stunning job of convincing voters that the schools were spending more than they needed to. In a town where the average family income was $14,818, according to the 1980 census, a starting teacher's salary of $11,500 didn't look so bad, even though New Hampshire teachers were some of the lowest paid in the country.

Littky was furious; didn't the new school board understand the implications of their vote? Where was the board going to make the cuts to meet the budget? There simply was no fat there, no place to cut that wouldn't cause damage. The implication was that existing staff and programs would get the ax.

TGIF March 22, 1985:
 . . . The cuts made in the budget are drastic. I am angry. We should all be angry (not my usual, "Let's have a positive

attitude."). Next week we will have to create some incredible solutions to solve the fiscal problems that are ahead of us. I'm not sure the people understood what they did. They will soon see the implications.

Shortly after the budget cut, a Thayer eighth grader wrote a letter to the board. After reading the letter, Littky said, "This kid has more on the ball than the new school board." The letter was neatly hand-printed:

School board members, towns people, friends:
   I realize that programs have to be cut to accommodate the new school budget, but why can't we cut them down instead of cutting them out?
   Programs like foreign language, the arts, and the apprentice program are all major factors in the growth of our students.
   You may think these programs are fringe benefits or extras that can be cut out, but we need these programs.
   Before Dr. Littky and others came here the dropout rate was high and the number of students going on to college was low.
   Now we have students going on to college or after an apprenticeship have a job waiting for them when they graduate.
   After someone comes out of 2 or 3 years of a fine arts class they might say "Wow. That's what I want to do."
   On the other hand I would rather find out now that I didn't like a profession, than when I'm out on my own.
   Please, if there is any way possible, keep these classes and help us find out where we can go in life.
   Thank you.

The school board planned to tell the community where it would make the cuts at the April 19 meeting, the second monthly meeting of the new board. Letters appeared in the *Keene Sentinel* from teachers, parents, and students urging

residents to attend the meeting. In a letter signed by the staff
of the Winchester Elementary School, teachers appealed to
the community to voice their opinions on the likely reper-
cussions of the budget cuts: serious decreases in staff, which
would mean an increase in the teacher-pupil ratio and the
elimination of special programs.

> TGIF Memo March 29, 1985:
> A very amazing week. We are expected to carry on as
> usual while 800 things are happening around us that will
> affect our lives next year.
> I am very impressed with how people have been pulling
> together and being supportive of each other and of me.
> The turnout of positive students, teachers, and supportive
> parents at last week's meeting was beautiful. It gave
> strength to me as I sat up front.
> Yes, we have a struggle ahead. No one ever said it would be
> easy. There are times when things seem to be going very
> well, and then other times when nothing seems as if it is
> going right. You know which time we are in now. We must
> not lose our perspective about who we are and the outstand-
> ing job we are doing. We may now have to look harder at the
> good and not let the negative influence us.
> Someone asked me, "Wouldn't the coalition be easier to do
> somewhere else?" My response was, "My concern is about
> Thayer Jr/Sr High and Winchester. The coalition came
> into being just as a support. The coalition is not my con-
> cern. My love and commitment is to the students, to the staff
> and to the town. Don't ask me why it is so strong, but it is."
> I do not think it is an ego trip—I'm too old to love pain
> for a chance at a little success. I feel we started something.
> We have believers, we have made big strides and I'm not
> about to back down and let all we have done go by the
> wayside.
> So thank you all for being strong and continuing to strive
> for the best. I believe our work will pay off.

During the three weeks after the district meeting, the new

board met twice at Bobby Secord's house without posting public notice. Only board members were invited. The budget was among the items discussed. An editorial in the April 24, 1985, *Keene Sentinel* slammed the Winchester School Board and the town's budget committee, which had also held private, unannounced meetings.

> While the chairman of the Winchester Budget Committee [Elmer Johnson] was asserting that he and his colleagues were above the law, members of the Winchester School Board were taking refuge behind faulty memories and "no comment" when it was learned they, too, had held two private meetings recently, at the home of a board member. Those meetings were also very probably violations of state law.

On April 18, thunder rumbled ominously, then rain and wind bit the region. Inside the Winchester Elementary School, tempers flared hot and mean. "We came here in good faith to get some answers. And you failed us. And you know it," said an angry town resident, David Donahue.

He was backed up by a volley of accusations from other residents condemning the board for unfairly excluding the public from board meetings. "You should be ashamed," was the consensus of opinion from the hundred-member audience.

If board members felt any inkling of shame, they didn't show it. Instead, Allen Barton tried to put the audience in its place: "You don't wash your dirty laundry in public. It just can't be done that way," he said. Once cuts had been decided, "we'll tell you everything."

Donahue was on his feet again. "I came here tonight expecting an answer. I think you should make your decisions now."

"Would you like to change jobs?" Barton replied. "You come up here, and you decide the budget. We'll get it done as soon as we get it done."

Cindy Nelson, now a member of the audience instead of the board, stood to make a comment. Ignoring her, Allen Barton shoved his chair back, stood, and walked behind Susan Winter and Bobby Secord, who also were seated at a long table at the front of the room. The three of them whispered to each other for five minutes before Barton returned to his seat. Nelson remained standing during the huddle, the third of its kind that evening. She waited for Barton to sit down, then she spoke, trying to keep her voice even.

"I think it's high time that the board makes its tough decisions," she said. "We're very frustrated and anxious, not only for our teachers, but for our children. We've got to get going. You cannot sit here and tell us that you can't make those decisions. Parents must know what their children's schedules will be next year. Teachers need to know if they're going to have a job next year."

Then she focused her attention on Barton and Winter. "Since the two of you spoke in favor of the budget cuts at the district meeting, you must know where the cuts can be made!"

Barton and Winter gave no response.

Former school board member Ken Gardner spoke up. "I think these people would like to be a part of the process to see what happens to the schools."

Barton shot back: "I don't know what the gentleman has in mind. I don't know how much experience he has handling budgets."

Board member William Strenkert spoke next: "The bottom line that the voters voted, in my opinion, will not run this school."

His remark was greeted with loud applause. The board then left the room to meet in private for an executive session. Forty minutes later, the board members resumed their seats and William Strenkert finally made a motion that most in the audience had been hoping to hear. He proposed that the administrative staff be rehired. The list, of course, included Dennis Littky. The Barton-Secord-Winter voting bloc defeated the attempt.

When the meeting ended, Winter would make no comment to the press about the events of the evening. She, Barton, and Secord left the room almost immediately.

Littky's head hurt. Rumor had it that Barton and Winter had joined the board for one reason—to get rid of him. Was the budget cut their first step at undermining the work he and the staff were doing? Was the bloc vote against rehiring the administrative staff aimed at him? Would they rehire him? One fact was clear: Barton, Secord, and Winter formed an intractable voting bloc, a troika. As long as they clung together, they owned the school board.

That night, Littky dusted off his journal. He hadn't felt the need to write in his diary since his solitary days as a mountain man. In the dim cabin light, he wrote.

I won't leave—I have a vision—I care not only about kids in general but for the kids in Winchester—I care not only for schools in general, but for Thayer High—it is the town in which I live. I care so very much for the teachers—they have struggled, they have trusted, they have changed, they have believed—I have a commitment to them—We have had a dream together & must not give up.

Anger over the board members' conduct mounted.

"I was shocked and dismayed to see such a display of rudeness by one of the school board members," one woman wrote in a letter to the editor. "We, the taxpayers and parents of children who attend the schools, did not go to this meeting to have our intelligence insulted by such an egotistical, pompous man as Mr. Barton apparently is."

Marcia Ammann got her pen out as well for a letter to the editor:

. . . I have no argument witn those townspeople who came

to the meeting knowing that they simply could not bear the burden of higher taxes. I have watched you work too hard all your lives to lose your homes to support the rising cost of educating our children.

My concern is with a small group of people who, for various reasons, deliberately set out to undermine the work that has been done at both Thayer High School and Winchester Elementary School. This was accomplished by distributing inaccurate budget figures and salaries, and by spreading rumors that reflect negatively on the school.

On April 25, the board announced its cuts in staff. One by one, beginning at 11:15 that night, the superintendent read the names of the teachers who would be laid off. Nine jobs were wiped out, more than anyone had anticipated. Part of the reason for the deep cuts in staff was that the board had opted to cover a $38,000 deficit from the previous year out of the account for teachers' salaries.

Littky was aghast. Nearly 20 percent of the fifty-member elementary and high school staff had been fired, though he was not among them. He was further dismayed by Secord's motion to preserve a $6,410-a-year job for a part-time janitor instead of the part-time kindergarten teacher requested by the elementary school principal. The message was clear to Littky: *education* was not this board's chief concern.

"It can't be true," Doc said. "I won't believe it."

Doc pushed toward the staircase. Terri Racine was heading down. He caught her eye. She half-smiled. She followed him to the office.

Doc shut his door behind her. "I just heard this nasty rumor," he said.

"It's true," Terri said simply.

"Oh, God. How—"

"I threw up the pills. I got stomach flu when I was in Florida." Terri's eyes filled with tears.

"I called Family Planning and told them I'd missed a

period and that I was throwing up and everything. . . .
They told me not to worry, that it's normal to miss a period
after just starting the pill."

Littky paced the floor. He pulled at his beard and bit at a
fingernail.

"What am I going to do?" she cried. "I'm fifteen and I'm
pregnant!"

Doc stopped pacing. He looked down at Terri's face. She
was president of her class. He shook his head and put his
arms around her. Then he cried.

Terri had come a long way since her first year with Doc as
a seventh grader. Then she was cocky, popular, never
lacking for an opinion, and she absolutely hated Dr. Littky.
She felt the same way about Jimmy Karlan, her science
teacher. Littky had hired Karlan his first year as principal.
To Terri, Karlan looked as though he'd been assembled by
the same mechanic as Littky. Even when he dressed up, he
could make a Brooks Brother suit look like it was ready for a
romp in the woods. He and Littky wore the same John
Lennon wire-rimmed glasses; their hair was woolly; beards
smothered the bottom of their faces like halves of the same
Brillo pad. Karlan wore his blue jeans ragged and his
shirttails out and stomped around the classroom in snowmobile boots. And, like Littky, he was a Jew. Terri saw
them both as "too weird."

Karlan had hoped that after a few weeks in his class Terri
and Melanie Nelson, her best friend, would give up their
antagonism toward him. His other kids were getting along
with him just fine. He was big enough to take a student's
dislike, but Terri and Melanie were leaders—he was afraid
their sour attitude would undermine his control of the
class. He had to get to the bottom of it, and he wasn't doing
so well on his own. He turned to Littky for help.

"Why do you think they're hostile toward you?" Littky
asked.

"I tell you, I don't know," Karlan said. "It's unprovoked. I sensed it from the first day. There's nothing I've done to them directly to trigger that kind of negativism."

"Are any of your other students antagonistic?"

"No, not that way. Occasionally there's an outburst, but usually it's resolved before class is over."

"And that's not the case with Terri and Mel?" Littky said.

"No. The strange part is, they're two of the brightest kids I have—especially Terri. Maybe I remind her of someone she doesn't like."

"Terri's been going through some rough times at home, with her parents' divorce and all," Littky said. "I know she's pissed off at her dad. Maybe she's taking it out on you."

Littky asked the girls and Karlan to meet after school to talk about "their problem." They were to collect in a classroom—"neutral territory"—some place other than Karlan's classroom or Littky's office. Littky had agreed to act as mediator.

As the girls shambled toward the classroom, Terri turned to her friend. "I can't stand these little truth sessions Mr. Karlan keeps putting us through," she said. "He wants us to be pals or something. It's not gonna work."

Karlan, already in the room, overheard Terri's comments and flinched.

Littky waved them in. "Take a load off your feet, girls." Littky straddled a chair backwards.

Karlan leaned forward. "Look, guys," he said. "I'm not out to hurt you. I just want you to do well. I don't get it— what is it you don't like about me?"

The girls shrugged.

"If it's because I'm too short, tell me it's because I'm too short. If it's my beard, tell me."

"Give the guy a break," Littky said. "Who knows, you might actually find something to *like* about him."

The girls had no response other than to roll their eyes.

Despite themselves, Terri and Melanie found themselves becoming engaged in Karlan's classroom activities. When they studied the eye, Karlan had his students spend an entire school day blindfolded, then a blind college student came in as a guest speaker. The section ended with student teams dissecting cow eyes.

As "Thingamajigists," teams of students invented simple machines using a clutter of objects on Karlan's desk—two batteries, a lever, a ramp, water, a pendulum, a moveable pulley, a motor, wires, a flashlight bulb, an electric switch, and a buzzer. The machine had to demonstrate a force working against the force of gravity and emit a sound that could be heard outside the classroom, and all parts had to be necessary to its operation. The Thingamajigists were allowed to touch their contraption only once during its operation.

Terri and Melanie invented a toothpaste-tube squeezer. When their Rube Goldberg dispenser deposited its first dollop of paste on a toothbrush, Terri and Melanie let out a victory whoop and hugged each other. After class that day, Terri stopped by to talk to Karlan.

"Hey, Mr. K. This whatchamacallit thing was a lot of fun!" She flashed a smile at him, turned and headed out the door toward her next class.

In ninth grade, Terri became a member of Doc's advisory. At first she was standoffish. She refused to attend the barbecue with her advisory at Doc's cabin that fall. The day after, when her classmates bubbled excitedly about the "great time" they had had snowmobiling, playing basketball in the snow, roasting hot dogs, singing, and cross-country skiing, she was sorry she didn't go. In the spring, Doc held another picnic at the cabin. As Terri watched the sun set, she turned to Doc. "I can't believe what a jerk I was about you and Mr. Karlan. Now I think you're my favorite people in the world."

Now, as a tenth grader, Terri faced the most difficult decision of her life. She didn't know what she wanted. Abortion, adoption, motherhood—she didn't want any of them. There was so much else going on in her life.

Just last week, she and her mother had driven to Keene in search of the perfect taffeta hoop skirt for the prom. She was serious about Mark—but not *that* serious. He was the first steady she'd had.

Terri's mother knew she was on the pill. It was Terri's stepmother who actually suggested she get some protection and drove her to the family planning agency in Keene. But Mrs. Racine approved. She knew only too well what pregnancy would do to a teenage girl: in her own senior year she'd landed a job at a rehabilitation center in Vermont. She was supposed to start work as soon as school was out, but she got pregnant. She had to resign from the job before she even started. She was crushed. Seven months later, Terri was born.

Mrs. Racine had high hopes for her oldest child. Terri had the ambition and the smarts to get out of Winchester and do something significant. She couldn't bear the thought of Terri ending up as she had—stitching shearling slippers at Bick Manufacturing.

Mark was adamant. He wanted Terri to have the baby. Mark's parents tried to remain neutral. They told Terri and their son it was up to them to do what they thought was best. Whatever they decided, Mark's parents were behind them.

Terri had known of girls before her in Winchester who'd gotten pregnant and had had their babies. A couple of them drew welfare and lived in the subsidized housing on Main Street. Nearly all of them had dropped out of school.

Would she end up like them if she had her baby? Would she drop out too? Make more babies? Go on welfare? What about her big plans to leave Winchester and explore the world? How could a teenage mother do that? Terri knew the answer. She couldn't—it was as simple as that. She couldn't. But she also knew she couldn't have an abortion or give her baby away.

As soon as word spread that Terri was pregnant, things changed for her. One by one, her friends stopped talking to her. Even walking down the hall, she sensed a change. Terri tried to laugh it off, but she couldn't. Even her good friends were distant and aloof. In advisory one morning, one of the boys came right out and said what was on his mind.

"How do you expect to be president and pregnant at the same time?"

"He's right," Terri thought. "Maybe it would just be easier to drop out."

She pictured her life as a young mother at home with her baby. While her friends planned the prom, she'd be changing diapers. When they talked about college, she'd talk about babysitters. Her life would be so different from theirs. They'd have nothing in common. Eventually, she'd be alone.

Mark, her family, and his family remained supportive. "If anybody's going to drop out of school, it's going to be me," Mark said. "You're a much better student than I am. You're president of the class. You can't give *that* up."

Littky talked with Terri every day. The next several weeks were crucial to her future, and he knew it. When she started to talk about dropping out, he came down hard. "Dropping out wouldn't make your life any easier—just the opposite," he told her.

"I just don't see how I can go to school and have a baby, too."

"It wouldn't be any different than being a working mother. There are millions of mothers who hold full-time jobs and raise a family at the same time. It'll mean you'll have to schedule your time a little more carefully. But for the sake of your baby, you need to think of your own future."

In the meantime, Doc did some campaigning on her behalf. One by one, he talked to her friends. He made them look at Terri's predicament from Terri's point of view. "She needs your support, not a cold shoulder. If you were in her shoes. how would you want to be treated?"

Terri began her junior year at Thayer High six months pregnant and president of her class. Now as she walked down the hall, her classmates reached out and touched her belly. It didn't embarrass her in the least. At lunch, her friends laughed with her and talked about going to the movies in Keene and playing miniature golf. "When your baby's born, you can bring her," they said.

Terri was thinking seriously about becoming a beautician. Jimmy Karlan, who was now the school's apprenticeship director, met with her to discuss setting up a job site at Village Beauty Salon, the beauty parlor next to Kulick's Market.

"I'm not sure this is what I want to do," Terri told Karlan. "But I figure it's the best way to find out."

As required, she wrote up a résumé describing her course work, grades, extracurricular activities, and prior experience as an apprentice working in the office at Bick Manufacturing.

Karlan had a standing rule: "Your résumé has to be letter-perfect before you can be interviewed by a potential site supervisor." Terri worked and reworked hers, grooming it word by word. Village Beauty was impressed.

By the end of the second week of school, Terri was spending two hours a day at the salon. She kept a daily log of her activities.

But as Terri's pregnancy became more conspicuous, her boss told Terri she thought it would be better if she didn't continue her apprenticeship through the end of the semester. Some of the older customers would be offended by Terri's condition and make her work there uncomfortable.

Terri was hurt. Though her schoolmates now accepted her, this blow hit her hard.

"Mr. K.," Terri sobbed, "I have to quit my apprenticeship."

"What happened?" he said.

Terri wrapped her arms over her distended belly. "It's because of this. Because I'm pregnant and unmarried. Those old ladies find me offensive."

"Let's try to keep this in perspective, Terri. Go home and get a good night's sleep. Tomorrow we'll brainstorm about alternatives. Think about how we can turn this whole thing into a positive experience. Remember, Terri—never back down."

Terri became the administrative assistant at the local community center, assisting the director with daily administrative procedures. Together, they developed an after-school activities program for elementary school students. Terri discovered that most of the children enrolled in the program came from single-parent families, mainly mothers.

All students enrolled in the apprenticeship program were required to complete a written project associated with their job site. Terri had been turning over ideas, brainstorming with Karlan about possible projects. "There are a lot of single mothers in this town," Terri said. "Why don't I try to do a project that deals with that and my own pregnancy?"

Terri and Karlan worked out the details, then cleared the whole project with Littky. Terri would design a survey, framing questions to assess townspeople's attitudes on teenage pregnancy. Then she'd circulate it and evaluate the information. The final phase of the project would be an in-depth paper about teenage pregnancy based on the survey, outside research, and her own experience.

Terri tackled her new assignment with unaccustomed zeal. She quickly exhausted all the relevant material at Thayer High and headed to Keene to tap the college libraries. She was flabbergasted to learn that every year more than a million American girls between the ages of fifteen and nineteen got pregnant—10 percent of all girls in that age group. The knowledge made her feel less alone, less like an outcast.

She prepared a list of questions.

"Should unwed pregnant teenagers have all the same rights as other teenagers?"

"Do you consider pregnant unwed teenagers as immoral people?"

She crafted her survey carefully, trying to word each question so as not to influence responses. She expanded her research to include the preparation and use of surveys and learned about demographics. She worked on her math so she could figure percentages and ratios.

She got permission from Shady Plifka's son, Butch, to distribute the survey at the supermarket. Shady, Butch, and Al Kulick owned the supermarket. At Bick Manufacturing, Terri cleared it with management; her mother posted the survey. Terri also handed out the survey at the high school after okaying it with Doc.

The noon whistle hadn't even sounded at Bick Manufacturing when Susan Winter, sitting at her desk at First Northern Bank in Keene, heard about Terri's survey. She was not happy.

On the other hand, it *was* good ammunition. Just the kind Barton, Secord, and Winter were looking for. Now Littky was promoting teenage pregnancy.

When Shady Plifka learned that his store was being used as a distribution point for Terri's survey, he blew up. Butch got the brunt of his anger for giving Terri permission.

The anti-Littky faction was outraged. The survey was labeled "an independent project for the Apprenticeship Program at Thayer High School." Now Littky was giving that girl *credit* for getting pregnant, they hissed. Some even suggested Littky was the one who got Terri pregnant.

"It's like putting her on a pedestal," Winter said with disgust.

Almost a hundred questionnaires were returned by the December 6 deadline. Terri devoured the information.

The responses ran the gamut: Some said that pregnant teens should have the same rights as other teenagers. A number of people indicated that they thought pregnant unwed teenagers were immoral.

Some of the comments cut to the bone:

"Yes, I think pregnant teens should be allowed to stay in school so that they can be an example to everyone else."

"How can you have a baby when you're just a baby yourself?"

Terri recognized the handwriting of one of her teachers. "I don't think unwed pregnant teens should be on National Honor Society, since the honor is awarded on the basis of superior character."

Such comments struck her as unreasonable and hypocritical. "Here I'm trying to be the best person I can be," she told Doc. "I didn't have an abortion. I'm working hard. I won't go on welfare. I won't be a burden to anyone. And people are telling me I'm immoral."

20
The New Right

VALERIE COLE OPENED HER ENGLISH classes in
September of 1985 the way she had for the past ten years.
She asked her students to take out a notebook and spend ten
minutes writing. Mrs. Cole didn't care what they wrote—the
only requirement was that they fill an entire page.

Many teachers at Thayer had their students keep journals,
but Mrs. Nolan told her youngest daughter, Kerry, not to. "I
don't mind if they keep journals," she said. "My objection is
that they must put down their deepest thoughts and feelings. That's not a journal. That's a diary."

Nolan sought to have the practice banned.

Through the conservative Heritage Foundation, she
learned about a two-page form letter that protested journal-
keeping in schools. The letters were originally composed by
a Maryland-based group called the Coalition of Concerned
Parents, but were picked up by the Eagle Forum, a far-right
organization based in Alton, Illinois, and founded by conservative crusader Phyllis Schlafly.

Nolan made copies and began circulating them. The ban
was being sought, according to those who signed the letter,
"to assure that their children's beliefs and moral values are
not undermined by the schools."

Marilyn Nolan saw the practice of journal-keeping as a
thinly veiled effort to pry into students' home lives. "The
teachers say they don't read them, but they do," she said. "If

a kid writes, 'My mother's so mean. I hate my mother,' next thing you know, welfare comes knocking on your door. That's an invasion of family privacy, that's all there is to it. And they don't care about what the student does to the English language. It can be loaded with misspellings, bad grammar, and punctuation and the student can still receive a high mark. It's appalling."

Cole defended herself and the educational merits of the journal assignments to a *Boston Globe* reporter. "This is the one time when they can write without fear of somebody standing over them with a red pencil. I like them to explore, to clear their minds. . . . I encourage them to use it for sorting out feelings, describing people, places, anything."

When state officials caught wind of the protest going on in Winchester, they stated publicly that the Eagle Forum letters were based on a misleading, if not erroneous, interpretation of the November 1984 Hatch Amendment, a rider on the federal general education act.

Officials said that the original intent of the amendment was to ensure that schools secure parental approval before conducting any psychological evaluation or treatment. The New Right had extended "psychological treatment" to include subjects such as nuclear war, values clarification, drugs and alcohol, abortion, human sexuality, evolution, and autobiographical assignments such as journal writing.

"They cannot teach those extra things to our children," Marilyn Nolan told the *Globe* reporter. "When they get started back to basics . . . then Johnny will be able to read again."

That summer about a dozen of the Eagle Forum letters landed in the superintendent's office. At the August meeting of the Winchester School Board, member Susan Winter announced her support for banning journal writing.

The school administration reviewed the matter, and concluded that the letters did not represent the whole community. No ban occurred, and journal writing at Thayer continued unabated. Kerry Nolan did her best to protest her teachers' journal assignments—she recorded weather reports, the time she got up in the morning, what she ate. She recorded nothing about how she felt, nothing about her inner thoughts, and she received full credit for her work.

Marilyn Nolan's crusade did little to dampen Littky's energy or enthusiasm about the start of the new school year. He regarded it as the work of a few narrow-minded people. To be sure, their objections concerned him—not because he thought they had any foundation, but because they were people whom he needed to try to reeducate, to try to show them how wrong they were.

He shook off Marilyn Nolan's negativism and concentrated instead on the positive things happening at Thayer.

TGIF September 6, 1985:
It has been an incredible week for me. The school has been very beautiful and calm. Watching some of the interactions between you and the kids have been heartening.

Yes I know we got a good start last year, but this year has been special. The seniors seem more content than seniors in the past, more appreciative. The teaming that is going on has been inspiring. There has been more teacher to teacher communication in our first week than all of last year. Watching teachers observing each other and sitting and figuring out curriculum and tactics to work with students has been beautiful—good models for kids to see—teachers using their minds—working together.

Indeed, by Littky's estimate, the school had matured considerably. Teachers and students were building on each year, becoming better and better learners.

Littky had hired Karen Thompson, now Karen Marsh, as a special education aide working with Don Weisburger. She had come full circle during the last four years. She'd grown from the recalcitrant member of the Group to a compassionate and responsible aide in Weisburger's self-contained classroom. That year, she and Don won the outstanding teacher team award from the state of New Hampshire. Ultimately, she had forgone college so she could marry her high school sweetheart and gain some more work experience in special education. Now, after working for two years with emotionally disturbed and learning disabled children at the regional collaborative program in Keene, she was back at Thayer.

Littky still had the note she'd written him as a senior:

> . . . You have done so very much for me and have made my junior and senior year at Thayer two of the most enjoyable years of my life. I owe a lot to you, Mrs. Knox and Mr. Weisburger for teaching me and giving me opportunities that I never thought I'd have. . . .

The transition from Thayer student to teacher completed the circle for Karen. The teachers she'd resisted and intimidated as a high schooler were now her colleagues, and she was trying to teach students who were as recalcitrant and tough as she had been. But her students and she shared a common ground that helped make her an empathic and effective teacher.

Littky had taken on another new project—a group of boys in the weekly Life After Thayer course. LAT, a requirement for all Thayer seniors, had evolved since Littky's first year as principal when he instituted the program. That year, the students had met every day. An evaluation the first year made it clear that daily sessions weakened the program. Littky scaled it back to once a week and also separated students by gender.

As the teachers gained experience, they became much

more adept at sorting out the key issues and problems that faced students who would be leaving high school at the end of the year. The gender separation made students more comfortable talking about personal concerns.

As he tended to do with his advisory, Littky chose the boys who were most unruly. Littky's LAT was more like a rap session than a class. The one hour he spent each week with his LAT class was sacrosanct. Nobody was to disturb it.

"This time's real important to me. I can't expect you guys to share with me if I don't share with you," he said. "*I* need this time."

Sometimes Littky went to his LAT session with a pre-pared agenda—teaching them how to balance a checkbook, make a budget, write a résumé. Sometimes he didn't follow any agenda. Once, when a couple of the boys came to LAT uptight about something, Littky had them all sit on the floor in a half-lotus position. He spent the hour teaching them how to meditate and relax.

For Littky and the boys, it was a time to unload, dream, ask questions. Littky saw it as a place that allowed kids to have a kind of "controlled vulnerability," a place "to share those vulnerabilities and trust."

"If you can dream it, why can't you do it?" Billy Higgins asked during LAT one day.

Billy had done a lot of growing since his first encounter with Doc four years earlier, in the ninth grade, raging drunk. His best buddy, James Beaman, had been drunk too. Billy Higgins was the class clown. The year Littky became principal, he was a third-time seventh grader. Billy's prob-lem wasn't a lack of smarts—he was just lazy, unmotivated. When Doc discovered the boys had been drinking, Higgins admitted to it upfront and apologized; Beaman, tough as a bull with a temper to match, denied everything, cursing all the way.

Now a senior, James Beaman was a tutor for an eighth-grade boy who had serious discipline problems and was failing school. After his first session with the boy, Beaman came to LAT, drained and exasperated.

"Teachers ought to get paid a million bucks. I never knew how tough it was to teach jerks like that kid," James said. "Tell me, Doc. Was *I* that bad?"

Littky nodded.

One day, James burst into LAT. "Tim put himself away," he said.

"Yeah, I know," Doc said. The student in question had admitted himself into an alcohol rehabilitation center the day before.

"Jesus, why did he do that?"

Tim was a drinker. He also smoked pot. But Littky knew there were others who smoked and drank as much as he did. He sensed their worry.

"We drink at least as much as he does," Billy said. "And he put himself away."

Doc leaned forward. "You know the crazy thing is," he said, "Tim talked to me a few days ago and said to me 'I always thought I could stop. I got sickeningly drunk last night, threw up, and said I'd never drink again. I got up the next morning and opened a beer. That's when I knew I couldn't stop.' "

Doc looked at James and Billy. "Do you think you guys could stop if you wanted?"

"We can stop anytime we want," James said without hesitation. Billy was quiet.

"Okay, let me make a heavy bet with you," Doc said. "If you stop drinking for two months, I'll give you each $100."

"Hey, man, you serious?" James said, his eyes lighting up.

"Of course I am."

"Sure, I'll do it."

"How about you, Billy?"

"I dunno. I'm not so sure I can."

"That makes me real nervous to hear you say that," Doc said.

"C'mon, Billy. You can do it," James said.

The other boys joined in.

"Sure you can, Billy."

"For a hundred bucks, you gotta do it."

"Okay," Higgins said finally. "I'll try."

Suddenly James had his doubts. "Oh, Jeez," he said. "My parents are going out of town. This was going to be party weekend."

"It'll be a good test," Doc said. "If you can do it now for a measly hundred bucks, it'll be a good lesson if you run into trouble later."

During the next several weeks, Billy and James stayed away from alcohol. Every week in LAT they'd report on their progress, the temptations they'd overcome, the invitations they'd refused. On the day that marked the end of the two months, Billy Higgins was home in bed. The night before, his eye had stopped a soccer ball from barreling into the goal.

Doc and the rest of the LAT class piled into Doc's jeep and headed for Billy's house. Billy's mother answered the door and stared wide-eyed as the troop of boys marched into Billy's dark room and sent a hundred crisp one-dollar bills into the air.

21
Troubled Waters

ENGLISH TEACHER JUNICE KENDALL WAS getting her hair done at Village Beauty Salon when she first heard the rumor.

"Francis Gutoski's going around town saying the board's finally going to straighten up the school."

"What'd he mean by that?"

"By getting rid of Littky."

Melanie Nelson, whose mother, Cindy, was ousted from her seat as school board chairperson the previous year, came home from school distraught over the news that Doc might not be rehired.

"Why would the board do that?" she asked.

"They have it in for Dennis," Cindy said. "I don't know why. But they do."

Bill Strenkert had resigned his position on the Winchester School Board that summer because he was moving to Florida. In March, the town would elect a new board member to fill the vacancy. In the meantime, the board would appoint someone.

When school began in September 1985, the board had its new member: Francis Gutoski.

Littky didn't know much about Gutoski, but what he knew concerned him. His sole interaction with him had occurred the year Littky revived the *Winchester Star*. He was the man who'd kicked Dennis out of his store because Littky had printed a negative letter to the editor about him.

At the first meeting of the new board, member Allen Barton made a motion to drop Thayer from the Coalition of Essential Schools. The motion died for lack of a second.

In November, Francis Gutoski made the motion again. There was no discussion. The vote was unanimous.

The action sent Littky and his staff into a tailspin. Why had the board done it? The Coalition was an important asset to the school. In response, the staff formed a crisis committee. Jimmy Karlan, committee chairperson, drafted a letter to the *Keene Sentinel*, which was signed by nearly the entire Winchester teaching staff.

> Contrary to the statement of board member Francis Gutoski who made the motion to withdraw Thayer from membership, no cost was incurred by the school or the town as a result of membership in the coalition. Nor is there any obligation to follow any line of thinking or theory advanced by that group or other member schools.
>
> In short, our membership in the coalition was a very positive arrangement for a school and town with our financial considerations.
>
> With this in mind, it seems that a motion (and subsequent vote) to withdraw the school "without explanation" is an abrogation of responsible behavior on the part of elected officials of this community.
>
> We are particularly concerned that a pattern of decision-making without input from staff or administration, delaying important decisions for no apparent reason, and refusing to offer reasons for decisions made, is leading to frustration and poor morale on the part of staff, concerned parents and students.

The Crisis Committee submitted thirty questions to the board. On December 2, the committee and the board met to discuss them.

Crisis Committee: "Why did the Board decide to abolish the high school's membership in the Coalition, against the advice of the administration?"

Allen Barton: "No comment."

Crisis Committee: "Why was it done without the input and advice of staff, students, and community?"

Allen Barton: "No comment."

Crisis Committee: "Explain the Board's perception of the Coalition and what Thayer's responsibility was to the Coalition."

Allen Barton: "It's essentially nothing."

Crisis Committee: "Which of the Coalition's principles do you object to or disagree with and why?"

Allen Barton: "The Coalition is a rehash. Sizer is using it to promote his own interests. I don't agree with his philosophy of education. It simply hasn't worked. Thayer doesn't have any responsibility to the organization. My point is a matter of philosophy. I don't like Thayer High School even considering such a philosophy."

Members of the committee pressed Barton and the other board members to state which philosophies they disputed. The board gave no answers. What really baffled the staff about the whole thing was that very board had unanimously accepted the staff's philosophy and goals just a few months earlier.

Despite the Crisis Committee's efforts to open the lines of communication, the board members remained cold and unapproachable. At meetings, requests from the audience for elaboration on positions the board took were answered by an angry stare or an abrupt rejoiner. At the December monthly board meeting, a man told the board it owed the town an explanation for voting the school out of the Coalition.

Francis Gutoski took such umbrage at the inquiry that he lurched to his feet, shook an angry finger at the man and offered this: "We don't owe you anything. If you couldn't see fit to attend last month's board meeting when the issue was decided, then we're not going to spend time with you now!"

"It wasn't on the agenda," the man protested. "You gave us no advance notice that the topic was even going to be discussed."

"That's not my problem," Gutoski shouted. "The board discussed it in executive session, and it's been decided. It's done. We owe you *nothing*."

As soon as meetings ended, Secord, Barton, Winter, and Gutoski left immediately. Reporters from the local papers had to run to catch them. Their standard response to most inquiries was, "No comment."

Next Littky came under pressure from the board about Terri Racine's project on teenage pregnancy; Susan Winter wanted it stopped. Terri and her mother braced themselves for the next school board meeting, and Terri voluntarily handed her outline to the board—three rough drafts of her paper, the surveys, and a list of the references she'd used. Susan Winter accepted the material with a shrug.

In January, on the day teacher Christa McAuliffe and the Challenger crew were killed in the space shuttle disaster, Littky and his LAT class spent their period in the library with several other classes. They watched in horror as television reports gave updates on the likely fate of the astronauts.

Christa McAuliffe was a social studies teacher from Concord, New Hampshire, just sixty miles from Winchester. Reporters from the *Keene Sentinel* scrambled to get reactions from students and teachers around the region. A call was made to Thayer High.

"Dennis," the reporter said, "Is Richard Pratt in school today?"

"Yeah. He sure is."

"Could you ask him to get some reaction photos?"

Pratt had served an apprenticeship at the *Sentinel* working with the paper's head photographer and had had several of his photos published. Pratt's photo of Thayer students intently watching the news of the shuttle disaster on television ran in the *Sentinel* the next day.

Not long after the edition was out, Littky heard the news: Bobby Secord "went crazy" when he saw the photo because it showed a couple of students wearing hats.

Littky shuddered at Secord's reaction. "That's the absurdity of it all. Christa McAuliffe and six crew members die, and what he sees in the picture is not people sad and stunned, he sees *hats!*"

This time, Littky wasn't blinded by his own optimism. Things were tense. Something was sure to break. The next target, he feared, would be himself.

At four o'clock on Friday afternoon, Marcia Ammann asked to talk to Dennis. She looked drawn, a little too serious.

"Gutoski's seat is up for grabs at the next election," she told him. "I'm going to run. It means I'll have to leave Thayer. It means I'll have to quit my job. But I'm going to do it."

For a moment, Dennis stared at Marcia. He knew how deeply she loved teaching. But she was standing before him saying she would give up her job to run for the board if that was what was needed. Tears came running down his cheeks. He couldn't talk.

Under stress, Dennis once again began to keep a diary.

March 10—
    Here is what I think will happen—I think the School Board will fire me (not renew my contract) the last week of March—I have prepared to hear their unanimous no's as Dick nominates me.
    I will be surprised if I don't get fired.

If Gutoski wins the 20th, there is no hope—no hope because the board then has 3 sure no's and one probably, plus they have brought the people out to beat Marcia & make their point—The voters will probably be the older people without kids in school.

If Marcia wins, like I think, then there is a small, very small hope—Basically Marcia will have a week to convince the board members to vote for me—not much of a chance—but miracles do happen—

Despite the troubles in Winchester, Littky was once again in the public light. *Harper's* magazine held a forum on education reform in New York City with Dennis Littky as one of its eight panelists. The panel discussed the topic "How Not to Fix the Schools—Grading the Educational Reformers." The discussion was printed in the February issue of the magazine.

In January, *Executive Educator*, a national magazine, named Littky educator of the month and featured him in a lengthy article.

The publicity brought with it job offers. Superintendent Roger Sundstrom and Assistant Superintendent Dick Mc-Carthy urged Littky to take one of them. Offers had come in from high schools and colleges all over the country. All of the jobs meant substantially more money than the $32,076 he was making at Thayer.

"Why fight?" they asked. "The board and their people just don't appreciate you. Why don't you leave now on your own terms? If you get fired, some people won't touch you."

"Why *am* I fighting this?" Dennis asked himself. "Is my time up in Winchester? How would I know?" At times of peak frustration with students and teachers, Littky found himself thinking: "This may be a way out for me."

When Dennis confessed his feelings to Marcia one day, she lit into him. "You better not back out," she bellowed.

"We have done great things, and we will continue battling!"

That woke Dennis up. At the next staff meeting, he told his teachers, "I will fight and win. I will stay."

The weekend before the March 20 district meeting, Littky left town. He wanted to try to clear his head, ease some of the tension that had been building in him in anticipation of Marcia's race against Gutoski and, of course, his own fate at Thayer.

On Monday, he went through the motions of his job, out of focus, a little numb. Tuesday he caught a cold. Wednesday his girls' softball team lost a game. Thursday he went to see a lawyer . . . just in case. The district meeting was that evening. When he arrived back at school, he saw the *Sentinel*. Front page: "THAYER'S PRINCIPAL MAY NOT BE REHIRED."

Something shifted inside him. Suddenly the issue was public. He read it again. "Thayer's principal may not be rehired." It did something to him. Reading it in the paper suddenly made it seem more real, almost inevitable.

Nearly everyone at school had seen the article. The energy in the building was strange—it was neither positive nor negative. It was confused. It seemed to Dennis that nobody knew how to act—least of all him.

Also in that day's paper was a letter to the editor from Val Cole.

> . . . According to school board member Francis Gutoski, the school board will vote March 27 not to renew the contract of Dr. Dennis Littky. On March 14, Mr. Gutoski told two members of the Thayer staff that Dr. Littky had been notified. As of March 17, Dr. Littky has not been so notified.
>
> . . . I wish to express my total support of Dr. Littky and the programs and policies he has seen instituted at Thayer.
>
> . . . Because so much school board discussion takes place behind closed doors, because notes of these meetings are not

made available, and because school board members seem averse to stating opinions publicly, I'm not sure why Dr. Littky will not be renominated. Rumor has it that "he's not right for Winchester."

He is not the kind of person one would expect to find as the leader of a small rural high school—his critics are right in that respect. He does advocate change in the American system of high school education—so does every leading educator today. He certainly doesn't look the part of a principal. Perhaps his often-discussed informal attire is his way of saying, "Judge me for my competence, not because I can dress the part." I have worked for several principals who effectively dressed the part but who couldn't measure up to Dr. Littky as an educator, an administrator or a leader.

In any case, ask your children about school. Ask recent graduates about the good jobs they might have obtained because of the apprentice program. Ask teachers and administrators for answers to questions you might have. Don't settle for second- or third-hand rumors or half-truths.

Insist that the board explain why they are failing to nominate Dr. Littky and ask yourself if you would like your supervisor to use those same reasons for failing to hire you for your job, especially when you have accumulated five years of positive recommendations.

If you think the quality of education at Thayer has improved over the last 10 years, or five, or even from last year, please express your support of Dr. Littky to the school board at the budget meeting March 20 and the school board meeting March 27, when nominations of faculty and administration will be voted on by the school board.

Littky had been on edge all that day. If Marcia didn't win the three-year seat on the board, his situation would be hopeless.

Just before the polls opened that afternoon, Marcia Ammann and a supporter, Jack Ainsworth, challenged the election, questioning the process used to collect absentee ballots. Each submitted a signed letter to Moderator Elmer Johnson charging that the school clerk's appointment of Peg Pinard as an assistant was illegal because Pinard was a vocal Gutoski supporter. New Hampshire law states that clerks and their assistants must remain apolitical.

"It would appear votes were solicited," Marcia contended.

In addition, several of the absentee voters' names were not on the checklist as required by law. Of the sixty-one absentee ballots cast in the election, four were not validated.

That added another measure of tension as Dennis watched people file into the gymnasium to cast their votes. He didn't recognize a lot of the faces. Many of them were older people, and most older residents supported Gutoski. Voters without children in the schools had to rely on what they heard. Who would they more likely trust: a well-known townie who'd held nearly every political office in Winchester or a beatnik principal?

For the first time in thirty-five years, the school board and the budget committee agreed on the bottom line of the proposed budget. The $2,287,855 budget would increase spending from the current year by 6.8 percent. But when Elmer Johnson called for the motion to be considered, a man stood up and requested an increase of $20,000 to hire a first-grade teacher. The proposed budget didn't provide for the position, which, the man said, was sorely needed. Several others in the audience echoed his sentiments.

Board member Secord, who was also on the budget committee, told the crowd to leave the budget alone. He said there was enough fat in it to take care of hiring another teacher if the need should arise. "We've finally done something right and I think you should support the budget committee," Secord said.

The man who proposed the amendment questioned how much fat could be in a budget that hadn't taken into account $107,000 worth of accumulated debt. The man was worried that putting off the allocation would "only put us further in the hole."

Johnson called for a stand-up vote. The amended budget passed by a wide margin, in one of the shortest district meetings on record. In the two hours following, some 520 election ballots were counted. Most of the audience stayed to hear the results.

By a 64-vote margin, Marcia Ammann won. Cheers filled the gymnasium. Teachers and students swarmed around Marcia and Dennis, hugging them. As Francis Gutoski headed toward the door, a reporter ran after him.

"Mr. Gutoski," she said, "were you surprised by the results?"

"No," he said. "It was a teachers' election. They got all their people out. That's what it was."

"Would you say that this election will make a difference to Dr. Littky and his future with the school district?"

Gutoski stopped dead in his tracks and turned to face the reporter. "I can be very frank with you now that I'm off the school board. When I live in a community and see a principal walking around with a gold earring in his ear, I see not so much professionalism involved. I think a lot of the people in this community look at it the same way. Next week, the board will show everybody what they really think about that man."

Littky was in the middle of the gymnasium, the center of a swarm of happy supporters. He was laughing when the reporter came up to question him. She glanced at his ears. No earring.

"Tell me, Dr. Littky," she said. "Do you now or have you ever worn an earring?"

"What?" he said, laughing.

"Mr. Gutoski has just questioned your professionalism because you wear an earring. Do you?"

Littky shook his head and smiled. "I can't believe it. It

was probably my glasses," he said, fingering the part of his wire frame that wrapped around his ear. "The plastic covering on the end here broke off. That's what it was; it just stuck out. I guess it might have looked like an earring."

The victory and the party afterward at Marian Polaski's house was a boost Dennis needed.

"I'm hoping I'll be able to talk some sense into their heads between now and the end of the month," Marcia said. "I'd rather have them support your rehiring because they *want* to, not because they're scared."

The ballot-tampering issue caused more bad blood between the pro- and anti-Littky forces. Littky supporters accused Littky opponents of election fraud. Phone calls were made back and forth between the sides. Littky supporters questioned the point of contesting an election they had in fact won. There was, of course, the principle of the issue. Deals were proposed: we won't turn the matter in to the state ballot law commission if the board promises to renew Littky's contract.

In the end, the allegations were presented to the ballot law commission, but the commission dropped the matter because it said it didn't have the resources to investigate.

During the weeks before March 31, the last possible date the board could rehire staff, the school board was flooded with letters from Thayer teachers, students, former students, and parents singing Littky's praises and asking the board to support him.

Dear Winchester School Board,
   Throughout the past five years, Dr. Littky has been faced with many paradoxes that seem to be inherent in every principal's role. Paradoxes in which success appears as failure; strengths are perceived as weaknesses; and fairness

is viewed as being unjust. The very nature of a principal's job places him in a "no-win" situation.

For instance:

We want a principal to be a leader, but we don't like to follow.

We want a principal to be brilliant, but others' brilliance reveals our ordinariness.

Dr. Littky is given the legal responsibility of disciplining other peoples' children, but then he's accused of interfering.

He expels a student who has repeatedly interfered with the rights of others to learn, and then he's criticized for being unfair.

He raises the academic standards of the school, and then he's accused of having expectations that are too high.

He develops an Apprenticeship Program and is then criticized for not preparing students for their life after Thayer.

When he treats students as individuals and with respect, he is then accused of being too lenient. But when he charges students for violating minimum standards of behavior, he's criticized for being too strict.

He attracts grants and monies to the school and is then accused of not working within the budget allocated.

And although he refuses to judge people by their external appearances, he was criticized for being unprofessional for wearing an earring he doesn't wear.

For circumstances beyond Dr. Littky's control, he has had to repeatedly face "no-win" situations, situations we can change by simply being more aware and sensitive to the dilemmas inherent in every principal's job.

I have worked with over a dozen fantastic employers, yet none have proven to be as committed, creative, approachable, sincere, intelligent, respectful, respected, and as effective as Dr. Littky.

I only hope that we don't have to live with the paradox of realizing the value of what we have after it's gone.

Sincerely,
Jimmy Karlan
Apprenticeship Director

Nearly every member of Littky's staff wrote a letter to the board urging it to reconsider its position.

Barb Eibell:

> . . . The threat of Dr. Littky's dismissal has already created turmoil and stress among the faculty, students, and within the town. The actuality would place at risk one of the best efforts of quality education possibly in the whole country and one in which Winchester should take pride. The consequences of your proposed action would adversely affect many lives.

Don Weisburger:

> . . . I fear it would be a grave mistake to remove Dennis Littky from the position of principal of Thayer High School. His energy and leadership is a source of constant inspiration for all people involved with Thayer High School.

Terri Crowl, 1984 Thayer valedictorian:

> Dr. Littky is the best principal that Thayer High has ever had. His tendency toward innovation has changed Thayer from a lackadaisical bunch of kids who went to school under protest to a community of enthusiastic students who care about the school, their work, and each other. . . . I truly hope that the school board will rethink its position before resorting to something as final as "firing" the central spirit-instilling, unifying element of Thayer High School.

Bruce Shotland, science teacher:

> . . . Seldom in my life have I had the pleasure of working with, and getting to know a man as caring and giving of himself as Dennis Littky. . . .

Karen (Thompson) Marsh:

As a 1983 graduate of Thayer High School and now a staff
member, I have worked with Dennis Littky for 5 years as a
student and now a staff member. He is a man who believes
in what he does and he puts 100 percent in everything. I
have seen so many significant changes take place. Dennis
Littky works with his staff to make Thayer High School a
place to learn and grow. . . . I feel removing him from his
position as principal would be an awful mistake.

There were many more letters. Petitions began circulating in the community calling for the board to renew Dr.
Littky's contract.

During a quiet moment in his cabin, Dennis wrote:

Deep down I think I will win. I don't like to say it,
because I don't want to seem naive if I lose. The groundswell has been great. . . . Getting fired is out of my reality.
That is why it is hard to understand—I have no bad feelings
about myself. I know how good I am & on the other hand I
expect Secord & Co. to let me go.

It will be a different year—I will be outwardly strong
with Marcia supporting from the inside—I will fight for
our goals, our programs, money, etc.

If I win, I must figure out how to capitalize on the
groundswell—how to keep Earl [Beaman] behind us—&
others—how to make us heros—& be able to get on with our
task, use the situation to ask for things—i.e. twice yearly
progress reports of us at conferences—participation at bd
meetings—How can I be out there more with kids, with
teachers—How to get people to talk up front, not behind
backs—Why am I so committed—it just seems like my work
is not finished.

People now know we are doing good things—we must
stand up & be proud. . . .

On Monday evening, people streamed into the elementary school library early. Everyone wanted to make sure they had a seat. When the seats were full, spectators lined the walls. Along with teachers, students, and community members came the media. Television cameramen set up their hot lights. Radio reporters wandered around thrusting microphones in people's faces. Newspaper reporters milled about, talking and scribbling in their notebooks. Everyone was there for the same reason.

For nearly an hour, dozens of people spoke in favor of Littky and his programs. Teachers talked about the educational strides the school had made under Littky's tutelage. Students testified to the warmth and caring they felt at Thayer and the friend they had found in its principal. Parents pleaded with the board to keep the man who'd had such a positive impact on their children and the community. Not a single word was spoken against Dennis Littky.

Terri Racine handed her baby daughter to her mother, then raised her hand. Chairperson Bud Baker called on her. She introduced herself as the junior class president, then read in a clear, strong voice:

"We feel it is in the best interests of Thayer High School and the students for Dr. Littky to continue as principal. He is a dedicated, sincere, hard-working leader. He has started many new programs that have improved the quality of education at Thayer. He has improved the self-image of Thayer High School and its students. We do not want to lose this respect. We feel justice is not being done when a person is removed from his position without consideration given to the quality of his work."

The crowd applauded. Terri walked to the front of the room. "This petition has been signed by 173 students," she said, and handed the board the stack of papers.

The board closed the "citizen's comments" portion of the meeting and went on with its business, then broke for a closed-door session "to discuss personnel." Littky, wearing a new tweed blazer and tie, was not invited to attend. When the board returned, the room was still thick with people. All that remained for that night's business was renewing staff contracts.

Assistant Superintendent Dick McCarthy read list after list of nominations for the 1986–87 staff. The board unanimously accepted every nomination, with no discussion.

Then McCarthy read the last nomination of the night— Dennis Littky. The room went quiet. Marcia Ammann spoke, her voice cracking at times: "As an educator and as a human being, Dennis Littky is the most caring and generous person I have ever known. Before he arrived, the school was in a state of crisis. In the five years he's been principal he's influenced a lot of lives for the better and turned our school into a model for others. I've had the pleasure of working with him and watching these changes. He's the best thing that's ever happened to this town."

Marcia scanned the crowd, taking in the room full of faces. So many were her friends. But there were a few people there she wasn't sure about. She drew a deep breath, trying to steady her voice. "I move that Dennis Littky be rehired for the 1986–87 school year."

Nearly the entire crowd rose to its feet and roared its support. The applause was loud and sustained. Winter, Secord, and Barton, bunched together at one end of the long table, whispered to each other through the thunderous applause. Ammann, Baker, and McCarthy sat quietly. Littky, at the other end of the table, bit his lip trying to hold back tears.

When the crowd finally quieted, Chairperson Baker called for the vote.

"Ammann?" Baker said.

"Yes," she answered.

"Winter?"

"No."

"Secord?"

"No."

"Barton?"

"No."

The motion failed. Dennis Littky had lost his job.

Over the boos and angry voices, a man in the audience shouted loud enough for all to hear. "Impeach the board! I think it's time!"

That prompted raucous applause.

Someone else shouted at the board: "Why don't you give us some reasons for your vote? Why don't you tell us why you've done this?"

Allen Barton stood up. "I move that the meeting be adjourned," he said.

When Dennis drove into the school parking lot the next morning, a thick mist still covered the valley like a shroud. It was six o'clock. He hoisted his leather book bag over his shoulder, walked up the front steps, and unlocked the door. The building was dark and empty. He flipped on the lights. He unlocked the front office, crossed the room to his office, stepped over the bag of softballs, bats, and gloves and sat down at his desk. He dug into his backpack and pulled out his journal.

April 1: The morning after the firing—I really don't feel any different. Either it will hit me later or the battle has just begun & I just feel it is another project to get on with. Weird—

Doc closed the book, tossed it back into the leather pack, and got on with his day.

Advisory was where he heard the rumblings first.

"They're talking about walking out," Terri Racine said. "They want to protest."

Doc shook his head. "Don't do it," he said. "That would just make things tougher for me."

He decided the best way to control the situation and short-circuit any students' plans of boycotting classes was to hold an assembly. He set one up for that morning.

Students filed into the gymnasium.

"I'm behind you all the way, Doc," a senior boy said as he passed through the doors.

"We know you're the best," a young girl said.

"The school board's crazy," a boy said.

When all the students and staff had taken their seats in the bleachers, Doc walked across the gymnasium floor. By the time he got to the center, the gym was stone quiet. All eyes were upon him.

"As I'm sure most of you have heard by now, the school board didn't renew my contract last night. This doesn't mean I have to pack up and leave today. I'm still your principal, and I'm going to fight with everything I've got to stay your principal." Doc's voice cracked. He was on the verge of tears. He choked them back.

"I feel an incredible commitment to all of you. I feel an incredible commitment to the people who have worked to make things better. My time is not up here. I believe in what we've done together and where we're going. It's definitely worth fighting for. I know a lot of you are angry about the board's action and want to fight it. That makes me happy. The best way for you to fight is to be good. I've heard some students talking about walking out. I know you want to *do* something, but that won't help. If anything, that would only hurt the situation."

Standing there looking at the faces of the people who had come to mean so much to him suddenly brought home the events of the previous evening. More than ever he felt Thayer High School was where he belonged. His time wasn't up there. Come what may, he would stay and fight.

Throughout the day, teachers and students pushed letters

under his door, in his mail box, or handed them to him directly. The phone rang constantly. People stopped by.

"I'm just calling to tell you I support you."

"If there's anything I can do, count on me."

Former apprenticeship director Judy Knox flew in from Colorado when she heard the news.

A young girl in Karen Marsh's special education class stayed after school so she could hand Doc a note she'd written:

Dear Doc,

I am real sorry about last night. People just don't know you for who you are. I am sorry. I like you alot. You will alway's be in my heart and I love you for every thing you did for me and other's.

Now I have no one to look up to because you have alway's been there for me and I love you for that. I want to wish you the best of luck and I hope you are here next year. This letter is coming from my heart. You are #1 and you will alway's be #1 in every thing you do. I love you as a principal and as a friend. Thank you for everything and thank you for helping me when I have problem. I just need help. You are the best and I mean it.

22
The Fight

JON MEYER, LITTKY'S LAWYER, WAS young and capable. He had prepared his client well for the procedure they would follow if Littky did indeed lose his job.

The first order of business was the request for a public hearing before the board and a written statement from the board explaining why Littky's contract wasn't renewed. Under state law, tenured teachers could request a hearing to contest a nonrenewal. If the board reaffirmed its decision not to rehire him—and Littky fully expected it would—he planned to appeal the decision to the state board of education, then to the state supreme court if he had to.

Meanwhile, the community was up in arms, split between those who supported Littky and those who didn't. The Littky supporters were by far the most vocal contingent and the bulk of the audience at every public school function. The show of support overwhelmed Littky. Hardly a day passed that a letter didn't appear in the *Keene Sentinel* applauding Littky and condemning the board. People Dennis had never met wrote him impassioned letters of support. A group of influential people in Keene started a fund to help pay for Littky's fight against the board. But the letters that affected him most came from the kids. They were the ones who really knew how things were at school.

David Carey had been one of the boys in Don Weisburger's alternative special education class the year Karen

Thompson was an apprentice. Now he was a tenth grader.
He wrote to the *Sentinel*:

> I am a student of Thayer High School. I have lived in
> Winchester most of my life. This has been one of the best
> years of my life because of all the things Dennis Littky has
> done for the school . . . .
> I am writing this letter to ask all residents to help us win.
> I have been at Thayer High School for three years as a
> student. Dr. Littky has helped the school a lot. He has
> helped a lot of kids like me. We want Dennis Littky to be
> our principal for the next five years if possible.
> He has cleaned up the school. You do not see drugs and
> drinking around the school anymore.
> He started the apprenticeship program four years ago.
> Because of this, I am still in school.
> Why doesn't the school board ask the kids what they
> think? They haven't come in to school to see how it is run.
> The board just sits behind a desk and makes decisions
> without asking the kids.
> Thank you for reading this letter. Please help Doc win.

About twenty critics of the board formed an organization
in town called the Committee for Good Schools. The group
was made up of parents of school children, teachers, and
former school board members, people who were fed up with
the actions and behavior of the board. The group was
circulating a form letter asking Barton, Secord, and Winter
to resign. More than a hundred letters had been signed thus
far. The plan was to collect signatures from as many registered voters as possible and forward the letters to the state
education commissioner.

The letter charged that the three board members had
"disregarded their responsibility to serve the will of the
majority; they have failed to communicate reasons for their
actions; they have embarrassed the community by acting in

a rash and unjust manner. I feel that these actions will jeopardize the educational process currently taking place in our school and will have adverse effect on our children."

But not everyone joined the bandwagon of support. On the night Littky was fired, a small coterie of people left the elementary school satisfied with the actions of the board. Ernie Royce was among them.

The article in the *Sentinel* made him mad. It made it sound as though the entire crowd was against the board. He called the paper to complain. The reporter urged Royce to state his side of the issue.

"Why didn't you or anyone else who's against Littky speak up at the public meeting?" the reporter asked.

"We didn't think it was the place or time to say anything," Royce said. "It would have been like throwing a hunk of raw meat into a cage of hungry lions. We don't want to say anything they can use against us. We're rounding up facts. . . . We've got plenty of facts and figures that support the board's decision."

Royce said that thirty to forty people were "actively participating day to day" in the effort to build a case against Littky, and fifty to sixty more were willing to help as well if called upon. He said he would get in contact with some of his ranks to see if they were willing to talk to the press.

When the reporter called him back, Royce had backed off a bit. He said his people—a group he called The Silent Majority—wanted to remain true to the name . . . silent.

"When you are at odds with the black dirt of psychology," he said, "you don't lay out your cards until you're ready to rake in the pot." They wouldn't "show their hand" unless the matter went to court.

"When you play with a person of his caliber, you have to be careful. He's a very smart man," Royce said. "He knows why he's being terminated, and it has nothing to do with his looks. It has to do with his philosophy. There is a philosophical difference between the education we would like and what that man is teaching."

When the reporter urged Royce to elaborate on those philosophical differences, he said he'd encountered Thayer students who tried to get a job at his store who were unable to spell the name of the town in which they lived.

"Do you feel Littky's methods of education are responsible for that?" the reporter asked.

"Look," he said. "There's no sense in me publicly defending our position now. It could jeopardize the court case. If it goes to court, you'll find out then."

Marilyn Nolan, however, wasn't much interested in waiting until the matter went to court to air her opinions about Littky. In a letter to the *Sentinel*, she wrote:

> . . . Dr. Littky is a clinical psychologist, and talks one hell of a game, but my considerable amount of research, facts, pertinent data and personal experience with the whole matter paints a different picture indeed.
>
> . . . In my opinion, I feel that one trained in the science of using a person's feelings, thoughts, actions, traits, etc., in order to achieve positive results, then the use of a person's feelings, thoughts, desires, etc., can be used to achieve negative and manipulative results.
>
> . . . We must remember that the students and teachers at Thayer Junior/Senior High School are also under an untried, unproven, experimental process of learning, thereby must be defined as "guinea pigs." How, then, should Thayer be defined? A laboratory? For one man?
>
> Those of us who started having valid reasons to question curriculum, personnel and lack of policy in September '85 found that our concerns were steadily increasing. . . . We conducted a campaign based on fact, truth and honesty, and the rest is history as of March '85. . . .

Littky was dumbfounded by the opposition to him. People had opposed him in the past, but they'd never been secretive about the reasons. After open dialogue and compelling success stories, the scales tipped in his favor. Many of those who vocally opposed him became some of his strongest allies.

But Winchester was different. The behavior of the Barton-Secord-Winter coalition was an enigma. Barton had never really talked to him. Why was he so against him? Winter had at first struck him as reasonable and levelheaded. Her eldest daughter seemed to thrive in the Thayer system, plus she landed a job at a Keene insurance company as a consequence of her apprenticeship. That should have served to make a case in his favor. But not only was Susan Winter against *him*, he also knew that she was against the apprenticeship program.

Then there was Bobby Secord. He'd been a skeptic, but he'd seemed to Littky like a man who would listen to reason. True, he'd spoken against Dovetail and the Two-Week Project. But differing points of view on a board were healthy. The one time when Littky confronted Secord about his alleged dislike of him, Secord had waved him off. It wasn't anything personal, he'd insisted. It was philosophical.

What about Gutoski? What about that gold earring business? The comment had come from so far out in left field that it seemed almost laughable to Littky at the time. On the other hand, it did speak volumes. At least for Gutoski, the issue *was* one of appearances. Dennis Littky was unprofessional because he didn't look right.

Littky thought the two were somehow tied together. Maybe they assumed he had a philosophy they found odious because of the way he looked. That got him thinking—

Some incidents in his past began to make sense, incidents he'd tried to let roll off his back and forget. Considered by themselves, they didn't amount to all that much, but collectively . . . maybe they could shed some light on his firing.

He remembered the Alexander Ginsberg incident. His former guidance counselor had a friend who was Ginsberg's interpreter. Three years ago, the interpreter persuaded Ginsberg, a Soviet dissident, to come to Thayer High School and speak about his life as a writer in the Soviet Union and why he had defected to this country. Thayer High School hosted the lecture, also attended by several hundred students from area high schools.

Afterward, Littky learned that Don Hubbard, owner of Don's Barber Shop, was bad-mouthing him as "a commie" for inviting "that commie" to town. When Littky heard that, his anger flared—nothing bothered him more than name-calling behind his back. He phoned Hubbard.

"I heard you called me a communist," Littky said. "First of all, if you're going to say things about me, say them to my face. Secondly, if you bothered to look into the situation, you'd find out Ginsberg's just the opposite of a communist. The man fled a communist country!"

Shortly after that incident, a Thayer student came up to him and said, "My mom says you're a spy for Cuba. She says you went to Cuba the first year you lived here."

Then there was the article that ran in *Yankee Magazine* in October 1983. In the eyes of many townspeople, the article had done a good job of making the town look backward and pathetic, while making Dennis Littky look like a hero.

> It was one of the poorest schools in New Hampshire. Its dropout rate was staggering. "Can't spell? You must have gone to Thayer School," was often repeated over the years. Then along came an amazing, bearded, casually dressed individual with some ideas about "education appropriate to the circumstance of rural poverty. . . ."

Longtime Winchester residents took the criticism very personally. Former Thayer High School Principal McNamara saw it as an attack on his administration. Other town officials responded the same way. Marcia found herself implicated in the whole thing because of her association with Dennis and was prompted to write a letter to him.

> The *Yankee* article and its weird effect on this town burned us badly. It's the one single event that turned the tide against us. It burned me in the sense that I've had to stand up for us and what we're doing against everyone who's been close to me all my life. I've severed some ties, put some friendships on the back burner, and avoided family who disagree with us. I've never been treated coldly by this town before, never had to take a stand against them. Sensitive soul that I am, that's been hard for me, and I despise any situation where someone has to win and someone has to lose.

Marilyn Nolan asked Cindy Nelson to come over to her house so she could show her "the evidence" she had pulled together about Littky's "master plan." Cindy brought Marcia Ammann with her.

Nolan had sat at her dining room table pulling out papers and files she had accumulated to prove her case against Dennis Littky. The files were neatly organized, taking up a sizable portion of her dining room.

"He's using you," Marilyn insisted. "He's brainwashed you into thinking he's the greatest and we're just a bunch of illiterate fools."

Marcia had eyed the stack of manilla folders in front of Marilyn Nolan. Her evidence, Marcia figured. Marilyn Nolan had kept talking, ranting about the inferior quality of Thayer's teachers and about the immorality Littky was teaching Winchester's children.

Marcia was hot and getting hotter. This woman was distorting everything the school and Dennis were about. Then Marilyn produced her first piece of evidence: it was an assignment by one of Thayer's English teachers that Marilyn said was fraught with errors. Marcia glanced at the assignment and saw two typographical errors. Suddenly Marcia's anger ignited. She threw her keys on Marilyn Nolan's dining room table. "That's enough!" Marcia shouted.

Cindy quickly reached over and grabbed Marcia's elbow. "Wait a second here, Marcia," she said, trying desperately to calm her friend. Cindy didn't want to leave Marilyn Nolan's house angry and defensive. Above all, she didn't want Marilyn Nolan to think she'd won. Marcia calmed down, but she remained standing. After a few minutes, she and Cindy left.

In April, Littky had received a particularly snide letter from a woman in town, who condemned Littky for making himself look good at the town's expense. "I told you some day that 'silent majority' would stand up and be heard. They have done just that, haven't they? . . . "

Did Marilyn Nolan and this letter writer speak for the town? He wondered. . . .

Littky planned to challenge the board's actions against him at a public hearing on April 21. But a key issue remained unresolved.

New Hampshire law required schools to notify teachers who had been on staff for more than three years if their contract wasn't being renewed. A teacher was then allowed to request a hearing, seeking reasons for the decision. The question was did the law apply also to principals? The issue had never been tested in court.

Meanwhile, the school board hired an attorney through the New Hampshire School Boards Association. The board planned to meet at the lawyer's Laconia office to discuss the Littky case on April 15.

The next day, Littky's lawyer received six reasons in writing, explaining the nonrenewal.

- He allows for a degree of familiarity with students that is inappropriate.

- He fails to interpret properly and enforce a dress code and other regulations.
- He permits student behavior that disrupts the learning process.
- He fails to remain in control over the high school building and its grounds.
- He exhibits a philosophy of management that is inconsistent with that of the board's.
- He fails to project the leadership image that the board feels is necessary.

When Littky saw the reasons, he had to laugh. All the areas listed, he considered his strengths. The hearing was the following Monday. He figured he'd have little trouble defending himself.

The board's response to Terri Racine's project early that school year was the first indication Jimmy Karlan had that the board questioned the merits of the apprenticeship program. But when his name was not on the list of teacher candidates at the March 31 meeting, he knew the future of the *whole* program was in doubt. Karlan repeatedly extended invitations to the board to visit the school and observe the program firsthand.

None of the board members came.

Instead, he received a letter from Assistant Superintendent McCarthy saying he wasn't renominated because the board wanted the program reviewed.

Since the board members would not observe the program first hand, Karlan decided he would bring the program to the board. He sent letters to apprentices' parents, site supervisors, and Thayer graduates informing them of the precarious future of the program and urging them to lend their support.

The response was overwhelmingly positive for both the

program and its director. The school board was inundated with letters.

"I have been impressed with Thayer High's singular efforts to acquaint students with what goes on in the real world. No other school in southwestern New Hampshire has anything like the apprenticeship program, and I believe it is to their detriment," wrote the executive editor of the *Sentinel*.

The director of the New Hampshire Department of Health and Human Services' Office of Alcohol and Drug Abuse Prevention wrote: "The fact that other school districts within New Hampshire are requesting information in order to replicate the program certainly speaks to the vision and forethought of project planners within the school. We applaud you all."

A letter signed by ninety-nine Thayer students concluded: "The apprenticeship program is allowing us to explore different fields and opportunities. If school isn't the place to help us decide on our future, then what is?"

Karlan would give a presentation to the board on Thursday, April 17, just four days before Littky's hearing. In anticipation, he wrote a letter to the board summarizing the program and providing pertinent information.

> ... This year there are two freshmen who are involved in the Apprenticeship Program. As a result of serious behavioral and motivational problems in one of their classes, an apprenticeship was arranged, only after lengthy discussion with and approval by the classroom teacher, guidance counselor, principal, and parents. Both of these apprentices are doing excellently on-site. It is my understanding, as expressed to me by these students and one of their parents, that without their apprenticeship experience, they would have undoubtedly dropped out of high school.

On Thursday evening, the elementary school library was

once again filled to capacity. Karlan arrived with a two-page agenda of his own. He gave a brief description of the program, then went through the long list of requirements for participation—the résumé, interviews, tests, papers, and so on. He said that ten out of the fourteen seniors currently enrolled in the program had been accepted at colleges or technical schools for next fall, and nine of those ten planned to pursue fields directly related to their apprenticeships. Three other apprentices had been offered jobs, two of them by their apprenticeship supervisors.

In all, thirty-five students and former students, parents, and site supervisors were listed on the agenda by name. Each spoke about the merits of the program. Students talked about assisting nurses, teachers, auto mechanics, beauticians, business owners, bankers, and writers.

Thayer graduate Rick Durkee emphasized the direct influence his apprenticeship had on his career. "My apprenticeship was as the physical education teacher at the Winchester Elementary School. Not as an assistant, not as an aide, but as the only physical education teacher they had. The major factor in making my decision to attend Keene State College as a physical education student was the apprenticeship program. . . . If you are an employer, what is the thing you look for most? Either experience or education, and the apprenticeship program is both. It is an educational experience."

Karen Thompson spoke about how her experience teaching second graders and working in offices at school and at the leather factory taught her that these were not careers she was interested in pursuing. Then she described her year as a teacher's aide in the self-contained classroom with learning-disabled and emotionally disturbed boys. She told the crowd about the award for outstanding teacher team she and Don Weisburger had won her senior year, about the job she secured with the regional special education program in

Keene as a direct consequence of her apprenticeship experience, and about her return to Thayer as a staff member.

"I often wonder," she said, "where my future would have gone if the program had not existed. Without it I am convinced that many students would not have the career opportunities that they have now."

Karlan had simply invited the community to come and speak about the program; what people said was left up to them. Of the more than thirty-five presentations given, not a single negative word was spoken about the program.

The board members asked no questions and took no action.

That, however, wasn't their disposition when they voted on Dennis Littky's contract. Susan Winter, bow tied at her neck, sitting bolt upright in her chair, made a motion. "I move," she said, "that Dennis Littky be offered a teaching contract in a position for which he is qualified."

A loud stir ripped through the audience. The motion caught everyone off guard. Neither Marcia nor the chairperson knew it was coming.

A man shouted: "You mean to tell me that man is not fit to be our principal, but you would allow him to teach classes?"

"A point of order," Allen Barton said. "This is still a meeting of the board. I won't vote until I'm sure there will be no interruptions from the audience."

The man shot back: "We wouldn't want the public in on it, would we?"

The contract offer was for $19,600. Littky, who was certified to teach elementary school, had never taught at that level before, other than during his stint working with elementary school students at Ocean Hill–Brownsville. He didn't even consider the offer.

The reason for the board's surprise reversal soon became obvious. If the board offered Littky a job in the district, it wouldn't have to hold the public hearing and would effectively remove Littky from the principalship.

The board had successfully blocked the hearing just four days before it was to be held.

The following Wednesday, the Committee for Good Schools met. Getting rid of the school board's anti-Littky majority was the main item on the agenda.

The committee hoped that public pressure would prompt the resignations of Barton, Secord, and Winter and had already collected nearly two hundred signed letters. If that didn't work, the committee planned to organize a special school district meeting to enlarge the board from five to seven members. The increase would effectively dilute the majority stronghold. The eighty-five people who attended the meeting were more than the 5 percent needed to call such a meeting. The group also discussed the possibility of filing a class action suit against the board.

On April 27, the *New York Times* ran a story about Littky and Winchester. Marilyn Nolan and Elmer Johnson were quoted as voices from the anti-Littky crowd.

"What we're worried about is all the waste of time on cockamamy things—film reviews, no study periods," Nolan said. "They would give you an A-plus for content but don't care if you can spell. Some of us are pretty upset."

Elmer Johnson's remarks concerned Littky the most.

"He's one of these liberal educators teaching all kinds of sex education, spending more time talking about dope addiction and things like that. He's got a lot of new ideas. He keeps wanting to send some of the kids to those expensive special schools for the emotionally disabled," Johnson said. "Discipline's way down. We finally got a conservative school board in there to call a halt to what he's done. Only he kept right on doing it. He looks and acts like a tramp.

You know, as far as the kids are concerned, the ones he says are emotionally unstable, all they need is a good kick in the butt. That special education is costing Winchester too much money." Johnson would later deny making those remarks.

The article triggered more national media attention. "MacNeil-Lehrer Newshour," NBC's "Today" show, CBS's "West 57th," *Newsweek* and *Time* magazine were all on the phone to Winchester. Producers of the "Today" show planned a segment about Littky, but had to cancel it because no one could be found to present arguments against him. The producers tried to reach Elmer Johnson, but he never called them back. "I've got other things to do. I've got to tend to my crops and so forth," Elmer told the *Sentinel*.

The media attention set off a ripple effect of criticism from the anti-Littky people.

"Littky's grandstanding."

"He's more interested in personal publicity than education for the children of Winchester."

"He's turned the school into a circus!"

The publicity *was* distracting. It did intrude on education at Thayer. When "MacNeil-Lehrer" asked for access to the school for its film crews, Littky said no.

Marilyn Nolan, meanwhile, sent out another hot letter to the editor:

My, how the plot does thicken as the fires of rejection are fanned anew with the bellows of ignorance and the fuel of revenge.

This whole mess threatens to be likened to a "shootout at the O.K. Corral" right here in downtown Winchester, N.H. 03470.

The battle lines have been drawn and sides have been chosen as yet another group has been formed in the name of "concern for good education." Of course, we all know that this meeting of the minds, held at the town hall on a recent Wednesday, was to gain support for Littky and to enlist more help to get rid of the three "notorious varmints" on the school board who dared to shoot the saddle out from under the leader of the pack. Wanted posters were placed around town announcing the date and place of the meeting under the headline, "Keep Dr. Littky as principal."

Now, the "generals" are former school board members who hired Dr. Littky and made sure that every wish and desire was a command. They are also responsible for the large deficit, over-crowded classrooms at the elementary school, and many other problems which they have accused the present board of. . . .

The "troops" are loyal Littky fans and parents of students who have benefited so wonderfully under Littky's regime and/or been made happy by his methods and experiments. . . .

The "chief of stuff" is very busy writing his press releases, inviting various film and magazine producers, and keeping the propaganda machine well oiled.

Meanwhile, back at the fort, we of the "cavalry" play a waiting game . . .

Isn't it a fact that the whines of war began last March because the new board refused to become a "puppet board" whose strings would be pulled by one manipulator? . . .

Littky didn't have a chance to resign? Littky shot down in cold blood for the way he dresses, after dressing the same way for years? If anyone believes these tales, I will start taking bids on a few bridges for sale next week.

The best is yet to come, folks. Wait until court time arrives!

Dennis had no recourse other than the court system. On April 31, Dennis Littky sued the Winchester School District for violating his constitutional rights.

The suit, filed in Cheshire County Superior Court, requested a hearing to allow Littky to challenge the board's stated reasons for not renewing his contract. It also sought a temporary injunction that would allow Littky to continue as principal for the next year and put a stop to the board's search for his replacement.

Littky's attorney, Jon Meyer, made three claims on his behalf:

- Littky's rights were violated when the board attempted to circumvent state law by offering him a teaching position to prevent the hearing. Nominating Littky as a teacher was not done because the board was looking for a teacher to fill a specific position, but because it wanted to get rid of him as a principal. Meyer contended that there was no educational justification for seeking a teacher.
- The board circulated charges against Littky at a time when he was expecting a public hearing, but then didn't give him an opportunity to defend his reputation as an educator.
- The board "invaded the prerogative of the superintendent" when it made the motion to nominate Littky for a teaching position in the district. Only the superintendent can make nominations; the board confirms and elects.

The *Sentinel* contacted the school board's attorney, Bradley Kidder, informing him of the lawsuit. The lawyer verbally countered each of the claims, saying that the state law that permits a hearing applied only to teachers and not to administrators. While he conceded that superintendents make nominations and the board elects candidates, in this case the board only changed Littky's assignment, "which is its right to do."

Once again, the library of the elementary school was full at the next board meeting. Once again, Barton, Secord, and Winter sat at one end of the table at the front of the room— the two men in suits and ties and Winter in a tailored suit with the usual bow. Next to them sat Marcia Ammann in a turtleneck and Bud Baker in his shirt sleeves.

The meeting was called to order.

Lisa Healey, a petite senior, raised her hand. Baker nodded to her and she stood. She cleared her throat and gripped tightly the paper she held in her hands to keep them from trembling. Reading from the paper, she addressed the school board: "If you feel Dr. Littky is too familiar with the students, how could you give him less responsibility and more contact with students by making him a teacher?"

"Would you pose that question without reading it?" Barton said.

Lisa swallowed hard, glancing at the paper, quickly trying to rephrase the question. "If Dr. Littky is too familiar—"

"I won't listen unless you pose the question without reading," Barton repeated.

"Answer her question," shouted someone in the audience.

"Why are you bullying her?"

The girl faltered, then put the paper down. Carefully, quietly, she reframed the question.

"I'm not sure you're in a position to evaluate," he said and turned his attention away.

Jack Ainsworth, chairperson of the Committee for Good Schools, raised his hand and stood. "Three members of this board—Mr. Barton, Mr. Secord, and Mrs. Winter—have embarrassed Winchester by acting in a rash and unjust manner. There are 428 letters here seeking your resignations," he said waving a handful of papers. "We think this represents a community mandate for your resignations."

He marched to the front of the room and deposited the letters in front of chairperson Bud Baker.

In his typical quiet and restrained manner, Bud Baker did something very atypical. He insisted that Barton, Secord, and Winter respond individually to the public mandate. "As responsible school board members," he said, "you should respond individually. We are elected by the people. We should be answerable. If we do not respond we are not doing our job. We cannot just sit here and hide in the closet. We can not just turn around and say, 'No comment.' "

The board and crowd were quiet. None of the board members said anything. Finally Baker spoke again. "Al," he said, looking at Barton, "would you comment?"

Barton grinned. "Not at this time," he said. "I need time to think about it."

The crowd responded to Barton with jeers.

Barton stared at the crowd. Then he spoke. For the next half hour, Barton delivered a wandering monologue in which he criticized the state of education in the United States, never once mentioning Littky's name.

He said that "teaching" is the major failure of education today. As a faculty member at Springfield [Massachusetts] Technical College, he said, he spent half his time teaching freshmen things they should have learned in high school. "They can't read, they can't write, they can't spell. They can't do ordinary arithmetic," he said. "These are the things that make for good students later on, instead of learning to play with computers. This doesn't teach anybody anything." Computers, he said, were just a fad.

Toward the end, he got specific about Thayer. "At next month's meeting, the school board should scrap Thayer's current teaching program and return to a core curriculum," he said. "I think we've already taken the first step. There should be more to follow."

Susan Winter spoke next. She also said the high school should "go back to the basics of reading, writing, and arithmetic." She said that in her work at First Northern Bank in Keene, "I talk to several businesspeople where some of our finished products go. They have some comments to make." She didn't elaborate.

Secord was brief. "There are 1,600 people in this town, and I represent the majority. I would not care to comment."

Then Susan Winter leaned forward in her chair and

pointed a sharp finger at Bud Baker. "I think it's about time you take a stand," she said. "You've been a fence sitter long enough."

The audience shouted at Baker to take a stand.

Baker prevaricated. "As chairman, I remain neutral except in the event of a tie."

The audience wasn't satisfied with his response.

"C'mon, state your position!"

Finally Baker answered. "I don't see anything wrong with the way the system is at the present time. I think all we're doing is jeopardizing the students by taking away an outstanding program that has been nationally recognized." Baker was critical of the three board members who voted against Littky and said he was disturbed by the thousands of dollars being spent in legal fees on the case.

On the Sunday before Littky would appear in court to fight for his job, he received an honorary degree from Franklin Pierce College for his accomplishments as an educator. He was the featured speaker at the college's baccalaureate.

"In the past forty-one days, I've read about my struggle in various newspapers twenty-seven times. I think the reason for this obsessive coverage by local and national media is due to the few individuals who are daring enough to defy the power structure in defense of personal values.

"I'm a winner because I'm fighting for what I think is right in education. Don't ever back down if you believe in something. If it's worth believing in, it's worth fighting for."

23
The Court Case

SUSAN WINTER STOOD IN FRONT of the bailiff in her blue suit, white blouse, red bow, and red, white, and blue shoes. Her close-cropped hairdo allowed for no strand out of place. Her makeup was Mary Kay perfect—rose-petal pink blush, two thin lines of lipstick, a generous sweep of blue over each eye. She placed one hand on the Bible, raised the other stiff at her shoulder, and swore she would tell the truth, the whole truth, and nothing but the truth. Then she sat down ramrod straight in the witness chair.

Jon Meyer, Littky's attorney—boyish, methodical, with an odd, even disconcerting, habit of punctuating his sentences by raising and lowering his dark eyebrows—questioned Susan Winter, his witness. The case was being heard by a single superior court judge at the Cheshire County courthouse in Keene. After all the evidence was submitted, Judge George Manias would decide whether Littky's constitutional rights had been denied him by the school board. After a few opening questions, Meyer began his attack.

Winter had just told the court that she believed both the superintendent and the school board should evaluate the principal. "I personally think it should be done every six months," she said.

"Should the evaluation be done in writing?" Meyer asked.

"Yes," she said.

"Why wasn't it done, then?"

"We've had other things to tackle."

"You never thought it would be a good thing to tackle before you voted for nonrenewal?" Meyer said, raising and lowering his brows.

"No."

"Until the board changes a policy, are you obligated to follow it?"

"It can be changed at any time."

"But *until* it is changed?"

"Yes, I would follow it," she said.

Meyer showed her the code of ethics in the policy manual and asked if she agreed with it. Winter said she did.

"According to this code, isn't it the duty of the superintendent to assign all personnel?"

Winter looked uneasy. "In most cases," she said.

"Doesn't section F, page 11, make the superintendent responsible for assignment of personnel?"

"Yes."

"Without exception?"

"Yes."

Fact of the matter was, Barton, Secord, and Winter had voted to reassign Littky to an elementary school teaching position without so much as mentioning it to the superintendent.

Meyer turned to the statement of goals that Littky and his staff put together in 1985. Winter agreed that the board unanimously approved them, that no corrections were made then or since, and that there was nothing in the statement she disagreed with.

"Have you ever seen the evaluations of Dr. Littky by Mr. Sundstrom?" Meyer asked, referring to Superintendent Roger Sundstrom's written reviews of Littky's administrative abilities. Sundstrom had testified on the first day of the court hearing that Littky deserved "the very highest recommendation."

"No," Winter said.

"On April 17, you found out that no evaluation of Dr. Littky had been done this year?"

"Yes," Winter replied.

"Shouldn't you have asked for an evaluation prior to voting for nonrenewal, or asked to see prior evaluations?"

"No," Winter said.

"So the evaluations of Dr. Littky wouldn't make any difference to you, one way or another?"

"What I have viewed of Dr. Littky's performance I'm certainly not pleased with," Winter said.

"It didn't matter what was in the evaluation; you would have voted for nonrenewal no matter what?"

"Yes, I would have," she said.

On the first day of testimony, Jim Burke, one of the school board's lawyers, had questioned Littky about a series of excerpts from the TGIF memos. Burke, tall and hulking, was an aggressive, caustic man who could deliver a line like "Have a nice day" as though he were pronouncing a death sentence.

"Do you review all contributions written by faculty for TGIFs prior to publication?" Burke questioned Littky.

"I usually see them, but not always," Littky said.

Burke had pointed to a passage that referred to two teachers as "Vince and Tuna."

"Vince is a teacher, Vincent Tom, and Tuna is a nickname for Barbara Toner," Littky explained.

Burke cited other passages. " 'I feel it is my main job to help each of you grow more and more,' " he read from a memo. " 'But if you feel that I am pressing you too hard, you should feel free to tell me to back off.' "

"Sharing feelings is how we try to build trust," Littky said.

Burke flipped through some more pages. "What is meant

by 'our great change this year?' " he asked referring to another passage.

"Faculty efforts to get kids to be critical thinkers and independent learners," Littky said.

Littky was baffled. Burke sounded like he was accusing him of something, yet Littky saw every passage cited as evidence of the good education taking place at Thayer.

Burke pointed to a memo written by Jimmy Karlan shortly after returning from a conference in Toronto, called Controversial Issues in Moral Education.

"Here's a potential moral dilemma that we may all face one day soon," Karlan had written. "The school board learns that one of our untenured staff members is a homosexual. They take measures to fire this individual because of his homosexuality. Irrespective of their legal grounds, this individual is fired. . . . The staff is considering walking out in support of this teacher. . . . What would you do and why?"

"Did you try to edit this piece?" Burke barked.

"No, I don't do that," Littky said.

"Do you adopt an attitude of 'anything goes?' "

"I do not edit my teachers' work unless it would be damaging to someone in the school. I would edit anything I felt was harmful to the school."

"You don't feel that was?"

"No," Littky said, and explained that the question was one Karlan carried back with him from the workshop. It was hypothetical. Its purpose was to challenge the staff.

Meyer asked Susan Winter if she'd seen Littky's thesis (she hadn't) or the TGIF memos (she had).

"Where did you get them?" Meyer asked.

"Mrs. Nolan," Winter said.

Marilyn Nolan had dug into her vast files and supplied the defense with a good deal of ts material. She had spent a

stunning amount of time, energy, and money stirring together a pot of "incriminating evidence" against Littky.
Her letters to the *Sentinel* had been her main outlet up until
then. Now, through the board and its attorneys, she
planned to show everybody the "obscenities" that Littky
permitted.

"Do you know what Dr. Littky's position is on basic
skills?" Meyer asked.

"He wants to stick to the basics," Winter said.

"Do you share his concern for the basics?"

"Yes," Winter said.

"What about increasing graduation requirements?"

"I support that," Winter said.

"Is that a liberal or a conservative idea?" Meyer asked.

"It's good education," Winter said.

"What about Dr. Littky adding writing, library skills,
and advanced courses?"

"It's good education," Winter said.

"Isn't that what's at stake here, just good educational
practices?"

"Yes," Winter said. "But school board policies need to be
followed."

"Are there any curriculum or other board policies which
Dr. Littky is not following?" Meyer asked.

"No," Winter said, shifting in her seat.

Meyer reviewed Littky's claims of reducing the number of
Thayer dropouts and increasing the number going on to
college.

"Do you dispute that?" Meyer asked.

"No," Winter said. "But the students who go on to college, I would like to know how many actually make it
through."

"Is enrolling in college a step in the right direction?"

"Yes," Winter said.

"Dr. Littky has made positive improvements at Thayer?"

"Yes, I would have to agree with that."

"Yet you voted for nonrenewal of his contract?"

"Yes," Winter said.

"Did you give any reasons at that time?"

"No."

"Dr. Littky asked for a hearing and a list of reasons for nonrenewal?"

"Yes."

"Did the board make a decision on his requests?"

"We talked with our counsel and made a list of reasons."

"On the advice of counsel, you decided to grant him a hearing?"

"No," Winter said. "Mr. Baker told the board we had to grant Dr. Littky a hearing."

"So the board decided to grant a hearing?"

"Only on Mr. Baker's say-so."

"*Was* the decision made?"

"Yes."

"Who made it?"

"Mr. Baker."

"And the others went along?"

"Yes."

"After your counsel had been contacted?"

"Yes."

"Two and a half weeks after you had voted to nonrenew Dr. Littky's contract, you rescinded that vote?"

"Yes."

"What was it in two and a half weeks which led you to change a decision you were so firm in?"

"We didn't know Dr. Littky had a teaching certificate."

"What role did your counsel have—why did you change your decision?"

"We learned we could transfer him."

"So it was your counsel who suggested the transfer?"

"Yes."

"Did you know anything about his elementary teaching experience?"

"Only now I do, from previous testimony."

"Does the fact that he has no elementary teaching experience make any difference?"

"Not as long as he is certified."

"Do you care anything about a teacher's experience?" Meyer asked. "Isn't that the first thing you check out about candidates, whether or not they've ever taught?"

"Yes."

"Has the board ever selected someone for a teaching position who wasn't experienced?"

"Not to my knowledge."

Perhaps for the first time since Winter's election to the board, her ice-woman demeanor was cracking just a bit.

"Who drafted the reasons given to Dr. Littky for his nonrenewal?"

"Mr. Secord and I did after talking with our counsel."

Meyer turned to the reasons, focusing first on the claim that Littky allowed for an "inappropriate level of familiarity with students."

"I don't like students calling professional people by their first name," Winter said. She said she'd attended basketball games and other school functions where Littky was called "Doc" and "Dennis."

"I consider that not professional," she said.

When Meyer questioned her, she could give no further basis for the complaint.

"Have you ever told Dr. Littky or asked Mr. McCarthy to tell him that you found it inappropriate for students to call him by his first name?"

"No."

"Yet you have no qualms about assigning him to teach at the elementary school?"

"I would just like to see Dr. Littky reassigned."

Meyer ended his examination of Winter after establishing that she could not recall any disagreements with Littky on academic matters, that Littky had reported regularly to the board, and that there were no problems with his reports.

Meyer's next witness was Bobby Secord. He handled him much the same as Winter.

"I've never seen evaluations of Dr. Littky. I never asked to see them," Secord said, answering Meyer's litany of questions much the same as Winter had.

On the issue of Littky's "familiarity" with students, Secord said, "I don't feel Dr. Littky handles himself the way he should at school sports programs. As principal, he should be the most respected person in town." Then Secord gave his example.

The girls softball team, which Littky coached, had just finished a game at Hinsdale High, and the boys game was beginning. Littky came over to watch.

"This man," Secord said, meaning Littky, "this man comes over and sprawls himself on a dirt pile."

"He sprawled out on a dirt pile," Meyer said, carefully enunciating each word.

"All sprawled out by himself," Secord said. "In view of half the town."

"Was the problem the dirt pile or the sprawling?" Meyer asked. "Would it have been okay if he had sprawled on the grass?"

"It was the dirt pile," Secord said. "I don't mind if he sits on the grass or the bleachers. I don't believe he conducts himself as a principal ought to."

There were rumblings in the audience.

Secord shifted in his seat and smoothed his red, white, and blue tie.

"So your underlying concern is that the principal be respected in the town," Meyer said.

Secord agreed.

"Isn't it true that Dr. Littky is widely respected in town?" Secord disagreed.

"After you voted not to renew his contract, how many petitions were presented asking you to resign?" Meyer asked.

"About four hundred," Secord said.

"Isn't it true that at the most recent school board election the total number of voters was five hundred?"

"I'm not sure," Secord said.

Meyer continued down the list of reasons. The last of the six was "He fails to project a leadership image that the board feels is necessary."

Secord again responded that Littky didn't act with enough dignity at sports events.

"Is there anything else?" Meyer asked, raising his eyebrows.

"Not that I can think of right now."

On the third day of testimony, the court room was again full. Many of the spectators wore black-and-white "We support Dr. Littky" buttons. One man in the audience fingered a glossy newsletter titled *The Phyllis Schlafly Report* that warned parents to watch out for "anti-parent" and "anti-religion" material in their local schools: "Is it anti-parent? Does it lead the child to believe that parents are ignorant, old-fashioned, or out of touch with the modern world? Does it suggest that the child not tell his parent what is taught in class? . . . Does it produce fear and despair in the child, instead of faith in his family and country, and hope in the future?"

On the back of the newsletter was an open letter to parents. In it Schlafly imagined a public school called Basic Fundamentals School where "parents are treated with friendliness, not hostility," and "the school is characterized by orderly classrooms, discipline, a strict dress code, and mandatory homework." This was the school of Marilyn Nolan's and Ernie Royce's dreams.

Barton took his seat and Meyer began. Again, Meyer went through the string of questions he had asked Winter and Secord.

"We haven't really been concerned with evaluation," Barton said. "To be honest with you, I didn't really know there had ever been any done."

On the statement of Thayer goals and philosophy, Barton said, "I don't remember how I personally voted."

"Was it approved by the board?" Meyer asked.

"Probably," Barton said.

"Does this mean that the goals and philosophy reflect the board's goals and philosophy for Thayer?"

"I suppose one may make that judgment based on the board's vote."

"Is there anything in that document you object to?" Meyer asked.

"Probably most of it," Barton said.

Meyer asked him to identify the parts he objected to.

"To give a proper answer," Barton said. "I have to talk in generalities, and my basic difference of opinion goes back to the philosophy of the educational process."

"The document emphasizes basic skills," Meyer said. "Do you share that emphasis?"

"I share the words. How one defines basic skills is the issue."

"Where is it that your definition of basic skills differs?" Meyer asked.

"It's a matter of judgment, of experience. The question is how do you achieve these things," Barton said.

"Dr. Littky increased graduation requirements. Do you agree or disagree with this?"

"It's a matter of semantics. What constitutes requirements?"

"Dr. Littky introduced an advanced biology course. Do you have a problem with that?"

"I have no problem as far as the words go—it's the achievement of competency that concerns me."

"What would you do?" Meyer asked.

"Change the administration. Change the curriculum and the policy of learning."

"What policy of learning would you change?" Meyer asked.

"There's no short answer," Barton said. "My concern is with quality education, a concern that's shared nationwide in the media, in business, in the NEA even. Everybody says the words, everyone wants to hear 'innovation,' thinks innovation means progress. I want students to be competent in whatever field they seek—in reading, writing, arithmetic, the old-fashioned goals. This is what concerns me. They put it in more flowery language. The modern secondary education system doesn't work."

Meyer raised his eyebrows. "Do you recall the question?"

"No," Barton said. "You'd better repeat it."

The question was repeated. Barton replied, "The philosophy is the method of achievement. I agree with the words."

"Isn't this statement a blueprint for good education?"

"In semantic form," Barton said.

"What other form is there?"

"I would write it differently," Barton said.

"I'm asking you to be specific in terms of Thayer," Meyer said.

"I disagree," Barton replied. "This case is concerned with the philosophy of the modern educational system."

"You're saying that what's on trial here is not Dr. Littky and Thayer High, but modern education?"

"I am certainly not carrying out a personal vendetta."

"How do you know what Dr. Littky's philosophy is?" Meyer asked.

"I know it from how the school operates and from what he's written."

"From what that he's written?" Meyer asked.

"From this document," Barton said, referring to the statement of goals. "Also from his thesis."

"When did you read his thesis?"

"I don't know—two or three weeks ago."

"After you voted to nonrenew him?"

"Yes," Barton said.

"So you read his thesis, written in 1969, but you never read his evaluations?"

"I am aware of Mr. Littky's background and of those in the educational establishment. My judgment is not based on any short-term decision."

"Do you have any problems with Dr. Littky's background?"

"These questions will not make me any friends. Everyone is entitled to his way of life. My feelings regarding education are not the result of a snap decision."

"Do you recall my question?"

"No," Barton said.

Meyer repeated the question.

"That's his problem," Barton said. "It's very complex. The problem is in the college departments of education which train teachers. It's also a problem for teacher unions—they recognize this shortcoming."

"Your problem with Dr. Littky is a philosophical one?" Meyer asked.

"I have no personal vendetta against him. . . . He is a modern educationalist. The philosophy hasn't changed. It comes out in different forms. The words are always the same—different innovations for the educational system. It's the same old thing."

"Is there any *specific* difference at all between you and Dr. Littky on educational philosophy?" Meyer said.

"It's as different as black and white," Barton said. "His background is education. Mine is in engineering. The two are violently opposed. Education is very unscientific."

Meyer had begun questioning Barton at 10 A.M. At 10:35, the judge cautioned Barton to answer the questions.

Once again, Meyer asked Barton to identify the difference between Barton and Littky.

"I want it structured."

"Dr. Littky doesn't want it structured?"

"It's not structured enough."

"Who establishes policy for the academic curriculum?"

"The school board," Barton said.

"In your one and a half years on the board, what has the board done?" Meyer asked.

"Nothing much," Barton said.

"Isn't the board responsible for the academic curriculum?"

"Yes."

"If you think the board should do it, why do you put the blame on Dr. Littky instead of on yourself?"

"We just want to change the system and do it our own way."

"What do you want to change?"

"We want a change of philosophy and of discipline and of administration," Barton said. "I can't get specific."

The hearing at Cheshire County Court had been scheduled for one day only. But on the third day of testimony, the defense had yet to call a witness. Littky's attorney had called ten and would call two more before the hearing's end.

On the afternoon of the third day, school board attorney Burke called his first witness, Nathan Spaulding, to the stand.

Nathan, a Thayer senior, had accompanied his father, Howard, to every school board meeting since the new board gained control. A rangy young man with thick black hair, dark eyes, and dark complexion, he provided an odd visual contrast to his father, who was small, white-haired, white-bearded, and pale-skinned. Nathan took after his mother, who'd left her homeland of India to be Howard Spaulding's wife.

Nathan was quiet. He attended school board meetings religiously, but never once asked a question or offered an opinion. If asked a direct question, he would respond awkwardly, uncomfortably. His father was the talker. Howard Spaulding made no bones about his antipathy toward Littky as an educator and his support of Barton-Secord-Winter. "Dr. Littky spends so much time pumping these kids up and telling them how great they are—so that they *feel good* about themselves. He wants them to have a *good time* at Thayer. When they get out into the world, they're going to find out the real truth. Then where will they be? It gives them false ideas." Spaulding regarded himself a principled conservative. By transference, one assumed Nathan's politics were the same.

Burke was questioning Nathan about conditions at Thayer. His father sat in the audience watching as his son testified. Nathan was saying boom boxes (large tape players) had been a problem at the beginning of school that year, but were "not as much now." He said that in three out of his six classes boom boxes had been played an average of "three times a week," but they were "almost nonexistent now."

He said that swearing "happens every day in most of my classes" and that in several of his classes, students slept.

Nathan complained about the movies shown in class, among them Ray Bradbury's *Fahrenheit 451*, which he described as "not very educational."

Under cross-examination from Meyer, Nathan admitted to taking TGIF memos from one of his teacher's desks and giving them to his father.

"Did you ask if you could take them?" Meyer asked.

"I figured he'd probably say no," Nathan said.

While Nathan testified, Allen Barton, sitting at the defendants' table, slept.

Later that same afternoon, the defense called another witness, Bobby Secord. The crux of the defense's case came down to this: creative writing and Eddie Murphy.

Mr. M. was Thayer's creative writing teacher. Energetic, highly creative, Mr. M. was making better writers of Thayer students. But Marilyn Nolan saw him as a scourge, glaring evidence of everything that was wrong at Thayer High. He was the man whose "obscenities" Littky permitted. In question were two assignments made by Mr. M. to his eighth-grade class, one member of whom was Kerry Nolan, Marilyn's youngest daughter.

The first assignment asked students to write a story based on a Dear Abby letter concerning a girl who had endured years of incest with her father. The board had discussed the teacher's assignment with Littky at the next board meeting. Littky had said he would monitor future assignments.

"Did anything else happen?" Burke asked Secord.

"Two or three weeks later we got another complaint from the same parent about a writing assignment with topics on 'murdering a child' and 'vomiting' and another on 'going to the bathroom.' "

Secord had decided to take matters into his own hands. He drove to Thayer that morning and waited for Susan Winter in the parking lot.

"While I waited in my car," Secord testified, "I saw half a dozen students listening to music. Some were dancing. They kept turning the music up, louder and louder, and finally, even inside my car, I could hear some of the words, something about 'sticking things up your butt.' Elementary students were passing by on their way into school while this was happening. I also saw some teachers walking in while the song was playing."

When Winter arrived, the two stormed into the building and went directly to Mr. M.'s room as students were assembling for class. They began questioning him about the assignment. A teacher dashed to tell Littky about the confrontation that was in progress. When Littky arrived on the scene, he insisted that Secord and Winter discuss their complaint in his office. School board policy, he informed them, required that outsiders go through the principal's office first. Winter said that, as a school board member, she felt she had a right to go anywhere she wanted in the school building.

"It struck me as kind of funny," Secord told the court, "that after Dr. Littky said he would monitor Mr. M., it was still happening. Then we started to leave the building."

"Did Dr. Littky express any concern or dismay?" Burke asked.

"No."

"Did Dr. Littky comment on the quality of Mr. M.'s teaching?"

"He said Mr. M. was a good teacher and he was behind him 100 percent."

Under cross-examination, Secord revealed that the assignment in question had come from a textbook on writing published by the reputable firm of Alfred A. Knopf, Inc. In addition to the writing topics in question, there were some thirty others on the page, none of which Secord found objectionable. The preamble to the lesson told students to write "without a lapse of taste." Mr. M. also had changed the item about "murdering a child" to "murdering a cat." In March, the board unanimously accepted the superintendent's nomination to rehire Mr. M. At the end of the school year, he resigned of his own accord.

"Did you expect Dr. Littky to prereview each and every assignment of that teacher?"

"He said he would," Secord said.

"You think a principal should review every subsequent

assignment every time there is a parent complaint?"

"Dr. Littky felt he would monitor Mr. M."

The tape that Secord had heard was by comedian Eddie Murphy; the song was "Boogie In Your Butt." Secord heard the tape again as he passed by the art room that day.

"I talked to the substitute teacher in whose class the tape was played and then sent him back to class," Littky said in rebuttal the next afternoon. "Later I went back to him. He admitted it was a mistake to allow the tape to be played. He is a dedicated young man who is preparing to be a teacher."

The day after the incident, Susan Winter showed up at Littky's office and demanded that he give her the student's tape. Littky refused, saying that it wasn't his to give, it belonged to the student.

"Do you as an individual board member have a right to go into school and take someone else's property?" Meyer asked Winter.

"Yes," Winter replied. "In this case."

At 2:10 P.M. on the fourth day of the hearing, testimony ended. After summary arguments from both sides, the judge thanked counsel for doing "a thorough job" and took the case under advisement. His ruling was expected in a couple of weeks.

24
Eye of the Tiger

LITTKY WAS BACK IN SCHOOL for the first time since the trial. It felt good to him to be away from the courtroom, away from the politics. His future rested in the hands of one judge now. He didn't like that lack of control. But it also gave him time to breathe, time to concentrate on school. He figured there was no sense wasting any more energy on something that was beyond him.

Barb Eibell marveled at Doc's ability to insulate the school from the political brouhaha. He managed to come to school still laughing and joking, still pushing and encouraging staff to grow, still providing a shoulder for everyone to lean on.

The past year had been such a roller coaster ride—successes, accolades, opposition, failures. Rarely did Doc discuss the political situation in school. Staff meetings were still the high energy affairs they had always been—collegial, absorbing, visionary. As far as Barb was concerned, her classes had never been better.

It seemed to her so long ago since that first meeting with Littky when he told her to throw out her books. She'd been bowled over by his energy and expectations. Foreign students, sending Thayer students to other countries, fundraisers—it had all seemed so far-fetched to her then. But she'd done it all. She'd brought in a foreign student during

Littky's first year and every year thereafter; at the start of
Littky's second year, Barb organized an elaborate interna-
tional festival successfully raising $1,500—half of what it
cost to send two Thayer students to Mexico for a semester.
Doc had commented to her just the other day how far she'd
come since the days she lectured her students. She knew that
if she left the room while class was in session, her students
could carry on without missing a beat. They weren't shy
about speaking in French or Spanish. They weren't shy
about telling Barb their opinions of *her* teaching techniques.

"You're talking too much, Mrs. Eibell. We're the ones
who need the practice!" a student quipped one day.

She and Val Cole were team teaching an English and
French class, daily combining lessons on language, literature, culture, writing, and oratory.

At staff meetings, when Doc threw out his classic question, "Summarize the essence of your class in one sentence,"
Barb had an answer.

"The essence of my class, the thing that makes it work . . .
I can describe it in one word—respect. If you've got it and
you give it, everything else follows."

But even with Doc's efforts to "carry on as usual," the
pressures were there for everybody. Barb was worried.
Would Dennis win? Would she want to work at Thayer if he
didn't? Would she want her children to attend school there?
Even if he did win, would the school board just keep undermining everything he did?

The trial had put Barb on edge. There were spies in the
school. She had nothing to hide, but the opposition seemed
to her to be masters at taking things out of context and
making them into something they weren't.

The pressures were definitely coming to bear on a number of staff members. In June, the guidance counselor
resigned.

Dear School Board Member,

"Power corrupts and absolute power corrupts absolutely"—Lord Acton

"Power like a desolating pestilence, pollutes whate'er it touches"—P. B. Shelley

"The greater the power, the more dangerous the abuse"—Edmund Burke

Effective June 23, 1986, I hereby resign my position as guidance counselor at Thayer High School.

The climate that has been created has made my position and duties most difficult to perform efficiently. The blatant disregard for healthy and productive education has affected me so greatly that it is no longer appropriate for me to stay on.

It is my hope that the school board and the school are able to come to an agreeable resolution of their problems so that the students can once again have a positive environment in which to develop and learn.

The school administration, Dr. Littky et al., have been nothing but wonderful to me, and the town is lucky to have these very professional people.

A half-dozen more teachers would resign for the same reasons.

The apprenticeship program remained in limbo.

At the board meeting that June, the Barton-Secord-Winter bloc defeated Marcia Ammann's motion to keep the program intact. Then Bobby Secord offered a plan that would effectively kill Jimmy Karlan's position as director. Secord proposed using an aide to run the program with the school's guidance counselor overseeing it. He also proposed allowing only juniors and seniors in the program.

"I want to make it clear I'm not against the apprenticeship program," Secord said, "but I think it can still be run if it's compacted somewhat."

There were groans and angry words from the audience.

Marcia Ammann spoke first. "I don't think you can ask a guidance counselor, who already has a full-time job, to take on something she knows nothing about."

Melanie Zwolinski, Thayer's art teacher, would take over as the new guidance counselor on July 1. When she heard Secord's proposal, she went pale.

"How can I handle both jobs?" she whispered to Barb Eibell.

Bud Baker told Secord his plan would gut the program. Littky, who seldom said much during meetings of this board, criticized Secord's plan, saying the program couldn't be run properly.

The vote never reached a conclusion. Secord and Winter voted yes and Ammann voted no, but then Barton asked the board to postpone action on the matter.

After the meeting, Jimmy Karlan fumed. "If I'm not offered a job by June 30 when my contract runs out," he said, "I'll sue the board."

In July, the Barton-Secord-Winter vote cut the program and eliminated Karlan's position. The three ignored suggestions from Assistant Superintendent McCarthy, Chairperson Baker, and Board Member Ammann to hold off on the overhaul until after the state completed its ten-year evaluation of the school in the fall.

"What do you think you'll accomplish?" Baker asked after Secord overrode Ammann's motion to leave the program unchanged until after the evaluation. "It's throwing everything to the wind, and we'll be losing more than we gain."

Secord was unmoved. Restricting the apprenticeship program to juniors and seniors would not kill the program, he said.

Barton added his two cents. He amended the motion to say that only juniors and seniors with a C average or better be allowed into the program. "I don't see that the apprenticeship program as it is now has much to do with educating kids," he said. "I'm still more interested in kids getting a basic education. The apprenticeship program is ripping off the kids. They're substituting play time with real time in the classroom."

Littky was incredulous. Hadn't Barton listened to the students, parents, and site supervisors at the presentation? How had he come to this conclusion?

Littky protested. Scheduling for next year was already completed, he said. Shifting apprenticeship students back to regular classes was impossible without crowding classrooms and adding more teachers.

Barton, who'd been shifting between staring out at the crowd and whispering to Bobby Secord, turned his attention to Littky.

"It might be you'll have to sit down and do a little hard thinking," Barton said.

"At this late date, it's going to be a disservice to change the program," Littky responded.

"It's not a disservice," Barton said. "It may be the best thing that ever happens to them."

"Why don't you wait until after the state evaluates the program?" McCarthy said. "You're going to get hard data."

Littky saw the apprenticeship program crumbling before his eyes. He couldn't let it happen. "I can't run that program under these changes!" he protested again.

Secord's face turned red. Slamming his hand down on the table, he shot back: "It isn't open for discussion!"

On the morning of June 20, a Cheshire County Superior Court clerk called Thayer High School and asked to speak to Dennis Littky.

"The ruling has been filed on your case," the clerk told Littky. "It's here at the courthouse if you want to read it."

Littky's face flushed hot. "I'm on my way," he said. As he

drove toward Keene, his mind was a blur. "This is it . . . this is it," he kept saying to himself.

At the courthouse, the clerk handed him the file. He was the only one there to read it. No one else had been notified yet.

Dennis scanned the documents searching for the answer.

"The state board has treated principals as teachers for at least 14 years, . . . The school board did not validly circumvent the plaintiff's procedural rights when it rescinded its nonrenewal vote and offered the plaintiff an elementary school classroom teaching position. . . . that served to deprive the plaintiff of his statutorily guaranteed procedural rights."

Dennis leaned against the table. He'd won.

The school *had* violated Littky's rights by denying him a hearing. The judge ordered that a hearing be held "in the very near future." Littky could keep his job until then or until the appeals process was exhausted.

So far, the school board's case against Littky had cost the school district $15,752. Littky was handling his own legal fees privately—through donations, membership in the New Hampshire Principals Association, and out of his own pocket. Townspeople were appalled at the school board's mounting costs and spared no words to let the board know that.

"How many teachers would that employ?" one man shouted.

"Enough for a director for the apprenticeship program?" asked another.

The school budget contained only $8,500 for school board expenses, which meant it would have to dip into other accounts to pay off the bill. As the case continued, the legal bills continued to mount.

At the special school board meeting four days after the

judge's decision was released, Chairperson Bud Baker planned to recommend that the board keep Littky as principal "and drop everything." He hoped Barton, Secord, and Winter would "listen to reason."

The trio was clearly unmoved by Baker's request during the 45-minute closed-door session. Instead it delayed action on the whole matter because the board's attorneys hadn't had time to review the decision thoroughly. But it was clear that dropping the case was not an option the trio was considering.

The fact remained that if the board followed proper procedure, it had the right to remove Littky from his job. The only thing the board had to do was provide a reason that was "not arbitrary or capricious."

Littky wondered, was calling him "too progressive" for Winchester sufficient reason? Was it reasonable to say he wasn't a good leader because he'd "sprawled out on a dirt pile?" If he appealed the case to the New Hampshire Board of Education, would that body agree with him?

Meanwhile, the Committee for Good Schools tackled the issue of legal fees. A Keene lawyer volunteered his services to the group to come up with strategies to recover the money the town had spent on the board's legal expenses and prevent the board from running up more. Options included suing the school board or individual members for the money.

The chairperson of the committee sent a letter to the editor, venting his anger:

> . . . How many textbooks, library books, supplies, uniforms and musical instruments could have been purchased? How many repairs could have been made to the high school? Because of this unexpected cost, what will it cost our children? What programs and services will be affected? Will this expense jeopardize the apprenticeship program or its director? Will the elementary school receive the extra

staff position that was added and approved by the voters at the March district meeting?

As an example of their wastefulness, it took a board member two hours to tell the court that, although his philosophy of education and that of Dr. Littky were "violently" opposed, he could not identify any words or phrases he disagreed with from the statement of the goals and objectives prepared by Dr. Littky and approved by the entire board last December. Two hours of court time with two lawyers working to represent the three board members comes out to a minimum of $400, to hear a board member ramble on.

Who is or will be responsible for the court cost? To the charge that it is Dr. Littky who is responsible for this court case we say that if the board had honored its commitment to give him and the people of Winchester an open hearing, this case would not have had to be heard in court.

Finally, the school board reached a decision. It would go ahead with a hearing. School officials speculated it would cost $20,000 to $30,000 to pay for it.

Marilyn Nolan fired off another letter:

To The *Sentinel*:
The saga continues at the old corral. . . .
The decision to allow Littky his public hearing has been made, much to the dismay of his generals and troop members. Now they are yelling about litigation costs thus far, and moaning about additional cost for the hearing.
"Well," one may ask, "isn't the hearing what Littky sued the school board for?" . . .
Littky had a battle plan all written when he rode into town. . . .
The plan consists of three basic steps: Learn about power—how to find and influence it; learn to discover the latent desires of the community, and how to work with these desires; learn to work within the system and solve logistical problems which could otherwise destroy one's work.

The first thing that Littky did was to "watch the town through the plate-glass window of the hardware store."

Next, he joined the PTA which consisted of 15 women. I suspect that they were awed by his tales of his accomplishments in Long Island, N.Y. Not to mention the thoughts of hearing what their poor, illiterate little community needed.

Then came the establishment of the local newspaper because he could see that the "worst thing about Winchester was the people's self-image," etc. (See step two in plan).

Then came Littky's appointment to the school board to finish a term left vacant by a resignation, and then a term as a legislator.

Last came his appointment as principal of Thayer. I find it quite interesting to note that many of the members of the PTA, the *Star* staff and the school board were all one in the same. (His little group has served him well and are his most loyal supporters today.)

Because of such loyalty and trust on the part of his little group, Littky created positions for some of them at Thayer so that they could all stick together.

Now Littky had to get the parents and the students to cooperate. . . .

Littky decorated the walls with murals, took out study halls, had movies available, rock music, and instituted an advisory program. The student adviser met with students so that any gripes or problems would be handled at school, and not become known about at home. Students who thought they had problems had a ready ear and sympathy when needed. Littky's philosophy in Long Island was, "only as a last resort should parents be notified.". . .

Littky admits to have had a free reign in running the school until March 1985, but he came prepared for opposition too. The plans for this event are also simply stated. When a school board opposes one's methods or projects, one first goes over their heads. If this doesn't work, go to the news media. If this fails, one tests the "nuisance value" of what the opposition decides the project is worth. One of the tests is to get people to march on the board. The rest of his strategy is now public knowledge.

Yes, indeed, folks! Littky wants that public hearing! If anyone hasn't had the opportunity to hear about his wonderfulness and importance, be sure and get a seat. And bring plenty of tissues because his troops will wring your heart with their testimony. Please leave your clubs and bats at home because some of us can't run very fast in hip boots.

Just pity us fools who just don't appreciate "progress" and greatness among us.

On the day before Littky's hearing before the school board, Terri Racine drove into the Village Hill Trailer Park to pick up her daughter from the baby-sitter's. Elizabeth was seven months old. As she drove past the lines of trailers, Terri noticed leaflets stuck in the doors. She parked her car in front of the baby-sitter's. As she got out, she spotted a girl and a young boy carrying fliers to a trailer a few doors away. A thin mustached man waited in a rusty green car nearby.

"Terri, have you seen *this*?" her baby-sitter called when Terri was in sight.

"Seen what?"

"They're all over town! They're shovin' 'em in doors all over town!"

Terri grabbed the flier. On the cover was a photocopied picture of Doc. Below it, in handwritten boldfaced caps: "WHAT HAPPENED? THE LITTKY STORY"

"The last few pages, Terri. Look at the last few pages."

Terri flipped to the back, her hands trembled when she saw her own name and the letter she had written to the school board on June 9.

Dear Winchester School Board:

Enclosed is a copy of the article I wrote for an independent project for my apprenticeship. I am sending this in regards to the concerns that were expressed months ago

about my project. Please feel free to make any comments on
this paper.
Thank you,
Terri Racine

Attached were the first several pages of her paper, those
in which she described her reaction to and personal experience with being pregnant.

"Oh, God!" she said. "They had no right to do this. It's
my paper! It's private! Who did this? Only Mr. Karlan and
the school board have copies!"

Then she remembered the green car. "That's the Nolan's
bombshell! It was Kerry and her father! They're out there
right now handing out my paper for everyone to see!"
Elizabeth started crying. Terri lifted her, cuddling her in
her arms.

Terri turned and ran out the door. She looked left and
right for the green car. It was nowhere in sight. She turned
back to her car, strapped Elizabeth in her seat, ran to the
driver's side, and jerked open the door. She slid onto the seat
and slammed the door. Elizabeth wailed as Terri cruised
through Village Hill Trailer Park searching for the Nolans.
They were gone.

Terri turned the car around, bound for home.

Mrs. Racine shrieked when she saw the flier. "That bitch!
This time they've gone too far! Terri, you don't have to put
up with this! I'm calling a lawyer."

Mrs. Racine stormed to her mother's house to use the
phone, because she didn't have one. She called Jon Meyer,
Littky's attorney—the only lawyer she knew.

His advice was brief and unsatisfying. "Wait," he said.
"We don't know for sure who's behind the pamphlet."

Meyer had told Littky the same thing earlier that night.
Littky was hopping mad at the whole thing. The last page
of the pamphlet, however, made his blood run cold.

The back page was littered with crudely drawn stick figures—some of them were supposed to be students, others were plainly Littky.

- One stick-boy carried a large radio—the words *Eddie Murphy* blasting out of the boom box.
- A stick-boy stood in front of a door labeled *Out*. "What duz dat say?" the stick-boy said.
- A stick-boy held a marijuana joint, smoke curling up around his head. "Wow!" his balloon read. "Am I High!!"
- A stick-boy slept at his desk. Another tilted a bottle of booze to his lips. "Glug, glug, glug," his balloon read.
- A stick-boy waved a certificate of merit at another stick-boy, who said, "What good is it? You can't eat it! And you can't spend it!"
- Stick-Littky was walking into a door labeled *Girls Shower*, saying, "Just checking you out girls. Te-he-ha-ha-."
- Stick-Littky floated in a bathtub shouting "Help!!" An arrow pointed to his ear, indicating an "earing" [sic]. The cartoon was titled, "Sink, Swim or Drano."
- A stick-mother and stick-father were crying big round tears. "Why wern't [sic] we told?" their balloons lament.
- Stick-Littky carried a stick-girl by the neck and leg. "Just a girl student," he said. Again, an arrow pointed to an earring.
- A Stick-building, presumably Thayer High, had stick-students on the roof and hanging out windows. One carried a boom box. A stick-boy on the sidewalk pointed to the scene. "Wow!!" he said. "Can I go to that school?"
- In the middle of the page was stick-Littky, seated at his desk. He wore a yarmulke, the skullcap worn by male Jews. Another arrow pointed to an earring.

Jon Meyer told Littky to calm down. "It's libelous, Dennis," he said. "No doubt about it. But unless we know for sure who's responsible for it, there's not much we can do."

The Littky pamphlet was the only topic in town the next

day. Reactions were extreme in both directions—from "appalling and disgusting!" to "Hits the nail right on the head, if you ask me!"

The eleven-page leaflet, signed by "The Silent Majority," began with a letter to the town.

WHAT IS OUR TOWN WORTH TO US???

Do you, as a parent, want Mr. Littky to control your child's mind psychologically? . . .

Parents and Grandparents—don't you think that it would be far better to teach the three R's than to waste our students time and minds listening to Eddie Murphy's filth? Or watching mandated movies rated PG and R?

Two years ago, we asked you to turn out to vote for a change in the school board, and you did—in an overwhelming majority!

Now we ask that you once again show your support by attending this very *important meeting—Littky's public hearing—on TUESDAY, JULY 22, 1986, starting at three P.M. At the THAYER HIGH SCHOOL GYMNASIUM. THANK YOU!*

An excerpt from Littky's dissertation followed. The paragraph highlighted three models "the author feels are important in making educational change in urban schools and communities":

Finally, if all attempts to work within the system are stifled and one's project is being hindered, the next step is to cause more aggravation and trouble than one's demands are worth. This may mean sitting in until demands are met or bringing community people to march on the Board's offices. The number of tactics used and their complexity will depend upon how important it is to the Board to stop someone from reaching his goal.

After that came a page entitled "LITTKY QUOTES." There was a list of quotes lifted from various publications, including the 1983 *Yankee Magazine* article and Littky's dissertation. "Watched town through store window . . . education appropriate to the circumstances of rural poverty . . . Must learn about power—how to find and influence it . . . finally moved on smoking in johns this fall—I hated it, but couldn't move on it before this year."

Next was an article clipped from the *Keene Sentinel* that listed Thayer as having the fifth-highest dropout rate in the state at 8.19 percent. Littky was quoted:

> The year before I came, in 1980–81, the dropout rate at Thayer High was between 16 and 20 percent. The next year, 1981–82, we cut the rate in half, to about 8 percent, actually bringing back students that had dropped out in previous years. The rate stayed at about 8 percent during 1982–83, then went up again slightly the next year. We realized the dropout rate was our most serious problem, and worked on it; then when we felt we had that under control, we took the next step. We toughened the standards of our courses. We lost some students because of that, which is to be expected.

The next page carried a letter to the editor sent to the *Sentinel*: "The saga continues at the old corral as we get ready for the big scene called Littky's hearing," the letter began. It was signed by Marilyn J. Nolan.

Sandwiched between Nolan's letter and Terri's paper was an article by Phyllis Schlafly. It seemed wherever there was opposition to Littky, someone somewhere would start waving copies of Schlafly's code of ethics. Like a chronic cough, there she was again, this time criticizing journal writing.

> . . . Although used in English class, journal writing has nothing whatever to do with developing the ability to read and write the English language.

The nitty gritty of journal writing is the content . . . "personal problems—family fights, divorces, death, drugs and alcohol, peer conflicts and love affairs. . . ."

Sorry, teacher, but most parents didn't authorize the school to pry into private family problems and affairs. Those are none of the school's business.

When Terri Racine read the Schlafly article, her outrage deepened. "Damn hypocrites!" she said. "I didn't authorize anybody to take my private paper and distribute it by the hundreds around town!"

There was some speculation that Barton, Secord, and Winter might have been behind the smear packet, but most of the speculation started and stopped on Marilyn Nolan's doorstep. When a *Keene Sentinel* reporter called Nolan to question her about the pamphlet, she retorted with a fusillade of insults and slammed down the phone.

Cheshire County Court had ruled that the school board had violated Littky's rights when it denied him the chance to defend himself in front of the board. The court had ordered that a hearing be held. If the school board, after hearing Littky's defense, once again voted to fire Littky, then he would appeal the case before the state board of education.

Littky's attorney opened the public hearing before two hundred people in the Thayer gym by holding up a copy of the pamphlet. "It makes a number of false and libelous accusations against Dr. Littky," Jon Meyer said, "the worst of which claims Dr. Littky to have assaulted a female student. It's a deliberate attempt to poison the atmosphere of this hearing. The publication is unsigned. The authors did not have the courage to sign their name."

Here Meyer directed his comments to the board members, who were seated behind a table in the middle of the gymnasium. "Dr. Littky has a right to a fair and objective hearing.

The matter must be reviewed objectively and not in terms of preconceived ideas. If any board members come in with preconceived notions, they have an obligation to disqualify themselves."

The state hearing officer met quickly with the board, then returned to say, "Each member assures me they had no role in authoring the pamphlet. The members feel they can rule dispassionately."

Meyer faced the crowd: "Would the person or persons who have to date hidden behind the cloak of anonymity have the guts to identify themselves?" There was absolute silence in the auditorium.

To eliminate any duplication of the court hearing and save the district money, the transcripts of the twenty hours of testimony given at the Cheshire County Court House would be submitted as evidence in about sixty days, the time the court expected to take transcribing the volumes of material relating to the case. Though this would prevent another drawn-out hearing, it also meant Littky's future with the district would remain in limbo for at least another sixty days.

James Burke, the tall, hulking lawyer hired by the school board, would call four witnesses—Dennis Littky and three students, including Kerry Nolan. Littky's attorney, Jon Meyer, would bring seventeen witnesses to the stand, including Ted Sizer. Many, many more had offered to testify on Dennis's behalf.

Burke questioned his first witness, a seventeen-year-old Thayer student who claimed she overheard Littky tell another person that her mother had spent, for personal use, student funds placed in a certificate of deposit in her name. Then Burke tried to establish that Littky had entered the girls' restroom while girls were in there.

"Not only is that question indelicate, it's outrageous,"

Meyer shouted. "We've allegedly been given *all* the reasons.
. . . I think that all of us as lawyers have a minimum
responsibility of decency and honesty."

Meyer's comments were met with vigorous applause.
Burke immediately withdrew the question.

Under questioning, Kerry Nolan discussed her experience
with Thayer's creative writing teacher, Mr. M., who had his
students write about "having sex with a parent, killing an
infant, vomiting, and a Dear Abby clip about a mother
breast-feeding her six-year-old son." She also talked about
watching R-rated films in class and attending a biology
class field trip to a hardwood forest. All of these she found
objectionable and not educational.

Under cross-examination, Kerry admitted she helped deliver the smear pamphlet, but swore she had no idea who
was behind it. She said she got the pamphlets from Francis
Gutoski, who later told a reporter that was true but that he,
likewise, did not know who the author was. Kerry said she
hadn't read the packet before she delivered it.

"Didn't you have any concern about delivering something
you hadn't read?" Meyer asked.

"No," Kerry said, "because I knew it was against Dr.
Littky."

Littky's witnesses came next:

A realtor testified that property values in Winchester had
gone up directly as a consequence of an improved Thayer
High School under Littky.

Eleanore Freedman, executive director of the New Hampshire Association of School Principals, said, "Although I
try not to play favorites among five hundred principals,
Dennis Littky is one of the most outstanding principals I
have ever known in thirty years of education. He has been
used as a model, as an example of what can be done with
real and inspired leadership."

Ted Sizer said the high school under Littky's administration "is a very demanding school, and a very warm school. This combination is very rare. He's one of the outstanding principals I know."

Terri Racine: "He makes sure your grades are what they should be. He's one person you know is your friend."

Val Cole: "I have learned a great deal from Dr. Littky. He encouraged me because he said I was good. He made me have confidence to think I could contribute to other people."

Marian Polaski: "My youngest son had an I-don't-care attitude about school. Dr. Littky helped him feel very good about himself. He's now in the U.S. Navy."

Karen Marsh: "He was there to help me decide my future."

Students, parents, and teachers lined up to show their support for Littky. When Meyer gave his closing statements, he told the board members to transcend their personal differences and look at Littky's performance. "The overwhelming bulk of evidence is overwhelmingly in favor of Dr. Littky."

In one great wave, the crowd surged to its feet, applauding thunderously for five minutes.

Then Burke made his closing statements, saying Littky had failed to enforce the no-smoking policy; that he allowed students to call him "Doc" and "Dennis," a degree of familiarity Burke called inappropriate; that he didn't adequately enforce the dress code; that he once failed to inform the board about the paving of a road on school property; that his educational philosophy was clearly at odds with the board's.

"Don't let Dr. Littky's credentials and awards get in the way of the real issue. This is an energetic man. Is he an innovator? Sure," Burke said. "But to truly understand a leader is to turn and look at his followers—teachers. Dr. Littky has allowed not just inappropriate conduct, but *outrageous* conduct from his teachers."

Burke's comments were met with silence at first, then about a dozen people in the audience applauded.

Two days after the hearing, Marilyn Nolan wrote a letter to the *Sentinel*. In it, she singled out Terri Racine:

> A student became a mother during the school year, and was welcomed back amid shouts and banners of congratulations. Of course, the student should not have been ostracized in any manner, but was this event considered an academic achievement? Of course it was at Thayer! The little mother actually received credits for the accomplishment as an apprentice! And—are you ready for this? According to her essay as an apprentice, she is not responsible for her pregnancy!

The two paragraphs that followed were not published by the *Sentinel*.

"Apparently," Nolan wrote, "the student had some upheavals and must have upheaved her Pill. Said student relates this cause as decreed by her case worker at Planned Parenthood, bless her heart. Further, the baby was to play a large part of her learning experience at Thayer also, but the darn rotters on the school board stopped that!"

The packet Marilyn Nolan mailed to the newspaper contained part of Terri's paper and her surveys. Attached to one of the surveys was a short, handwritten note by Nolan: "Miss Racine always takes her baby to the school board meetings and sits in the front row. No one else takes their children, and this makes some older kitty-cats purr 'does the baby look like Littky?' "

25
Institution Rattling

ELMER JOHNSON WAS SOMETHING OF an institution in Winchester. Town moderator for thirty years and state legislator for twenty, at one time or another Johnson had held just about every elective office in town.

Elmer's opinion of Dennis Littky was well known to the people of Winchester. According to many locals, he'd been bad-mouthing Littky for years—calling him a communist and a socialist agitator ever since serving with him in the state house. Lately, they said, he'd been telling folks Littky was a home wrecker, that he'd slept with a former school board member and broken up her home. It was the kind of thing that the locals mulled over at Don's Barber Shop or down the street at Pisgah Diner.

But even in the absence of a well-greased rumor mill, Elmer's opinion of Littky would have been no secret. He'd broadcast it to the *New York Times* and *Newsweek*. "He's the highest-paid individual in town and, instead of setting a dignified example, he acts like a tramp," Johnson told a *Newsweek* reporter. "Us old-timers resent liberal newcomers coming in and telling us how backwards we are."

The fact was, Littky was messing with *his* town and Johnson didn't like it.

Elmer Johnson, a sixty-six-year-old bachelor, was a lean, silver-haired man. His thin face and sharp, refined features were aristocratic. But he had the dry, weathered skin of a

344

man who spent long days working in the sun and wind. His shoulders and upper back were painfully, unnaturally bent. In the summer of 1966, one of his bulls gored him. Now he carried his infirmity like a badge. A few years ago, he lost the tips of two fingers in his hay elevator. He bandaged them up and returned to the barn to finish his day's work.

Johnson owned a fair-sized chunk of Winchester. His sprawling cattle farm, situated at the base of Pudding Hill, ran clear into Massachusetts. Three generations of Johnsons had farmed the land known as Pleasant Valley. It was lush, verdant, beautiful. Elmer had spent his life there. He lived in the same house where he was born and which he had bought in 1940 from his father, who had bought it from his father in 1920, who had bought it in 1889. Though he'd recently sold off some of his land, Elmer maintained five hundred acres of cropland and three farms in Pleasant Valley. Elmer collected farms the way others collect coins. One of his farms, opposite his home on Warwick Road, he rented to Marilyn Nolan and her family.

Elmer could look across his property to a line of stately pine trees that separated his land from fifty acres belonging to the school. Johnson would wave a proud finger at the trees and remind whoever was present that he had planted the seedlings as a member of Thayer High School's agriculture class of 1931.

During his quarter of a century as Winchester's state representative, he became notorious for striking cattle deals with fellow representatives in the state house parking lot before moving inside to conduct the state's business. But it was his property that got him into state politics: his vast landholdings brought with them substantial tax liability. So he became a state lawmaker and the chief sponsor of a "current use" tax bill, which allowed farmers to pay taxes based on the value of their property assessed at the land's present, rather than its potential, use.

In addition to state representative and town moderator,

Elmer had been a member of the budget committee since 1950, frequently its chair. He'd also served a couple of stints as town selectman and as a member of the planning board. In the last election, someone posted a sign on the outskirts of town that read, "Johnson City, 1 mile."

Johnson's knowledge of parliamentary procedure was legendary. His voice cut like an ax—sharp, clear, penetrating. He made decisions unwaveringly and rarely allowed challenge from the audience, settling disputes with a whack of his gavel. He would adroitly call the shots, squelching criticism of projects he liked or fanning criticism of those he didn't. Every now and again, he'd throw in his own opinion for good measure. During lulls, when ballots had to be tallied or something else delayed the meeting, Elmer Johnson would recite poetry (often his own) from memory. For the most part, the townspeople obliged him on the theory that he must know what needed to be done because he'd been doing it for so long.

Elmer Johnson and Bobby Secord were both running in the state election in November 1986. But Winchester locals had formed a bipartisan coalition to unseat them, an outgrowth of the Committee for Good Schools.

In addition to their disdain for Bobby and Elmer's regard of Littky, coalition members were also critical of them for another school issue. When the legislature passed a new school funding formula that benefited Winchester and other property-poor towns, neither Secord nor Johnson voted. It was a bill Littky had worked on during his two-year stint in the Legislature.

But Johnson stood by his record. "I was there for all the important votes that made any difference," he said.

A little more than a week before school was to start that fall, the Winchester School Board filed a petition with the New Hampshire Supreme Court. The petition sought to keep Littky out of Thayer High while the board waited for the transcripts from the court case.

"I can't believe it," Littky said when he heard about the petition. "A week before school starts, and the board wants the doors to open without anyone in charge or, at best, with a new principal?"

More than half the twenty-five-member staff was new that year. Many of the teachers who had left did so because of the political situation. It was the biggest turnover in staff in Littky's five-year history with the district.

The petition claimed that if Littky remained, "the person in charge of the high school on a daily basis, the school board's right hand, will be a person in whom the school board has no confidence. This is unjust, and it will cause irreparable harm to the school district."

The board's attorney blamed Cheshire Superior Court for delays, saying that the board had fully expected the Littky matter to be resolved before school began. The court, in turn, fired off an angry letter to the school board's attorney Bradley Kidder. "This office and Judge Manias went out of their way to accommodate this case and to provide the parties on both sides with a speedy hearing and a well founded order.... This Petition ... unjustifiably blackens the name of a system that has afforded your client speedy access and resolution of the issue."

In addition, the principal, the school board chairperson, the superintendents, and board member Marcia Ammann didn't know about the petition until they read of it in the newspaper. Even Bradley Kidder, the attorney whose name appeared on the document, didn't know about it.

So, everybody wondered, who authorized the petition?

"The board did, I guess," Kidder said. Eventually, it became clear that Kidder's associate Jim Burke had actually handled the petition, but for the moment he wasn't saying much. Nor were Secord, Winter, or Barton.

Efforts by reporters to talk to the three board members had long ago become absurd. Secord, perhaps the most accessible of the three, refused to answer any questions. Winter, who got an unlisted phone number shortly after assuming public office, did not return repeated phone calls to her office. Barton's gambit was not to give his name. Instead, he'd ask who was calling him. If it was the press, often he'd say he wasn't home.

Four days before school started, the state supreme court turned down the petition.

On September 10, the date of the GOP primary, voters knocked Secord out of his New Hampshire House seat. His loss was seen as directly linked to his actions against Littky. School board legal fees in the case had reached $24,456.

On September 22, shortly after the school board received the transcripts of the court case, the board planned to meet to reconsider its decision on Littky's job. There seemed little doubt what the board would do. The question that remained, however, was whether the trio represented the townspeople. If they went by the volume and force of protests emanating from the community, the answer would clearly be no. But was there really a silent majority? Was there a lot of background support from people who chose to remain quiet because of fear of retribution?

That Monday, the Winchester School Board met in closed-door session to discuss Littky's future with the district. The hearing officer appointed by the state to monitor the case spent forty-five minutes discussing procedures with the board. At the end of his presentation, he and Baker opened the discussion on reasons for not rehiring Littky to the other board members.

"None of the three board members had anything to say," Baker would report after the session.

Baker, who voted along with Marcia to renew Littky's contract, said that the three never reviewed the transcripts of the Cheshire County Court testimony. "They never even looked at it," he said.

Within a week after the refiring, Littky appealed the case to the New Hampshire Board of Education, and the school board sent its appeal of the lower court decision to the state supreme court.

In the meantime, Littky was in no hurry for the state school board to consider his case. He and his supporters had their sights set on the school board election in March, when Bobby Secord's term expired. If Littky supporters could find a strong candidate to defeat Secord, there would then be a pro-Littky majority with Marcia and Bud, and Littky would be assured of keeping his job.

Elmer Johnson's bid to resume his state House seat looked like it might be an omen. Five candidates were vying for three seats. Johnson was one of only two incumbents, and all four candidates condemned Johnson for his stand against Littky. When the votes were in, Elmer Johnson—a ten-term Republican lawmaker—lost. It was the major upset of the election.

That March, the people of Winchester would have a chance to decide the Littky issue themselves.

The pro-Littky group needed to promote a candidate who was well-known in the community, someone who was trusted, liked, noncontroversial, and a Littky supporter. The same name kept coming up. Marian Polaski.

Everybody liked Marian. Even members of the opposition would have a hard time speaking against her. She was a short, round, gentle woman who'd spent nearly every Monday for the past fifteen years teaching catechism at St. Stanislaus. She and her husband lived in a small yellow ranch house within sight of the high school. Two of their three boys had graduated from Thayer under Doc, and, by Marian's estimation, benefited immeasurably from their relationship with him.

Marian liked to make friends and liked to "do" for them. She hand-delivered casseroles to the sick and offered a soft shoulder for the sad to sob on. She worked hard at being "an honest, decent person."

In Marian's front yard was a yellow grapefruit bag tied to a branch of a century-old spruce tree. It had become a fixture in her yard, just like the yellow ribbons tied to so many other mailboxes, houses, and trees in town. The ribbons were a symbol. They would remain as long as Doc was under siege. Marian didn't have a yellow ribbon, so she used the grapefruit bag instead.

Still, Marian was hesitant about running for the board. Her kids were all out of high school. "I've served my time," she said. "I just think it's time for someone else, someone with kids in the school."

She remembered the frustrating battles with the town's tightfisted budget committee, the sometimes hostile confrontations with dissatisfied parents and taxpayers; she remembered the number of nights she wasn't home to spend time with her children or her husband. What bothered her even more were the events of the past year, the hard feelings, the hatred that had descended on her town—she just wasn't sure she wanted to be in the center of it.

"If you don't run," Dennis told her, "you might as well kiss me good-bye."

When the filing period for school board candidates closed on February 17, Marian L. Polaski was one of six candidates. Bud Baker was on the list. So were Bobby Secord and Francis Gutoski.

26
Mudslinging

DOC WAITED FOR THE APPLAUSE to die down before motioning to Shane, who was sitting near the top of the bleachers. Most of the attention was riveted on the group of boys on stage whose rock'n'roll gyrations were just barely on the clean side of risqué. They imitated the real-life rock stars with something close to scientific precision—strumming, jumping, spinning. Doc caught Shane's eye and, with a sharp jerk of his hand, motioned him to come. The eighth-grader shot a look back that said, "What'd I do?"

Shane stomped down the bleachers, his tight muscle shirt making his arms look especially long and sinewy.

"Follow me," Doc said, heading toward the door to the hallway. Shane couldn't read his tone and half bristled, half laughed as he followed him. Doc directed Shane to a darkened corner. Conspiratorially, he whispered, "Gimme your shirt." Doc was already unbuttoning his own.

Shane caught on to the plan. "Awwwwright!" he said and handed Doc his muscle shirt. In an instant the switch was complete, and Doc ran down the hallway to the main office. Both secretaries giggled when he dashed in, pointing at where the muscle shirt left off and his chalk-white belly picked up. Doc hastily scanned his wall of hats, grabbed the coonskin, and pulled it over the balding spot at the top of his head, filling in one of the few spaces from his shoulders up that wasn't a pother of hair.

Doc ran back down the hall, through the gym door, and leapt on the stage just in time for the final number. "Smokin' in the boys' room," the boys shouted, mouthing the words. Doc grabbed the microphone, joining the freckled-faced lead singer who accommodated him without missing a beat. "Smokin' in the boys' room," Doc mouthed, closing his eyes and tilting his head back. He turned on his heel, then danced his way to the electric organ and started pounding on the keyboard with the spasmodic energy of an Elton John or a Dr. Jekyll turning Hyde.

The collection of junior high students and teachers roared its approval.

When the music was over and Doc had traded high fives with the performers, he jumped off stage, signaled to Shane, dashed back to the office, tossed off his costume, and changed back into his shirt. Doc was back in the gymnasium a moment later, just as the winners of the Thayer Junior High lip-sync contest were being announced. He stood at the sidelines, calmly, with his arms folded.

During his brief performance, Dennis had noticed one of the gym doors slightly ajar. Someone had been watching from behind the door. He couldn't see who it was. A teacher told him he had seen school board member Bobby Secord park his black Cadillac in the lot and walk to the elementary school just before the performance. The elementary school was located right next door to the gymnasium. Dennis wondered if it'd been Secord behind the door, watching. The thought perturbed him, though not enough to make him regret his antics.

As the kids filed out of the assembly, he tried to read their reactions to him. They looked at him with eyes that said, "You're cool—not too cool, not one of us cool, but cool enough."

It was the last meeting before the school board election. A cold clear winter night. The Pinards headed into the elementary school just as the meeting was about to start. They sat down close to the front because of Mr. Pinard's hearing trouble. Sitting in front of them were Howard Spaulding and his son Nathan.

The Pinards and the Spauldings had become fixtures at school meetings. Their presence was as reliable as the bow tied at Susan Winter's neck, Allen Barton's natty sport coats, and the pin-striped suits that clad Bobby Secord's beefy slab of a body. They were the trio's rooting section.

Bud Baker called the meeting to order and asked if there were any comments or questions from the audience.

A small, attractive woman raised her hand and stood up. She introduced herself as Nancy Paight, candidate for the school board. She said she had some questions she wanted Dennis Littky to answer. "I'm not here as a school board candidate. I'm here as a parent," she said in a strong, clear voice. "Last weekend my husband and I chaperoned at a dance. My son is Henry Archibald, president of the junior class. I saw some things I didn't like. Kids were dancing and their hands were in places they weren't supposed to be. These kids were wrapped tight around each other; they were kissing and necking like there was no tomorrow. I know you saw it. You were closer than I was. What did you do about it, Dr. Littky?"

"Don't tell me what I saw," Littky said looking straight at her. "We expect that if you're there as a parent chaperon that you're there to supervise the kids, not to spy."

The woman tensed. "I didn't want to cause a commotion, so I didn't say anything. To me you're supposed to be a role model for these kids, are you not? If I hadn't been there my kids would have been right there with them, but because I was, they toed the line."

"Mrs. Paight, as a chaperon, if you saw this going on, why didn't you do something about it?" Littky held his anger in check.

"Because . . ." she paused. "I didn't say anything. I

wanted to see how far it would go. You had to be blind as a bat if you didn't see it. We might as well say what it is. We might as well say public petting, because that's what it was."

"Mrs. Paight, I didn't see whatever it is you're talking about. I've been going to dances here for six years and I know teachers that have chaperoned for twenty, and that dance was no different than any other," Littky said.

Bud Baker, in his halting, congenial tone, asked her "Is this your first dance as a chaperon?"

"Yes," she said.

Nancy Paight had a list of complaints. But she saved the biggest for last.

It concerned the anonymous surveys on homosexuality that Barb Eibell and Melanie Zwolinski had passed out in their Life After Thayer class, surveys that the teachers collected and destroyed after class. All but one, that is. One of Barb and Mel's students slipped a survey out of class and passed it to Nancy Paight.

"My kids know what homosexuality is. They know what lesbians are. They don't need this," she said. Paight said she was devastated when she saw the questionnaire. Contained in it were true-false questions such as, "Cruising is equally engaged in by gay males and females" and "Homosexual males and females have more interest in sex than do heterosexual males and females." The survey sought opinions on statements such as "I would feel uncomfortable being seen in a gay bar" and "I would feel I had failed as a parent if I learned my child was gay."

"If you ask me," Paight said, narrowing her eyes at Littky, "this sounds like it's for your own personal information. When my daughter handed me this, I said to myself, 'Is this man a homosexual?' Are you?"

Littky closed his eyes and took a deep breath. Though taken aback by the indelicacy of her question, Littky chose not to dignify it by answering no. "I'm a professional," he said. He paused a moment to subdue his mounting anger.

"Those are questions that the kids need to think about," Littky said. "The course is our opportunity to help prepare the kids for life after school."

Then he pointed out that parents of students in the course were told during a special meeting at the beginning of the school year that homosexuality and other touchy issues would be part of the Life After Thayer class. It was a *personal* decision if students participated or not.

Barb Eibell and Melanie Zwolinski, who were both in the audience, attempted to defend the assignment. The attitude surveys, they said, photocopied from a textbook called *Human Sexuality*, were distributed after a viewing of *The Times of Harvey Milk*, a documentary about a gay San Francisco city supervisor who was murdered by a board member who hated homosexuals. No names were on the forms, they said, and participation wasn't mandatory.

Al Barton wasn't listening. "It's a no-win situation for students," he said. "A high score on this test means you're a homosexual yourself. A low score means you have a fear of the issue. Nowhere in the questionnaire was there a word about decency, moral values, and a sense of right or wrong," Barton said. "I'm talking about normal people, not queers. 'Queers' is what I've known them by for years. I know 'gays' is more popular these days."

Barton's comment drew shocked expressions from some in the crowd. He continued.

"If we're going to talk about sex, I know the answer to that," he said. "I'd hire a professional prostitute and let her teach the facts. She'd tell them the truth of the matter."

Barton made a motion to restrict the use in school of "any subject matter pertaining to AIDS, queers, and sex until it has been approved and reviewed by the school board."

Superintendent McCarthy said he'd have to check into

the legality of the motion, since the state had recently imposed a requirement for sex education in schools.

"As an editorial comment," McCarthy said, "the United States Surgeon General has gone on record as indicating that schools should get into curriculum development relative to the subject of AIDS."

"You know my feelings on state mandates," Barton responded.

The board approved Barton's motion.

Terri Racine left before the meeting was over. "I can't believe it," she said as she exited. "First they accuse Doc of being my baby's father. Now they're calling him a homosexual."

In that Friday's TGIF, Melanie Zwolinski offered up her perspective on the events:

> At this point in my life, I have realized a new commitment to continue to carry out the responsibilities that being an educator demands. After the meeting Wednesday night, I thought again about our L.A.T. class. Our students watched *The Times of Harvey Milk*. They became aware that this individual was murdered because another individual didn't approve of his homosexual lifestyle. As a means to address this issue our students completed an anonymous questionnaire that gave insight to their own tolerances about people who are different than they. Also included were minorities; specifically, Blacks, and Puerto Ricans; the multiple handicapped, and the mentally retarded. It is all of our basic value to accept that these people have rights like anyone else. After all, this nation was founded on that precept: All men are created equal and have been endowed with certain unalienable rights. Based on this belief, any education without this value, is valueless.

The homosexual survey proved to be great fodder for Paight's campaign. The Paight camp, which included Mar-

ilyn Nolan, put together a five-page packet titled "TRUTH
IN EDUCATION," claiming on the cover, "All facts contained in this brochure are true and can be substantiated!"
It reprinted eleven questions from the homosexual survey
and followed up with this:

> This test, plus another one, was given to seniors in L.A.T.
> class. A film about homosexual Harvey Milk was also
> shown. None have anything to do with A.I.D.S.! This is
> psychological manipulation.
> This incident, lack of proper supervision at school dance,
> and drugs at school were topics of concern voiced by Nancy
> Paight at the school board meeting. Do you believe every-
> thing that you read in the *Sentinel*? If readers knew what the
> *Sentinel* did not print, Thayer H.S. would be well on its way
> to becoming a good school, since the March 1985 election!

The packet repeated many of the charges from the board's
defeated court case as evidence of Littky's moral turpitude.

> Students are shown movies that portray men acting as
> women and vice versa as in the film, "All of Me," as well as
> movies rated PG or worse that have nothing to do with
> academics. Movies about the Viet Nam War are shown for
> "moral and psychological effect." Yet, sex education should
> be taught without the moral and psychological effects. . . .

The packet questioned figures Littky claimed showed a
decrease in dropout rates since he'd been principal. It was
critical of the apprenticeship program, citing five cases in
which Littky allegedly had deprived students of basic
courses or pushed them out of school.

Bobby Secord and Francis Gutoski engaged in some mud-
slinging and distortions of their own. They also took credit
for playing "key roles" in paying off the $106,000 deficit in
the school budget and creating a surplus of $52,000. In fact,
the windfall came as a result of the new state law that

redistributed state aid to property-poor towns such as Winchester. It was the legislation Littky had worked for during his two years as Winchester's representative. For his part, Bobby Secord hadn't even bothered to show up for the vote.

In another campaign blurb, the Gutoski-Secord campaign noted that "Robert Secord was the FIRST VOLUNTEER for the committee to study making more room for pupils at the elementary school." However, Secord never attended a single meeting of the committee.

Marian Polaski waged a telephone and door-to-door campaign that stressed her experience as a seven-year board member. "I want nothing to do with a negative campaign," Marian insisted over and over. Her attack, if it could be called that, was tame at best. She emphasized "Educational orientation rather than political orientation," "Return of harmony to the Town of Winchester," and "Needs of children top priority."

Bud Baker, ever the low-key politician, did no formal campaigning: "The people of Winchester know who I am."

In a last-ditch effort to mediate a solution to Littky's firing, the state's educational commission met with Littky and the school board's attorney. If some agreement could be reached, the state board wouldn't have to conduct a hearing. No accord was possible. Both sides remained far apart.

Ten days before the election, Jimmy Karlan filed suit against the school board seeking reinstatement and back pay as director of the apprenticeship program.

27
The Election

AN HOUR BEFORE THE POLLS were to open, voters had gathered in front of the school. It was a bleak, cold March day. What little snow remained was blackened by road dirt. Both sides of the road were peppered with Gutoski-Secord signs.

Littky supporters such as Marcia Ammann had been knocking on doors all day. Marian probably had four hundred votes—but was it enough? That morning, Marcia had read Marian Polaski's cards. "I don't know what this means," Marcia had said as she studied the cards. "You're going to win *twice*. I see two victories here." She'd also seen a dark-haired man, whom she took to be Bobby Secord, going away very angry.

The line of voters stretched from the gym door across the entire length of the lobby. At 4 P.M., when the polls were scheduled to open, there was a commotion over the whereabouts of the ballot box. The box was not in its usual place in the town hall, which was undergoing renovation. A search party formed; teacher Henry Parkhurst dashed to the school office and came back with a box barely big enough to store a hat. Elmer Johnson, there in his official capacity as town moderator, sneered at Henry.

"I guess you just don't send a boy to do a man's job."

Henry barked back, "I'm not your servant, Elmer."

Finally the box was found. The polls opened twenty minutes late.

The queue folded back upon itself into the lobby, eventually inching single file along the perimeter of the gymnasium. The procession moved forward quietly, seriously. During the first hour, the number of votes cast exceeded the total in most previous elections. One man, who had stood in line to vote for nearly an hour and a half, shook his head. "I ain't ever seen anything like it," he said. "I've been voting in Winchester for forty years and I never seen it this crowded."

On Route 10, the main street into town, posters stuck in the ground and mounted on trees broadcast the same message: "Vote Secord and Gutoski for Better Schools!" Polaski and Baker had put up their share of campaign posters, too, but by noon they were gone.

A stretch limousine, bearing Secord-Gutoski signs, transported elderly residents to the polls and dropped them off afterward for coffee and refreshments at the home of Mrs. Secord's grandmother on Mechanic Street. The limo service had been donated by Susan Winter's brother. It came complete with a wet bar, television set, and telephone.

Gil Seldes, a reporter from the *Keene Sentinel*, conducted random exit polls.

"Excuse me," he said to a group of women standing near the school parking lot. "What do you think of this turnout?"

"I think it's great," one of them said. "It just means people want some changes. There's too much crap going on and not enough education."

"Can you tell me how you voted?" Seldes asked.

"We're voting Littky out of here!"

In the front yard of the high school, placards announced that no campaigning would be permitted within one hundred feet of the polling place. Francis Gutoski, wearing a suit, tie, and beige trench coat buttoned over his huge gut, hunched over to help an old woman out of the limousine. Taking her by the arm, he escorted her into the school, past the line in the lobby, straight to the supervisors of the checklist, then across the gym to the head of the line at the polls. She marked her ballot and handed it to Elmer Johnson. Then, holding onto Gutoski's arm, she returned to the parking lot to await the return of the limo.

Ernie Royce stopped to shake Gutoski's hand, cracking a broad, toothless smile, then talked to a reporter as he walked up the sidewalk to the lobby. "Even if we lose, we're not giving up," Royce told the reporter. "We've been working to get rid of that man for three years. You don't think it's going to end here?

"It's going to be like getting rid of a Department of the Army civilian," Royce said. "And we have a saying about those, that they were just like the rockets—they won't work and you can't fire them. And that's pretty close to the truth.

"You have to establish what's called 'a paper trail,' and sometimes it takes five years to establish a paper trail of adequate documentation before any action can be taken. It will take the form of legal action at the end of the paper trail. There would be legal action coming out the ying yang then." At this point, however, the pile of paperwork Ernie and his cohorts had gathered did not constitute much that was "legally actionable," as he put it.

"Some of it's legally actionable, but I'm old army. I believe in old George Patton's tactics: You hammer 'em and hammer 'em and hammer 'em and hammer 'em, and then when you get done you say, 'Okay now, do you want to give up or do you want to fight?' "

Inside the gym, Marian Polaski greeted people after they filed past the table manned by Mary Johnson and other checklist supervisors. Marian smiled broadly, shaking hands, chatting with voters, and sucking on a Halls Mentho-Lyptus.

The line moved forward slowly under the harsh gymnasium lighting, which cast a purplish pallor on everybody's skin, turning their veins dark. The scene was funereal.

Erica Ryll, the high school home economics teacher who'd married Marcia Ammann's brother a little more than a year earlier, exchanged worried looks with Marian Polaski. Like other Littky supporters, she was stunned by the number of elderly people who had turned out to vote. "I don't know, Marian. I don't know most of these people. It makes me nervous."

Marian's hand slipped deeper into her suit pocket, working the jade green rosary she had brought with her. It was her most important rosary—her Irish one, the one her sister had given her. Around her neck hung a gold pendant, shaped like a three-leaf clover and adorned with a green translucent stone. Hers was an admixture of faith and charm.

An elderly woman Marian had never seen before, a woman who looked as if she had seen some hard times, filed toward her. Marian smiled. The woman smiled back, focused squarely on the green carnation corsage at Marian's lapel.

"You know what just happened to me?" she asked the carnation excitedly. "I just rode in a limmzeen! My relatives will never believe it! I just rode in a limmzeen! I'm votin' for Secord and Gutoski."

Marian was chagrined. She knew the tactics the opposition had used to get people out to vote. She knew the lies they were telling about Dennis, calling him a socialist agitator, a mind manipulator, a "black dirt psychologist." The latest rumors had him beating up a woman on Warwick Road—depending on which rumor you heard, it was either an old woman or a female Thayer student—and having sex with a former school board member. The opposition registered people who hadn't voted in years or had never exercised their franchise, saying if they didn't get out to vote, Littky's special programs would drive their taxes out of sight; they could lose their homes.

Marian was also suspicious about the way they were handling absentee ballots. Twice she had asked clerk Ruth Lawrence to send absentee ballots to two shut-ins who wanted to vote. One man had no legs; a woman was badly crippled with arthritis. Ruth said she wouldn't deliver the ballots, but said she would deputize Marian so that she could.

"I can't, Mrs. Lawrence," she had said. "I'm a candidate."

"I'll send them if they send me a written request," she responded.

When Gene Clark, a supporter of Marian's, heard about Lawrence's refusal, he got himself sworn in so he could deliver the ballots directly to the shut-ins. They mailed them back immediately. The clerk said she received them too late. They couldn't be counted.

In spite of all of this, Marian managed to dredge up a Christian disposition. "I just believe honesty will prevail," she would say.

Others were less kind.

Frankie Amarosa minced no words. "My stomach turns every time I think about it," he fretted. "These people have lied so much, they wouldn't know how to tell the truth even if they were to profit by it."

It'd been almost ten years since Dennis arrived in Winchester. Frankie no longer regarded him as the fledgling mountain man who needed tending like a child. "He's tougher than a pine knot now," Frankie said.

Bobby Secord, Susan Winter, her husband, and a handful of their supporters, including Marilyn Nolan's husband, huddled together near the exit talking to supporters.

In a gymnasium filled with people wearing work shirts, jeans, and winter coats in shades of brown, blue, and dark green, Susan Winter wore a bold floral print suit with fuchsia blouse and bright pink pumps. When Allen Barton walked in, she strode directly to him, greeting him with a big smile. Together they joined Bobby and group at the exit.

Dennis's parents had flown 3,500 miles from their home in Los Angeles to be with their only son for the conclusion of the year-long battle. His father was seventy-five and his mother sixty-eight, but both looked younger. Someone later commented, only half jokingly, that they looked younger than their son.

Here, surrounded by his friends and family, Dennis felt better than he had all day. He distracted himself by telling stories, joking and commenting on the goings-on.

Mrs. Littky fluttered comfortably about the gym as if she were the hostess of a big party, talking proudly about her son. Her California tan, fashionable black and white dress suit, and sweeping skirt clearly labeled her an outsider. Dennis's father, an amiable and soft-spoken man, let his wife do most of the talking.

When the polls closed at eight o'clock, 918 ballots had been cast and the tedious process of counting the votes began. About half the crowd left; the remainder milled about the gymnasium, talking, gossiping.

Seven town officials—the clerk, the moderator, and five supervisors of the checklist—recorded the count. Elmer, reading the results of each ballot, was double-checked by three officials. On the other side of the table, one man wrote down the results on a tally sheet. Two other supervisors checked him.

Occasionally, the woman marking the tally would tell Elmer to slow down. A few times, Elmer misread ballots and was corrected.

As Elmer continued reading off the names, it became very clear there would be no run-away winner. Baker-Polaski and Gutoski-Secord were neck and neck.

Suddenly, a commotion arose from the counting table. Something about absentee ballots. As Elmer Johnson read off the names on the ballots, Jack Ainsworth was systematically challenging each one. More than fifty had already been accepted. Now he contested the twenty-seven remaining ballots.

"Why were ballots distributed to people whose names weren't on the checklist?" he demanded.

Ruth Lawrence, in her twentieth year as clerk, feebly explained she didn't have a checklist at the time the ballots were sent out. The same thing had happened last year.

The anti-Littky forces were in an uproar over Ainsworth's challenges. "What's he trying to prove?" Susan Winter sneered to another woman.

When the counting was done, Elmer Johnson picked up his papers and walked to the podium to read off the results.

Dennis held his breath.

"Baker—456," Elmer said. "Gutoski—324. Kelly—84. Paight—75. Polaski—432. Secord—423 . . ."

Before the last number was read, a roar filled the auditorium. Susan Winter, Bobby Secord, Francis Gutoski, Nancy Paight, and their small clique of supporters headed for the exit. The crowd rallied around Dennis, hugging him, slapping him on the back, cheering, jumping up and down.

Mrs. Littky gripped her son in a tight hug. Her voice trembled with excitement. "I love you," she said.

Val Cole, Cindy Nelson, and Marian Polaski embraced. Barb Eibell, who came in moments after the announcement was made, shrieked when she realized the outcome; big tears slid down her cheeks.

"I wasn't worried. I wasn't worried," Winnie Amarosa chanted.

Don Weisburger, wearing his satin Thayer jacket, wheeled Dennis about by the arm, then gave him a hug.

But the cheers of victory soon gave way.

"Why only nine votes?" Marian groaned as Marcia hugged her.

Littky, too, suddenly realized what that meant. His smile faded. "There's going to be a recount," he said.

Marian and Bud approached Elmer Johnson for the swearing-in, but Elmer refused.

"We have a right to be sworn in," Marian said.

"I don't know," Elmer said. "There's only nine votes difference. Twenty-five votes have been challenged. That's what I don't know."

As more people realized what was happening, a commotion erupted.

"We'd like to have it done now," Marian Polaski insisted. "We've been legally elected."

From the crowd, angry voices shouted at Elmer.

"Why are you doing this?"

"He's refusing because it didn't go the way he wanted it to go."

"You've been elected to perform a duty, Elmer, now do it!"

Officer Herm Winter radioed the police station that there was trouble at the high school and called for reinforcements.

Elmer backed away from the crowd. "I see there's a possibility of a recount," he said. "Twenty-five ballots have been contested."

"I withdraw my contest," Jack Ainsworth shouted. "If it will make a difference, I officially withdraw!"

But Johnson would not be moved. "I have never sworn in a town officer until it was clear it wouldn't be challenged," he said.

Someone remembered that any justice of the peace could perform the swearing-in ceremony, and a call went out to Marge Austin, the town clerk, at home.

Would she come down and swear in the new board members?

But Austin refused. "One more day won't hurt. I'm not going to walk in there and disrupt Elmer's jurisdiction tonight. But call me back if you need to."

Elmer turned away from the crowd and began walking toward the door.

Carolyn Nicholson ran toward the gym door ahead of him, then slammed it closed to prevent Elmer from leaving. "I will not be disenfranchised by this man!" she shouted. The crowd clapped, rooting for her. But Carolyn couldn't lock the door, and Elmer brushed past her, escorted part way by Susan Winter's father-in-law, the policeman. Other policemen had stationed themselves unobtrusively around the area.

Mrs. Littky followed Elmer to the lobby door. She came back saying, "He met three people in the parking lot."

Marian Polaski was teary-eyed. "Anything to ruin our celebration," she said.

Bud Baker looked at her. "We'll take care of that tomorrow. I will get a hold of you tomorrow, Marian. We'll take care of it."

28
Mind Jogger

THE ELECTION-NIGHT PARTY AT Barb Eibell's house had been billed as either a celebration or a good-bye party for Dennis. It turned out to be neither.

No one could celebrate wholeheartedly. They had won, it was true. But the election was too close, and Elmer had refused to swear in Marian and Bud.

High up on the hill, lights were on at Bobby Secord's large green house. The driveway and the parking area near the house were loaded with cars.

It was after midnight when the two dozen or so guests streamed into the Eibell's small ranch house and crowded into the basement. Most of the women had brought trays of finger foods—deviled eggs, cold cuts, sandwiches. Two bottles of pink sparkling wine appeared as well, and thimble-sized portions were dispensed in plastic cups.

Dennis came down the steps. There were hoots and applause. He still wore his herringbone sport coat, but his tie hung loosely around his neck, and he wore his Detroit Tigers baseball cap.

Dennis was tired. But, true to form, he propelled himself around the room, shaking hands, throwing his arms around shoulders and waists, talking, joking, laughing.

Deep down, though, he felt a worry he couldn't shake. At that moment, the ballots were in the school clerk's hands. The clerk had taken them home with her just as she had after twenty previous school board elections.

368

Dennis tried to make light of his worry.

"Frankie is going to break into her house," Dennis announced loudly, slapping Frankie Amarosa on the back. "He's going to steal the ballots, get caught, and get tossed in jail with the ballots so they'll be safe."

Littky supporters believed the clerk was in Secord's camp. Those in Secord's camp thought she was a Littky worker. What side she really supported, if any, was information she kept to herself.

Two of Marian's campaigners had followed the clerk home to see if anyone from the opposition met her. No one was there when she drove up her driveway, nor did anyone arrive during the several minutes the two waited. Then they felt foolish for having followed her at all.

The telephone rang. Barb's husband answered it. "It's for you, Dennis."

Dennis strutted over to the phone and shouted boisterously, "Hello, Mr. President."

Everyone laughed.

It was Littky's attorney, Jon Meyer. He confirmed that any justice of the peace could swear in the new board members.

When Marian Polaski descended the basement stairs, she was buoyed by a chorus of congratulations. Winnie Amarosa handed her a bouquet of flowers and hugged her hard. Marian cried.

"Don't let them get to you," Cindy Nelson said, giving her an affectionate squeeze around the shoulders.

"Marian, just remember one thing, you've been elected. That's it," Marcia said.

Marian's face was the best barometer of the confusion she felt. One moment happy, the next crying, the next blank.

"Elmer was so ugly to me," Marian told Winnie. "I went over to him and told him, 'You hurt my feelings. I thought I really respected you.'" Winnie nodded.

"Quiet, everybody," Barb shouted from the other end of

the basement. "I'd like to make a toast. This is spontaneous, but it's the best I can do. I want to toast to Marian for her hard work, to Marcia for her valiant effort last year, to Dennis, the best boss I've ever had, and to all of my favorite colleagues and all of my neighbors who have worked so hard to finally begin to do and show what 'Truth in Education' really is."

Thirty minutes later, the party started to thin out. It was after 1 A.M., and most of the guests had to be back at school in six hours. Dennis eased himself onto a small sofa and closed his eyes, listening to the din of voices around him. He'd had a headache on and off all day, and now it was back, throbbing.

The echo of cheers, victory toasts, and laughter still rang in his ears, but he didn't feel victorious. Bobby Secord had lost by nine votes. Francis Gutoski wasn't far behind him. They had gotten to the older people in town, people with whom Dennis had very little contact. The rumors still smarted. He'd been made out to be some sort of ogre or sexual pervert or socialist agitator, or what all else, he didn't know. What he did know was that it hurt. The people had not delivered the mandate he had hoped they would in getting rid of Secord.

Dennis could hear his mother talking spiritedly with a teacher. His father was laughing at someone's joke. He looked around the room. Melanie Zwolinski, Don, Barb, Marcia, and Marian—he was surrounded by friends.

Yet, in the midst of all this celebration, he could summon up no sense of release. At that moment, he felt no different than he had during the election buildup. The fight was not over. It would go on and on. Why had it all become so wild, so ugly? A few minutes later, the party broke up.

Outside, it was a windless night. A light snow fell. Bobby Secord's house was dark.

The next morning, the ballots were moved out of the

clerk's house and locked up in the town safe. A number of town officials had access to the safe.

Bud Baker went down to the town hall that morning to inspect the ballot box. The box was as he remembered it the night before—taped on all sides, with his, Elmer's, and the clerk's signatures across each piece of tape. But Eugene Clark, also at the town hall that morning, wasn't so sure.

Bud drove to Marian's. Though still jittery himself, it was he who offered words of support.

"The box wasn't tampered with," he said. "Let's just worry about getting sworn in."

But Marian didn't want to make any mistakes. She called her lawyer first. "It's absolutely your legal right to be sworn in," he said.

Marian followed that phone call with one to the secretary of state's office, who told her to hold off getting sworn in because there might be a recount. It would be better to take no action until that was known, he said.

Maybe she ought to wait, Marian thought to herself. Maybe it would be better to wait until after the weekend. But when she expressed these thoughts to the group at her house, everyone implored her to do it as soon as possible.

At six o'clock that night, the town clerk reluctantly swore in Bud and Marian. Fifteen minutes earlier, the school district clerk had received Bobby Secord's written request for a recount.

On Monday following the election, Francis C. Gutoski filed his request with the New Hampshire Ballot Law Commission seeking a new election. He listed seven reasons for the request. Among his assertions:

- The polls opened late. The man who helped prepare the voting place was a candidate in the election and also a school teacher.
- Ballot very confusing.
- All absentee ballots were challenged by Mr. Ainsworth.
- Non residents were allowed to enter the voting place.

The ballot recount was held one week after the election. For most of that time, the ballots and the ballot box had been impounded at the county sheriff's office. The box was brought out for examination by the moderator, the clerk, and the chairperson of the school board just before the recount. The cardboard box had been sealed with wide tape on all sides on the night of the election. The moderator, the clerk, and the board chairperson had each scribbled their signatures across the tape. All three examined the box and agreed there appeared to have been no tampering. But the tape lifted off the box easily, without tearing.

Because the recount was held at 10 A.M. on a weekday, only a dozen or so spectators attended. A few had taken the day off work, but most of those present at the town hall that day were retired persons or housewives. Bobby Secord was out of uniform. Instead of a suit and tie, he was wearing work pants and a green windbreaker.

Also out of character, Bobby was publicly voicing his anger. "You can't sit there! You get away from the table!" he yelled at Marian Polaski, who had positioned herself close to the recount table. "I want everybody down there at that end of the gym," he demanded, pointing a stiff finger.

A crowd of people remained at the recount table.

Secord raised his voice and his face turned florid as he demanded that they move back.

Marian stood her ground. She spoke evenly, politely.

"Now, the law says I can sit within six feet. I'm within my rights, and that means everybody has a right."

Her attorney busily thumbed through the statutes. "Six feet," he confirmed. "Spectators can come within six feet of the counting table."

The tables and chairs were pushed back to form a box around the counting table. Marian chose to have her attorney take her place at the recount table.

All candidates and board members were permitted to

observe the board of recount. Ammann, Baker, Secord, and Gutoski were present. Susan Winter and Allen Barton did not attend.

Marian sat at a table on the sidelines, surrounded by her supporters. She had two tape recorders running. Reporters and photographers milled about. The Pinards sat in the first row of chairs, just behind the rope.

The clerk held several absentee ballots that had been received too late. "If I didn't get them before the eighteenth at five o'clock, they aren't valid," the clerk said.

The board of recount checked the postmarks and agreed they should not be accepted.

"You folks jump right on me if I'm going too fast," Elmer said.

"I will," Marcia said emphatically.

Elmer reached into the ballot box and began the tedious process of reading off 918 ballots.

"Paight. Parkhurst."

"Gutoski. Secord."

"Gutoski. Secord."

"Baker. Polaski."

"Kelly. Secord."

And so the counting went for nearly an hour.

"Polaski-Secord, Polaski-Secord." Elmer opened another ballot. Before he read off the names, Marian's lawyer said he objected to the ballot. Elmer placed the ballot in a pile with several others that also had been contested. Every now and again, Elmer misread some of the ballots.

"That should have been Baker-Secord, so now you've got one extra for Polaski," Elmer said, correcting himself.

A worker in the town office relayed a message that Secord had a phone call. The counting stopped while he answered the phone. Marian's attorney leaned forward. "It's very close," he said to Marian and her supporters. "There are about ten to fifteen disputed ballots."

"What's this phone call about?" Marian asked.

"I think it's about their petition to superior court."

"I think there's something else up their sleeve," she said.

Secord returned to his position. Elmer quietly read the names and the columns of figures. Because of the distance from the recount table and Elmer's subdued voice, it was nearly impossible for anyone in the audience to hear him without strain.

Elmer: "The next one is Polaski: 88, 56, 97, 83, 100. Right?"

"Right," came the response from the other side of the table.

Elmer: "Secord: 77, 60, 94, 100, 91. Right? Have I got those right?"

"Yes."

What the board of recount knew—but what nearly no one else did—was that Polaski had 424 votes and Secord 422.

Secord was agitated. "There were six ballots received that weren't counted," he said.

"They were received after 5 P.M. on March the 18th," Marian's attorney said.

"Did they come in after the deadline, Mr. Secord?" Marian said. Secord stiffened but ignored her.

Secord, still in his green windbreaker, kept his hands on either side of his huge girth as he pressed his second point. "What about the contested ballots?"

Thirteen ballots had been set aside because it wasn't clear what was meant by the markings.

The meeting was recessed until 1:30 P.M.

Shortly before the meeting resumed, Susan Winter and Allen Barton appeared. *Sentinel* reporter Gil Seldes asked them if they had been called down to participate in the vote on the contested ballots. Susan, whose office at First Northern Bank in Keene was twenty-five minutes away, said she was on her lunch break and had just happened in. Barton, looking like he'd just come in from the farm, said he, too, just happened to be in the neighborhood.

Angry comments from the audience protested that Elmer was reconstituting the board for his own convenience. Barton and Winter took their seats on Elmer's side of the table. Elmer explained that Barton and Winter had been part of the board of recount all along; it didn't matter that they hadn't participated in the earlier proceedings.

During the recess, Elmer had talked to the secretary of state, who had informed him that the recount that day was the only recount Winchester could hold on the election. Cheshire County Superior Court could probably rule on the thirteen disputed ballots.

"I think we're all agreed on the others," Elmer said, taking up the contested ballots. "I will rule on the ballot first and give my reasons. This is challenge number one. Are you ready?"

Elmer studied the ballot.

"Parkhurst. Polaski," he said and passed it to the clerk.

"Parkhurst. Polaski," she said and showed it to Barton.

Barton took hold of the ballot.

"You're not supposed to handle ballots. Ruth and I are the only ones who are supposed to handle ballots," Elmer said congenially.

Barton took his time. "Most people would put a check. I can't distinguish if it's Polaski or Secord."

Marian's attorney looked over Barton's shoulder. "I think it's pretty clear," he said.

"I don't care what your opinion is!" Barton snapped. Then he said, "I can't guess at what someone intended." He read one vote for Parkhurst, opting to ignore the second vote.

The contest went on; the next batch of ballots were called for Secord-Gutoski.

"May I speak?" Marian's attorney said. "I think I have a

right to speak." The attorney was holding a document from the secretary of state's office that showed examples of how to rule on ballots with confusing markings. The picture he offered was identical to the ballot then being considered.

"I don't have a right to tell you how to vote, but I have a right to speak. This is the very thing the secretary of state says to throw out," the attorney said, thrusting the handbook toward Elmer.

"Are you on the board of recount?" Barton said.

"No, I am not," the attorney said.

"Then be quiet!"

Again the ballot went around. Again the vote was split. Again the vote went to Gutoski and Secord. So did the next two.

"Where's our tally sheet," Elmer asked. Someone handed it to him. "Three for Baker, right? Two, four, six, eight, nine for Gutoski. None for Kelly. None for Paight. One for Parkhurst. Four for Polaski. Nine for Secord."

The audience did not stir. Secord had won the recount by three votes. No announcements were made. Elmer rambled on about the absentee ballots that were postmarked after the 18th.

"Ruth handled them properly," he said. "The ballots will be in the town safe. If Superior Court orders them to be brought to them, the state police will be called to deliver them. We're all in agreement on the first 905 ballots. There were only 13 ballots contested. They have five days within which to request a recount or they can ignore it. That's a bridge they're going to have to cross."

Barton, Secord, Winter, and Gutoski left almost immediately. Marian's supporters rallied around her, lending words of encouragement. Elmer worked on the ballot box.

"We were under a tremendous amount of pressure," he said. "In an election this close, it's anybody's guess. There was a lot of stress and a lot of noise there that night."

The ballot box was resealed, and Baker bent over to sign the four strips of tape.

Peter and Peg Pinard lingered at the entryway of the town hall. "I'm pleased. I'm very pleased," Peter said.

Frankie Amarosa, who had stopped by several times during the course of the recount, was leaning against the outside of F. J. Amarosa Jr. & Son's Hardware. He watched Gutoski and Secord leave the town hall together. Both of them looked happy.

"Damn crazy, crazy world," he said.

Inside the store, Winnie looked up at her husband, her eyes moist. A tear slipped over the edge. "What do they have against Dennis?"

Without missing a beat, Frank turned, jerked a tissue from a box and handed it to his wife.

In spite of the crush of people in attendance and the undercurrent of tension, the board meeting that night was comparatively uneventful. Neither Marian nor Bobby took a seat on the board. By law, three days must pass before Bobby could resume his position. Gutoski and Secord had succeeded in obtaining the injunction preventing the board from taking any action on Littky's contract for the time being.

The board renewed contracts for all the teachers without discussion. A resignation was accepted from a long-time Thayer teacher. The assistant superintendent read from his letter: "I am sorry to have to submit my resignation. My years as a teacher under Dr. Littky have been the most rewarding years of my career. Dr. Littky has created a spirit in the high school unlike any I've ever seen."

At home that evening, Dennis picked up a die and shook it back and forth in his hand. He was sitting on the floor of the cottage he rented on Forest Lake during the winter months, slouched against the couch, smoking a pipe. It was a position he hadn't varied much since getting home that night. He leafed absentmindedly through a book, a modern-day version of *I Ching (The Book of Changes)*. He turned to the back, where there were blanks to be filled in by the user, pausing at a few pages that already had been filled.

Dennis had purchased *Mind Jogger* about a year earlier for his Life After Thayer class as a problem-solving tool. The book came with the twenty-sided die he held in his hand. Each roll of it was designed to help him work through a problem, just as the fall of the coins or forty-nine yarrow stalks were designed to help the I Ching user solve his. The book asked him to state the problem.

"Too much shit. Too many lies. Too much distraction," he wrote in big, careless letters.

He shook the die, enjoying the gentle motion against his palm, and tossed it on the floor next to him. Fifteen. He picked up the book, turned to guide 15, and read.

"INTUITION. . . . In the problem you presently face there is a struggle between trusting your intuition and turning to experts or other authorities. That is the root of the problem."

He took a deep draw on his pipe. "That's certainly true," he thought to himself. "The school board is the authority, and I have no control over it."

He wrote, "Imbalance between my self power & power of higher authority."

He rolled the die again. Twenty. This guide was labeled "THE STORM. . . . As an inner storm passes, give yourself time to mourn the loss of important beliefs, feelings, a place, or even a person you have lost. Accept the loss of an old way. Let go."

He wrote, "Accept loss—let go."

His final roll. One. "TRADITION. . . . Study the past and you will discover new knowledge. Alternatives will become clear when you acknowledge tradition and forge new paths that avoid errors which others have already made."

Dennis wrote, "Study the past—avoid errors & learn from it."

Each roll of the die brought him closer to a conclusion he hadn't until then believed a real possibility. He might lose. Despite his undying faith in himself and his unwavering optimism—he was registering for the first time the possibility that the school board might succeed in firing him.

Mind Jogger was a guide, a system. On a couple of other occasions, he'd used the system to help friends formulate thoughts and work out their problems. But this time it seemed more than that. It seemed prescient. For Dennis, the acts of rolling the die and reading the guide congealed in a moment the months and months of rumblings in his subconscious. He was compelled to acknowledge for the first time that he might fail.

Nothing in Dennis Littky's history or his composition had prepared him for failure. From his boyhood on, everything he had tried had been blessed with success. He was the wunderkind, the favored child, the boy voted most likely to succeed by his elementary school class. He had spent his life steeped in success. He took a job at Ocean Hill–Brownsville because education was his thing, and in 1968 Ocean Hill–Brownsville had had everything: poverty, depravity, conflict, experimentation, innovation, excitement. If it was happening anywhere, it was happening at Ocean Hill–Brownsville. So that was where he went. Ideals, implementation, conflict, success. He had repeated the process over and over again—at Stony Brook, at Shoreham–Wading River Middle School, in the mountains. It was a pattern he was used to, a pattern he repeated like a karma: ideals, implementation, conflict, success. This karma had sustained him through the past year. He had been so sure that if he just stuck it out, whatever pain and torment he had to endure would be worth it in the end. Because certainly he would win. He always had.

But now things were out of control. He had done all the

fighting he could. He had kept the school together and kept as far from the political fray as was humanly possible. He had maintained his cool, maintained his perspective—his job was to be a good principal. He was proud of the fact that if a stranger had walked into the school that day, he would have had no idea it was under siege. Leave politics in the boardroom, he had thought to himself; ignore the hole it's burning in the pit of your stomach.

It was not that he had never entertained the possibility of loss before. He had, but only intellectually—only because, as a realist, he had to acknowledge the abstract possibility of it. So many people were on his side. So many had said to him the election would be the litmus test that would tell the rest of the world that most of Winchester was not crazy—just a few fanatics, a handful from the lunatic fringe, but certainly not a majority of the townspeople.

"What will I do?" Dennis asked himself, rubbing the smooth pipe bowl. It had taken every bit of self-control to attend the board meeting that night. He had called Assistant Superintendent Dick McCarthy shortly after hearing the result of the recount. He didn't remember much of their conversation. What he did remember was that he had lost control. He cried. Dick had been unnerved.

"You don't have to come to the meeting tonight, Dennis," Dick told him.

He couldn't do that—not to show up would be to let them get the better of him. He was the principal; he attended any and all school functions he could. It had taken an enormous amount of effort to sit at the same table with Winter and Barton and treat them civilly. Oddly, even the urge to tell them how he really felt about what they had done to the school, to tell them what hypocrites they were, eluded him that night. He was a shell—spent, empty.

Maybe he would be better off out of Winchester. No more public abuse, no more prying into his private life, no more

hatred and calumny. He had been serious for so many
months, too serious. That's not how he was. That's not how
he liked to be. If he was forced to move on, so be it. He could
write that book he'd always wanted to write. He could work
with the Coalition at Brown University. He could travel. He
could have fun, take it easy, be himself. Six years at Thayer
was a long time. He owed no apologies. He had given
everything he had to the school for those six years. Having
never entertained the idea of being anywhere else, now he
wondered if his fighting so tenaciously to stay on had less to
do with a commitment to the school than with his hatred of
failure. He hated the thought of being forced out. He'd even
thought about talking to Secord, offering a deal: if Secord
agreed to withdraw from the race and let Marian be the
board member, he would quit the principalship. That way,
the town would be assured of a good board, and he could
leave Winchester without damaging the school.

Finally, the smell of overcooked salmon steak reached his
nostrils. He struggled to his feet to retrieve the now indis-
tinguishable object that was his dinner, carried it back to
his place on the floor, and ate. Chewing, but not tasting.

29
Roller Coaster Ride

ON APRIL 15, CHESHIRE COUNTY Superior Court Judge Philip Holman reviewed the contested ballots and made some changes in the calls.

When the votes were tallied again, the count was Marian Polaski 427, Bobby Secord 427.

"I feel like I'm on some kind of roller coaster," Littky said when he heard the news. "First Marian wins and Secord loses. Then Marian loses and Secord wins. Now they're tied. . . ."

According to state law, any tie in an election would be decided by the flip of a coin or some other chance method. But because of election "irregularities" cited by both sides, the judge opted to give Winchester forty-five days to decide the matter on its own. What form it would take was up to the town. If no alternative solution were found, a coin would serve as arbiter.

The candidates, every one of them, wanted the voters—rather than fate—to decide the outcome. State Representative Eugene Clark put together a bill calling for a new election, which, if passed, would supercede anything decided by the ballot law commission. That would keep the matter in Winchester's control. The bill passed the house with no problems, but on May 14, the day it was to be considered by the Senate, it got lost. Somewhere between the legislative conference committee and the senate floor, the bill simply disappeared.

Eugene Clark knocked heads with Junie Blaisdell, Winchester's senator, and went in search of another bill to attach it to as an amendment. The next day Clark succeeded in getting legislators to agree to attach the amendment to a house bill dealing with vocation-technical education. Unfortunately, the house adjourned before the bill came up that day. Which pushed the matter to Friday.

On Friday, the house and senate passed the bill calling for a new school board election. Only the governor's signature remained to turn the bill into law—but the governor was out of town.

On Wednesday, the day before the deadline, the bill was still unsigned.

"A bureaucratic miracle will be needed to enact the bill before the judge's deadline," Eugene Clark said. "It doesn't look good. We have to get it signed by the speaker and the president, and we have to hope they're in town."

Finally, late Wednesday night, New Hampshire Governor John H. Sununu signed into law Senate Bill 64 legalizing a new vote.

In the midst of it all, a new controversy erupted. Now the school board wanted to prevent Littky from participating in the graduation ceremony that spring.

At his second Thayer graduation, Doc had endeavored to personalize the event by reading a paragraph or two about each graduate—his recollections of the student's achievements and foibles, and his or her special contribution to Thayer. The personal notes were such a hit that students and families insisted that Doc make them a graduation tradition.

"I personally would like to see graduation conducted in a more professional fashion," Susan Winter told the packed audience at the May 21 board meeting. "I really feel that in some places last year's graduation turned out to be a circus."

Winter also criticized the T-shirt the senior class gave him that year with "Our Principal" on the front. The student who presented the T-shirt had said, "He's a very special friend to us. Whether he leaves or stays, he's our number one principal."

Allen Barton, newly appointed board president, agreed with Winter. "The three or four lines spoken about each student—I didn't think it was appropriate. Graduation is kind of a solemn occasion. . . . I think it should be strictly without emotion."

Social studies teacher Henry Parkhurst rose to his feet. "I have been helping out with graduation going on thirteen years," he said. "I think I walk away every June with a dignified feeling. For relatives who come for miles to see their family members graduate, the highlight is to hear that one or two or three lines by their principal about the child that they may not have known. Please leave this part of the program in."

The applause came hard and fast.

Then Bud Baker and Marcia Ammann spoke in favor of Doc's participation in commencement. Assistant Superintendent Dick McCarthy, vowing that administrators would not let the 1987 graduation become a "political revue," said that Thayer seniors supported Doc's role in the ceremony in a recent senior class vote. He also submitted a letter signed by most of the parents of the thirty-eight graduating seniors asking that Doc be allowed to give his speeches.

Allen Barton turned to McCarthy. "Do you have sufficient direction?" he said, without inviting a motion.

"Yes," McCarthy responded.

"I think that concludes that," Barton said. Doc could give his speeches after all.

The tension was beginning to wear. The ups and downs, twists and turns, had gotten to Marian Polaski. She wished sometimes that she'd never gotten involved.

Teachers, too, were bending under the strain. Karen

Marsh, in her second year as a special education aide and pregnant with her second child, was more than a little concerned about the future. If Marian lost and Doc left, she'd leave the school, too.

When it seemed clear that one way or another there would be a second election, it was all Marian could do to get up the energy to call her campaign workers together for a meeting at her home.

About ten of the election stalwarts gathered at the Polaski's yellow ranch house. Marian, wearing a blouse, pants, and white tennis shoes, alternated between squatting on the floor next to the big fish tank in her knotty pine–paneled family room and bustling to the kitchen for coffee and lemonade.

Dennis, sitting under a wooden cross and a heavily shellacked picture of the Last Supper, remained subdued throughout the meeting. Actively campaigning for Marian was just a little too close to campaigning for his own job. It was their election. *They* had to win it. He was there for support . . . but no more.

As the end of the school year neared, there was no softening of tensions. The political situation was unresolved and would remain so until after summer vacation began. Doc's guess was as good as anybody's on whether he would have a job next year. Talk circulated that "the opposition" planned to sabotage graduation. It was said the salutatorian planned to deliver a speech condemning Littky and Thayer High School. On top of it all, the state was conducting a ten-year evaluation of Thayer to renew its accreditation.

Doc poured his energy into running the school, trying to insulate it from the political wrangling. At the opening-night banquet welcoming the evaluation committee to Thayer, he greeted the evaluators, parents, board members, and staff.

"We do this every Sunday," Doc said, laughing. Yellow

daffodils adorned the center of each table; plates were
loaded with food. A cricket somewhere in the room sang
loudly. "There will be bingo until midnight," he said. "The
pool and sauna also will be open." The group laughed
with him.

Then Don Weisburger spoke. "This is our presentation
on the school and community," he said. "This is the students' work. It's their own words, their own feelings, and
their own writing and speaking style. This is the culmina-
tion of several months of work."

Two students manned the slide projector and sound system. Music played as the scenes flashed—a church steeple,
the town hall, the covered bridge, the library, Amarosa's
Hardware, kids walking in the shade of Parker Street, the
brightly painted geometric on the front door of Thayer
High School. The scenes stopped and a spotlight shone on
the face of a student.

"For two years I have been in a combination class of
science and writing," he said. "We, the students, call it Sci/
Wri. This period is no longer; it is just divided time between the subjects. For example, in our class we used science to build mechanical machines and writing skills to
take notes and record what we did that day."

The slides continued—the flag in front of the school, the
geodesic dome, the post-and-beam barn. Spotlight: "Something that makes Thayer real special," said freshman
Butchy Jones, a member of Weisburger's advisory, "is our
advisory system. The advisory can be a one-on-one conference with your adviser. It takes place in the morning before
school or right after school. You talk about your subjects
and how you are doing in your classes. If I'm having a
problem, then the teacher comes to my adviser and we, as a
group, work it out so it eliminates having to use the principal. If it keeps happening, then we use the principal. My
adviser and I go skiing, to see the Red Sox, and also go out

for dinner together. My adviser is not just an adviser. He is also my friend."

More pictures—students working on the newspaper, kids carrying a teacher on their shoulders, a boy playing the drums, teachers dressed up as cheerleaders, a group of teachers and students laughing. Spotlight: Stephanie White, another member of Weisburger's advisory. "Thayer provides an atmosphere that encourages me to put my best into all of my work," she said. "This atmosphere is created by the teachers and the classroom environments. The teachers challenge me to think and solve problems. I am never *given* the answers to problems. I am constantly encouraged to seek the solutions on my own."

Pictures—broken cafeteria tables, dirty walls, stained ceiling tiles, graffiti. Students painting lockers and affixing new tabletops in the cafeteria, Nick Collins painting the wings of the Pegasus. Spotlight: Mike Howe. "As I look back upon my six years of being at Thayer High School," he said, "it becomes very difficult to calculate the improvements made to our school building. You hear so much in today's world of teenagers and their lack of respect toward school property. Yes, there are those that just don't care in every school. But when it is evident that a majority of the students in a school show that they care about what their building looks like, it truly becomes exhilarating.

"As you walk through the halls of Thayer High School, you will see reflections of how we feel about this building. As you walk into the cafeteria, you confront a mural of the winged horse Pegasus and when you walk into the gym, it's nearly impossible to ignore our symbol on the wall—the tiger. When you walk through the front door, you will see murals displaying great artistic ability. You might be tempted to say, 'Dr. Littky sure must have spent a lot of taxpayers' money having a professional artist paint such murals.' . . . In fact, all these artists are or have been students at Thayer High School. Students here really care what our building looks like. No, you don't see graffiti or vulgar language on the walls, but only artistic beauty.

"With the evidence before you, you can see that we students of Thayer High School care about what type of environment we live in for six hours out of the day. For the care from the heart stimulates the brain to learn."

The evaluators were hugely impressed with the presentations. Marian Polaski, Marcia Ammann, and Bud Baker joined in the enthusiastic applause. Board members Susan Winter and Allen Barton were conspicuous by their absence.

Howard Spaulding stood near Thayer High with a home video camera on his shoulder, rolling the film as his son Nathan, in cap and gown, stepped his way to his seat below the outdoor stage. Ernie Royce, in rumpled work clothes, stood next to his young son, in spotless dress whites.

Men behind large television cameras jockeyed for position. Newspaper, television, and radio reporters moved through the crowd armed with microphones, notebooks, and cameras.

Mrs. Racine pointed up at the podium. "Elizabeth," she whispered into her granddaughter's ear, "do you see your mommy?"

Terri Racine, senior class president, adjusted the mortarboard on her head and turned to face the crowd that had assembled. "On behalf of the senior class of 1987, I'd like to welcome you to the sixty-fifth commencement ceremony at Thayer High School," she began. "Each one of us has a scrapbook, real or imaginary. I would like to turn a page or two of my scrapbook and share some of my memories."

Terri recalled the eighth-grade production of the *Wizard of Oz*, fund-raisers, the prom, the senior trip to Cancun, Mexico.

"The sun was rising and the waves were breaking over the rocks below us," Terri said, recalling the trip. "It was then that I realized that this was to be one of our last times together as a class. We were watching the sun rise, but the sun was really setting on our memories. I looked around at every person and I remembered something special that I'd shared with that person at one time or another. Even through some rough times we've always managed to keep our friendship strong. This year we've all grown together. But now the time has come to put aside our memories and get on with the rest of our lives.

"My wish for the entire class of 1987 is that you will all push yourselves beyond what you believe to be your limit and that you lead a happy, fulfilling life. We must all promise one another to never say goodbye."

Terri's throat tightened and the tears ran as she read her last line. "I'm proud to say that I'm a member of the Thayer High School class of 1987." She felt embraced by the applause that followed.

As the salutatorian walked up on stage to read her speech, Doc braced himself to intervene in the event it turned into an attack. If it did, he planned to announce to the audience that the comments were not part of the speech she had cleared with the senior class advisers, but that she would be allowed to continue.

But the speech cast no aspersions. She ended saying, "No matter where you are or what you do, don't forget your days at Thayer."

The sun was setting behind the stately pines as Dennis Littky walked up on stage. He wore a brand-new suit and tie and gripped a couple of dozen pages ripped from a yellow legal pad. He addressed the seniors.

"You are a class with dignity, a class that's learned to speak up for what you think is right. But you were always respectful with your actions. You're a class that worked hard so you had choices. I love to hear you say, 'Should I take this job or go to this college?' You were in command. Each of you has made a decision. For some, working was just right; others need time off; over half of you are going on to further schooling. It's your choice. Everyone is excited about what they're doing. Nobody has been backed into an option.

"I will read a paragraph or so that I wrote on each of you. What you'll see is the spark, the individuality, the fun, the hard work. For these are our special young men and women that we, and I, love and care for."

One by one, he read his messages out loud. Long before Doc got to hers, tears streamed down Terri's cheeks.

When Doc was done, he rubbed his woolly beard, now more gray than red. He didn't see the cameras; he didn't see the crowd of parents and well-wishers. His attention was focused on the Thayer High School graduating class of 1987.

"You are special, every one," he said, "to me, to your family, to your friends, to your teachers. Keep your dignity and respect, because in our hearts we will always be together."

In one great wave, the graduates and audience stood and applauded Dennis Littky, their principal.

30
Back to Basics

IT RAINED ALL DAY THE Saturday before the June 30 election. Chris Frado stationed herself at the Winchester town dump with an armload of campaign literature.

"Don't forget to vote Tuesday," she yelled, waving a Baker-Polaski sign and balancing an umbrella over her shoulder. She'd brought her wolf puppy with her. Now more mud than fur, the pup was doing battle with an empty Kellogg's Corn Flakes box.

Chris was new to town, but already she knew that the town dump was the cross-cultural collecting spot on any given Saturday in Winchester, and was, therefore, fertile stumping soil. She'd joined the Polaski-Baker campaign a few weeks earlier after voting for Bobby Secord in the first election. She'd cast her vote for Secord because she knew he owned the strip mall on Route 10. She had figured a businessman made a good political prospect. At the time she knew nothing of the battle raging in Winchester. When she found out, she was horrified that she'd cast her vote for Secord. To make up for her blunder, she pledged her support to Baker and Polaski's campaign.

Ever since the governor signed the bill that nullified the March election, Bud and Marian's campaign had been building a head of steam. Recruits and volunteers brought new energy and enthusiasm. Jan Gamache had spent sev-

391

eral days going door to door, talking to voters. "I just couldn't get over how much those people wanted information," she told a collection of campaign workers a few weeks before the election. "Going door to door, I just got so excited! I could have gone from now to June 30. It's so easy. It's so black and white."

They had taken out newspaper ads endorsing Marian and Bud, sent a barrage of letters to the editor, several of them questioning Secord's long-term commitment to the town, given that he was in the process of building a large, lake-front home for himself and his family in Swanzey, well outside the Winchester School District, and that his own children, enrolled in a private Christian school, had never attended Thayer.

In addition, Baker and Polaski workers held a rally, collected signatures for publication of Thayer grads who supported the pair, held community coffees, posted yard signs.

"Besides," one Polaski supporter said, "it's going to be tough for the opposition to attack Marian. It'd be like attacking Mrs. Santa Claus."

Even Secord and Gutoski's literature acknowledged that. "Just for the record," read one long-winded leaflet, "Marian is one of the most attractive and likeable ladies in our town. What's more, she's very sincere about her beliefs. It's just too bad that what she believes is so cockeyed. She actually believes in the worth of the liberal education concept that is not only old hat and discredited but has a good chance of ruining our high school."

It continued,

MARIAN has a wonderful personality and the ability to communicate, but isn't it too bad she is using them to promote ideas that she may want to forget later when she sees the result of them in KIDS WHO CAN'T EVEN FILL

OUT ORDINARY EMPLOYMENT APPLICATIONS or
GET INTO THE BETTER COLLEGES BECAUSE THEY
CAN'T MEET THE STANDARDS. . . .

MARIAN has a good eye for what is attractive and she
must feel that the "murals" (some people call them graffiti)
smeared on school walls look good. After all, the kids get a
chance to "express" themselves. But how come Michelan-
gelo was able to paint his masterpiece on the ceiling of that
chapel in the Vatican without going to Thayer High?

"LET'S GET BACK TO THE BASICS," another flier shouted,
"inspire our kids to love their country, their state, their
town . . . and love and respect their parents instead of being
turned against them by transparent devices. . . . The present
principal believes in the 'buddy' system. This adolescent
retread from the days of 'progressive education' is based on
the idea that an educator is a kind of 'pal' when anybody
with even minimal education in Psychology knows that the
kids privately yearn for STRONG PARENT FIGURES.
They can get all the 'buddies' they want on any street
corner."

James Beaman and Billy Higgins, two of Doc's former
Life After Thayer students, hit the muddy back roads of
Winchester that rainy Saturday before the election to distribute Baker-Polaski fliers. James, who now attended community college, had nearly come to blows with his father,
Earl, over the Littky issue. Earl Beaman, whose lumber
business grew from his father's little sawmill into a multimillion-dollar lumber operation, dairy barn, and vast landholdings, was the largest employer in town. Twice he'd flip-
flopped on which side he supported. When Susan Winter
and Allen Barton made their bid for school board seats in
1985, Beaman was a supporter. But he changed his mind
after three of his four children experienced school under
Littky.

"I feel Doctor Littky does care about the kids," Beaman told a *New England Monthly* reporter, "every damn one of them. He's done a good job of convincing those kids that if, goddamnit, they're going to be there, then they're going to do something."

That public posturing did not sit well with some of his oldest associates, Elmer Johnson among them. Just before the March election, Beaman shifted his allegiance once again to the anti-Littky forces. Publicly, he said the change of mind came after watching the division in town damage Winchester's economy. Privately, it was said that Johnson was applying pressure by way of a piece of land Beaman had wanted to acquire for a long time.

When James placed a Baker-Polaski sign on the Beamans' front lawn, Elmer Johnson blew the whistle.

"It's my boy's sign," Earl told him. "It's his yard, too."

Even before the polls opened Tuesday morning, the white GMC van decorated with twelve small American flags and half a dozen Secord-Gutoski placards had made several sweeps of Main Street. For the remainder of the day, it would be parked in front of the town hall. Across the street, in the large plate-glass window of Amarosa's Hardware, was a Baker-Polaski sign, the first political sign ever to appear there.

Outside the high school gymnasium, Francis Gutoski greeted voters entering and leaving the high school gymnasium. Marian Polaski was also there, surrounded almost constantly by campaign workers and well-wishers who chain-smoked, gossiped, and speculated about the outcome.

Howard Spaulding stood near one of his rebuilt Mercedes Benzes in the school parking lot, one of four or five relics he owned, talking to a reporter.

"The current board's insights are superb. It's their performance that's dismal. Their most important insight is to get rid of this farce, this man who calls trash excellent, saying this is quality when this is bilge. Children have no perspective. He builds them up with false motivation. They say a person should have high self-esteem, make them feel good about themselves. You don't pat someone on the back for doing a bad job. He uses those hype words, those superlatives from morning to night. 'Everything is great, everything is wonderful.'

"Instead of standing tall, what he does is get on the ground and grovel on their level. That's his stock in trade. If he's sincere, what he should be saying is 'I am your role model. I'm going to show you character, strength and, by God, you come up to *my* level.'"

Police Chief Harrison, in uniform, milled about the school, making sure things were under control. He remembered how it used to be, walking up the front sidewalk and being battered by insults from kids. That didn't happen now. The community center had helped. His own police department had gotten bigger and his men better trained. But he couldn't deny it—the school had played a large role. Things had gotten much better since Littky had become principal.

Inside the gymnasium, the New Hampshire secretary of state and assistant secretary stood behind Elmer Johnson, monitoring the ballot collection. The stream of voters was constant, but, unlike the last election, there was no wait to vote. Everything was orderly. All day the voters streamed in. Just a few minutes before 7 P.M., Ernie Paight rode into the high school parking lot on his Harley Davidson motorcycle, walked into the gymnasium, and cast the last ballot in the election. Nearly 70 percent, 1,750 of Winchester's eligible voters, had cast a vote; it was the biggest turnout in the town's history.

Secord, Gutoski, and their supporters cleared the gymnasium when the counting began and headed off to Secord's house, overlooking downtown Winchester, to await the results. Only Secord's uncle and campaign manager, Richard Secord, stayed behind. Amid the sea of pro-Littky supporters, Richard Secord stoically endured the two and a half hours it took to complete the count. Each ballot was monitored by the secretary and assistant secretary of state. A dozen or so reporters from radio, network television, newspapers, and magazines moved from person to person, collecting information for the stories they would write.

There was a nervous energy about the place. Val, Barb, Karen, Frankie, Winnie, Mel, Don, Terri, Marcia, Marian, and Bud waited with Littky for the results, at times talkative, at times pensive.

Shortly before 10 P.M. the votes were tallied. A great hush came over the crowd. Dennis's ears buzzed at the sudden quiet. He caught his breath and held it. This was it. This was it.

Elmer Johnson gathered up the results and walked to the microphone. "Baker 725," he said. "Gutoski 409—"

The hush broke. Marian gripped Marcia's hand, Marcia gripped Barb's, Val squeezed Doc's arm. Johnson's next words would reveal the winner and the fate of the town.

"Polaski 692," he said. "Secord 482—"

In a deafening roar, the people gathered in the Thayer High School gymnasium that night proclaimed to the world that they had won.

Epilogue

SUSAN WINTER resigned from the school board on July 1, 1987, providing no public explanation for her decision.

That summer, First Northern Bank in Keene accused her of skimming $500,000 in loan payments during her twenty-year employment there. After FBI investigation, Winter pleaded guilty in early 1990 to nine counts of embezzling bank customers' money totalling $54,525. U.S. District Court prosecution dropped six additional counts. She was sentenced to two years in federal prison and ordered to repay $100,000 to First Northern. She will serve five years probation and 750 hours community service. The civil suit filed by First Northern alleging she stole $500,000 is still pending.

BOBBY SECORD turned his historic Winchester home into apartments that summer and moved to a new home he'd been building in neighboring Swanzey. In March 1988, New Hampshire Governor John Sununu nominated him to serve on the 11-member State Fish and Game Commission. The nomination drew considerable public opposition. "I can tell you this, about nine out of ten are opposed (to Secord's confirmation) because of his involvement in Winchester," said a New Hampshire Executive Council member Bernie Streeter. The council voted down the nomination.

ALLEN BARTON resigned from the school board on August 21, 1987. Assistant Superintendent McCarthy, speaking on Barton's behalf, said Barton resigned for "personal reasons and his farm, he doesn't have time for the school board." Barton refused to put his resignation in writing. The board appointed Richard Cechvala, a retired Massachusetts public school teacher who moved to town a year earlier, to replace Barton.

FRANCIS GUTOSKI, contacted at his store, Big S Discount Co., the day after his June 1987 defeat, said, "Littky did everything he wrote about in his [doctoral] thesis. He overthrew the school, and he's overpowered the community. I wonder what he plans to do next. He's a very clever man." Just before Christmas 1988, Gutoski died.

JIMMY KARLAN dropped his suit against the Winchester School Board on July 2, 1987, saying, "I cannot justify penalizing a majority of the town for wrongdoings committed by the school board's old majority." He now works at Landmark School in Vermont, an institution for adults with learning disabilities.

NATHAN SPAULDING was among five candidates seeking the appointment to fill Winter's seat on the board. In August, former school board member Ruth Norton, who had helped elect Polaski and Baker, was appointed.

DON WEISBURGER and guidance counselor MELANIE ZWOLINSKI held a three-day workshop that summer for twelve Thayer students chosen as peer counselors, among them Lee Gamache. The workshop helped prepare the students to be good listeners and advocates for their peers who might be uncomfortable approaching an adult about a problem. Zwolinski left Thayer the following year to serve as a guidance counselor at Fall Mountain Regional High School in Fall Mountain, N.H.

Weisburger completed Antioch University's educational administration program while still a teacher at Thayer. In the fall of 1990, he began working as assistant principal of Woodsville Elementary School in Woodsville N.H.

ELMER JOHNSON became a principal mover in the Thayer High School Alumni Association. In March of 1989, Johnson completed his last term as Winchester's school moderator. He said he forgot to place his name on the ballot by the deadline and then failed to win the position. in a write-in campaign against pro-Littky activist Ed Zitta.

MARILYN NOLAN continued to monitor goings on at

Thayer, as well as education in general, in the rest of the country. She wrote a letter to the *Sentinel*, which ran June 23, 1989, discussing the degradation of the quality of teachers and student performance in America. She continued to contact pro-Littky supporters in town regarding Littky's activities. Her youngest daughter, Kerry, graduated from Thayer in 1989, the only one of her six daughters to do so. By then, two of her five other daughters had passed graduation equivalency exams and earned their high school diplomas. About two weeks before the hard-cover edition of *Teacher* was released in November 1989, Marilyn Nolan died.

VAL COLE became one of three teachers in the new student-centered Spectrum program, integrating science, math, and English. The program approached learning by theme, rather than by subject. For example, one section called Adaptation and Change focused on the study of Darwin, the novel *Inherit the Wind*, which deals with the conflict between Darwinism and Creationism, and mathematical notions of change. The curriculum was designed to compel students to draw connections among the disciplines. In addition, the students were required to design and present exhibitions of their learning, including videotaped speeches. The forty students involved made use of the Dovetail barn for collective activities. Unlike Dovetail, the emphasis was academic rather than vocational. Littky called it the most successful program of integrated studies at Thayer to date.

ERICA RYLL and her junior high home economics students became involved in local government, working to prevent the establishment of a controversial regional landfill in Winchester. Erica and her students joined science teacher Dan Bisaccio and his students in fighting the landfill. Through soil borings and other tests, the students revealed that the site was above a major aquifer that connected to the Ashuelot River. They asked questions and presented their findings at a public hearing, where their efforts were met with applause from some 250 people in attendance. Ultimately, the students were instrumental in convincing county and state officials to find another location. In 1988 the Cheshire County Conservation Commission named Winchester "Conservation Community of the Year," largely based on the students' work.

Erica also implemented the nation's first sustainable lifestyle curriculum at Thayer. She designed the curriculum to make students aware of ecological concerns that affect the family, such as use of renewable versus nonrenewable goods. Through a state grant, Erica published her curriculum, which is now in use in classrooms across the country and Canada. In 1988 and 1989, the entire school participated in various week-long sustainable lifestyle projects. One group, for example, designed and built a nature trail in town. Ryll has since returned to graduate school to earn a doctorate in education.

MARCIA AMMANN became chairperson of the school board in 1988 and is serving her second term on the board. She worked at the Monadnock Volunteer Center in Keene as volunteer coordinator before entering graduate school in education at the University of Massachusetts.

KAREN MARSH quit her job at Thayer in January 1989 to open a licensed day-care service in her Winchester home so she could be with her two young children during the working day. She returned to Thayer in 1990 as a teacher aid in the Chapter 1 program.

TERRI RACINE completed one year at Becker Junior College in paralegal training, then took a full-time job as a teller at a bank in Keene to finance her return to school. She is now in Florida studying to be a nurse.

ERNIE ROYCE maintained his disregard for Littky's brand of education. "I still don't like him. I still don't like his tactics, and I still don't believe the children are getting anywhere near an adequate education. And, on top of it all, taxes are out of sight."

Royce maintained that more money would not solve the

ills of education. "What I want to see is across-the-board competency testing of teachers every two to three years. . . . Even though we lost the battle here in Winchester, it will be won elsewhere. It has to be won. If it isn't, this country is heading for disaster."

DENNIS LITTKY was unanimously rehired as principal of Thayer by the school board on July 16, 1987. On August 6, the New Hampshire Supreme Court unanimously upheld the June 1986 decision of Cheshire County Superior Court that the Winchester School Board violated Littky's statutory rights when it denied him a public hearing. The precedent-setting decision ruled that principals have the same rights to their jobs as teachers. The supreme court also ruled that the board acted in bad faith in dealing with Littky and ordered that he be allowed to collect attorney's fees and costs incurred during his court challenge.

Thayer's ten-year evaluation was released shortly after, filled with pages and pages of praise. It also urged an end to the divisiveness between the board and the school, which still existed at the time the report was made. "There needs to be harmony between the school board and the school. The condition that has existed for the previous two years creates a real danger to the educational process."

The evaluation committee was hugely impressed by what it saw at Thayer:

Thayer Junior Senior High School offers a warm and friendly atmosphere to all members of the school community. School rules emphasize mutual respect, and are clearly stated and uniformly enforced. . . . All viewpoints are considered, and the sense of mutual responsibility is reinforced. . . .

Evidence of excellent staff/student relationship is plentiful. Students are made to feel important, and they appreciate the personal touches, the individualized curriculum approach, and the extra attention they are given via the advisory program, small classes, and after-school activities.

. . . Their care for their school is manifested in the responsibility they have taken for its appearance.

On October 22, 1987, Theodore R. Sizer asked the Winchester School Board to rejoin the Coalition of Essential Schools. The following month, its approval to do so was unanimous. The following summer, Littky was highlighted as one of the country's most effective leaders in a PBS special by Tom Peters called "The Leadership Alliance."

Littky describes his most recent year at Thayer (1988–89) as "the best of my career." Ten teachers, nearly half the staff, taught in teams. In its first year, the Spectrum program was working effectively in helping students integrate subject matter. In an alternative program, seniors tutored seventh graders who were experiencing academic problems. Thayer began a gifted program in English and science. The school held a steak dinner for honor students and their parents. Thayer teachers were hired as consultants by schools and colleges all over the country.

That summer fourteen teachers attended a three-day workshop at Littky's cabin to discuss teaming and curriculum integration. Four more attended a critical skills workshop at Antioch New England. The entire staff spent two days at an inn in Chester, Vermont, planning. Teacher volunteers planted flowers around the school.

At the close of the 1988–89 school year, Thayer High School had only two dropouts, less than one percent of its 325 students. More than half of the graduating class was bound for college—believed to be the highest percentage in the history of the school.

Littky, in a letter to his staff that summer, wrote: "Last year was incredible, almost scary how good it was for so many people. As we sat around the library the last day sharing, I was amazed at how many teachers said it was their best year. We have crossed a very important line. We are good, strong, confident, which should lead us to our next steps."

Recommended Reading

Dewey, John: *Experience and Education*. New York: Macmillan Publishing Inc., 1938.

Lipsitz, Joan: *Successful Schools for Young Adolescents*. New Brunswick, NJ: Transaction Books, 1984.

National Coalition of Advocates for Students: *Barriers to Excellence: Our Children at Risk*. Boston: National Coalition of Advocates for Students, 1988.

Sizer, Theodore R.: *Horace's Compromise: The Dilemma of the American High School*, Boston: Houghton Mifflin, 1984.

Wiggington, Eliot: *Sometimes a Shining Moment: The Foxfire Experience*. Garden City, NY: Anchor/Doubleday, 1985.

Sher, Jonathan, Education in Rural America